COUNCIL BLUFFS, IOWA

HISTORY & STORIES OF THE JEWISH MIDWEST

Journal of the Nebraska Jewish Historical Society
Volume 15, Summer/Fall 2017

333 South 132nd Street
Omaha, Nebraska 68154
njhs@jewishomaha.org
www.nebraskajhs.com

THIS BOOK
was made possible through the generosity of

Ellie Batt

Patty Nogg

The Ted Seldin Family Fund

The Special Donor-Advised Fund of
The Jewish Federation of Omaha

The Nebraska Jewish Historical Society would like to extend a special thanks to all of those who shared their memories of Council Bluffs.

WE FEEL TRULY honored to have been a part of this edition of Memories of the Jewish Midwest. All of us who have ties with the Council Bluffs Jewish community are grateful these stories are finally told. Sadly, during this long process we have lost some of our participants who were an integral part of the Bluffs' narrative. They were a joy to work with and shared their stories with vigor. Thankfully, their memories are preserved for us and future generations.

Thank you Ted for your insight and desire to have these stories documented. On behalf of the Nebraska Jewish Historical Society, we are privileged to memorialize the history and the stories of Council Bluffs.

So, let's raise a glass of wine and toast to the people and places of Council Bluffs — a delightful town forever seared in our hearts. *L'Chaim!*

RENEÉ RATNER CORCORAN
& JOEY HOFFMAN

ABOUT THE AUTHOR

JOEY HOFFMAN is a freelance writer whose work has appeared in The New York Times, The Washington Post, The Huffington Post, Condé Nast Traveler, and New York Magazine. She received a Bachelor of Arts degree in Journalism from the University of Wisconsin-Madison. Joey lives in Omaha with her daughter Daisy and two kleptomaniac rescue dogs, Sadie and Nala. She is working on a memoir about single momdom and her journey from transplantation to transformation -- a die-hard New Yorker with *shpilkes* who finds meaning and calm (sort of) in the heartland.

INTRODUCTION

I WAS A twice-a-year-Jew. Growing up in Larchmont, New York, 27 miles north of NYC, temple to me meant stockings (too tight), sitting ("Mom, may I please hide in the, er, go to the bathroom?") and sermons delivered by our J.F.K. Jr. look-alike Rabbi Rick Jacobs, now president of the Union for Reform Judaism. Yes, I had *shpilkes*, yet once I settled in I'd practice a favorite pastime: people watching. A husband would drape his arm around his wife, she'd lay her head on his shoulder as their children whispered and I'd wonder, what's their story? Novelist Umberto Eco said, "To survive, you must tell stories."

Like a Polaroid, my Jewish story developed over time. In my mid-20s, I became a writer living in Greenwich Village where there were more Jews in my apartment building than there are in Nebraska and Iowa. Since I'd had just one year of Hebrew School and a family who fast-forwarded through seders, pausing only for the farfel kugel portion, my education was limited. But it's our culture, community, spirit, and *kibbitzy* ways which have helped shape Jewish me.

In 2003, I gave birth to Daisy. My muse. She lived for seven months in a New York City Neonatal Intensive Care Unit as she was born with gastroschisis, an intestinal anomaly which caused her organs to malfunction. Craving a connection to my faith –– and a way to stay semi-sane –– I befriended the NICU Rabbi.

"How do I get closer to God?" I asked.

"Perform a mitzvah," he said. "Light Shabbat candles."

I did. The golden glow balmed my soul.

In 2006, we traveled to Omaha where Daisy received a small bowel, liver and pancreas transplant at Nebraska Medicine. Our intended short stay turned into, now, 11 years. Unlike my faith-free girlhood, Daisy attended Hebrew School since she was six and while studying for her Bat Mitzvah in January of 2016 at Temple Israel, I witnessed my daughter, chant by chant ("*Mi chamocha...*") walk her Jewish journey, absorbing the privilege of being part of our local and larger community. Daisy's dive into Judaism allowed me to go deeper into the waters of our faith, by proxy. Story and song strengthened my faith –– a bridge to our lineage.

There are no coincidences. When Reneé Corcoran, Executive Director of the Nebraska Jewish Historical Society, asked me to write a book about Jews from Council Bluffs and their family stories, it was like coming home. Together, we have laughed, cried, broken bread at Christy Creme and Pizza King, strolled Bikur Cholim Oakhill cemetery and attended B'nai Israel's Friday night and High Holiday services.

As a New York writer, the city was my beat. I covered The Best (fill-in-the-blank), reviewed restaurants and interviewed high-watt subjects. Yes, it was glam and fun for my palette, yet no project has given me more *nachas* than hearing your stories. I feel nostalgic for a time and a town in which I never lived.

Thank you. Thank you for inviting me into your lives, for allowing me to bear witness to your history, Council Bluffs chapter. My prayer is you will read, and re-read, these stories, share them with your kin, and theirs...May they shroud you in the love of your ancestors. You, their legacies, brought them to life. *L'chaim*!

JOEY HOFFMAN
Author

CONTENTS

1.	COUNCIL BLUFFS' JEWISH HISTORY	11
2.	BIKOR CHOLIM & OAK HILL CEMETERY	21
3.	THE PEOPLES STORE BY SUE MILLWARD	27
4.	HADASSAH BY OLIVER POLLAK	37
5.	SECOND LIEUTENANT IRVING COHEN	51
6.	THE SELDIN FAMILY	53
7.	DOUG & GAIL KRASNE	61
8.	REBECCA BLOOM	81
9.	MICHAEL GALLNER	89
10.	SOL KUTLER	105
11.	PAUL SHYKEN	121
12.	MARCIA TEPPERMAN KUSHNER	131
13.	JANIE FOX KULAKOFSKY	141
14.	HAROLD ABRAHAMSON	151
15.	CHICKIE PASSER LINSMAN	161
16.	MARTY NERENSTONE	167
17.	SISSY KATELMAN SILBER	173
18.	MILLARD R. SELDIN	187
19.	JERRY SLUSKY	195
20.	JAN SCHNEIDER LUND	203
21.	GARY KATELMAN	219
22.	SARA WOLF EPSTEIN	227
23.	BOB SULVALSKY	235
24.	MAYNARD TELPNER	245

25. SUE FRIEDMAN MILLWARD	257
26. HAROLD BERNSTEIN	273
27. MARK EVELOFF	285
28. YALE GOTSDINER	291
29. BOB FOX	301
30. JOE FINKLE	309
31. LEO MEYERSON	315
32. DAVID GOODMAN	329
33. DON NOGG	339
34. PATTY LEE NOGG	351
35. DR. ISAAC STERNHILL	367
36. BETTIE & LIBBIE GROSSMAN	369
37. SHIRLEY GOLDSTEIN	373

COUNCIL BLUFFS' JEWISH HISTORY

Council Bluffs Synagogue in 2016

LEAVE IT TO a *Levite* to pen the first page of Council Bluffs' story. Alexander Levi -- a descendent of the esteemed family lineage who acted as a bridge between priests, Kohenim and the Israelites -- was the first Jewish man to settle in the Iowa Territory. It was 1833. Levi, aptly-named as the Hebrew meaning is "joining," became the state's first naturalized citizen.

Following Levi's lead, a small group of Jewish men and women, left their lives and the instability of Western Europe -- Germany, France and Austria -- with their families, faith and a future unknown. The group would plant roots in the area around Council Bluffs. In 1881, a second wave of largely Orthodox Jewish immigrants followed, fleeing Eastern Europe and the *pogroms* of Tsarist Russia. They settled in Council Bluffs and formed Congregation Bikhor Cholim. The group rented a small building on Main Street in Council Bluffs, four officers of the 25 charter members included M. Brohlich, (President), Abraham M. Marks (Vice President) and O. Hochman (Secretary). The group was so small they had no rabbi.

The congregation realized the community needed a traditional burial ground, so in 1880, members of Bikhor Cholim arranged with the Council Bluffs Hebrew Society to divide newly-purchased Holy Acres into two sections, Orthodox and Reform, creating a cemetery with a dual name: Bikur Cholim/Oakhill. Orthodox families were interred on the Bikur Cholim side, while reform families were buried in the Oakhill section, as it remains today.

The Council Bluffs Hebrew Society further supported the community by sponsoring religious services which were first held in locations like the Danish Hall and the Grand Army Hall, until Temple Emanuel on North 7th Street was purchased. After that synagogue was sold, High Holy Days services were again held in various halls once again. Omaha's Rabbi Frederick Cohn visited Council Bluffs every other Sunday and The Sisterhood of Temple sponsored a Sunday school. However, due to lack of membership, the Temple disbanded and the remaining funds in the treasury were given to the Chevra B'nai Yisroel Congregation which was organized on October 21, 1903 and incorporated one month later.

Chevra B'nai Yisroel purchased a lot at 618 Mynster Street in northwest Council Bluffs and built a wood-framed synagogue at the cost of $6,000. The congregation's first officers included President Isaac Gilinsky, Vice-President George Whitebook, Secretary M. Frieden and Treasurer M. Solomon who, with fellow congregants, laid the cornerstone on June 19, 1904. Unbeknownst to them, 27 years later, on March 5, 1930, a fire would set the synagogue ablaze, razing the building. But *Baruch Hashem*, thank God, members of the congregation ran into the burning building and saved the Torahs.

A building committee including George Whitebook, B. Gilinsky, Abe Gilinsky, Morris Hoffman, Dave Fox and Simon Shyken hired local architect J. Chris Jensen to design a new *shul*. The original cornerstone was salvaged and an inscription for the new synagogue was added. January 11, 1931, the new 500-seat sanctuary was completed. The cost? $26,000.

Setting the corner stone of B'nai Israel Synagogue, 1930

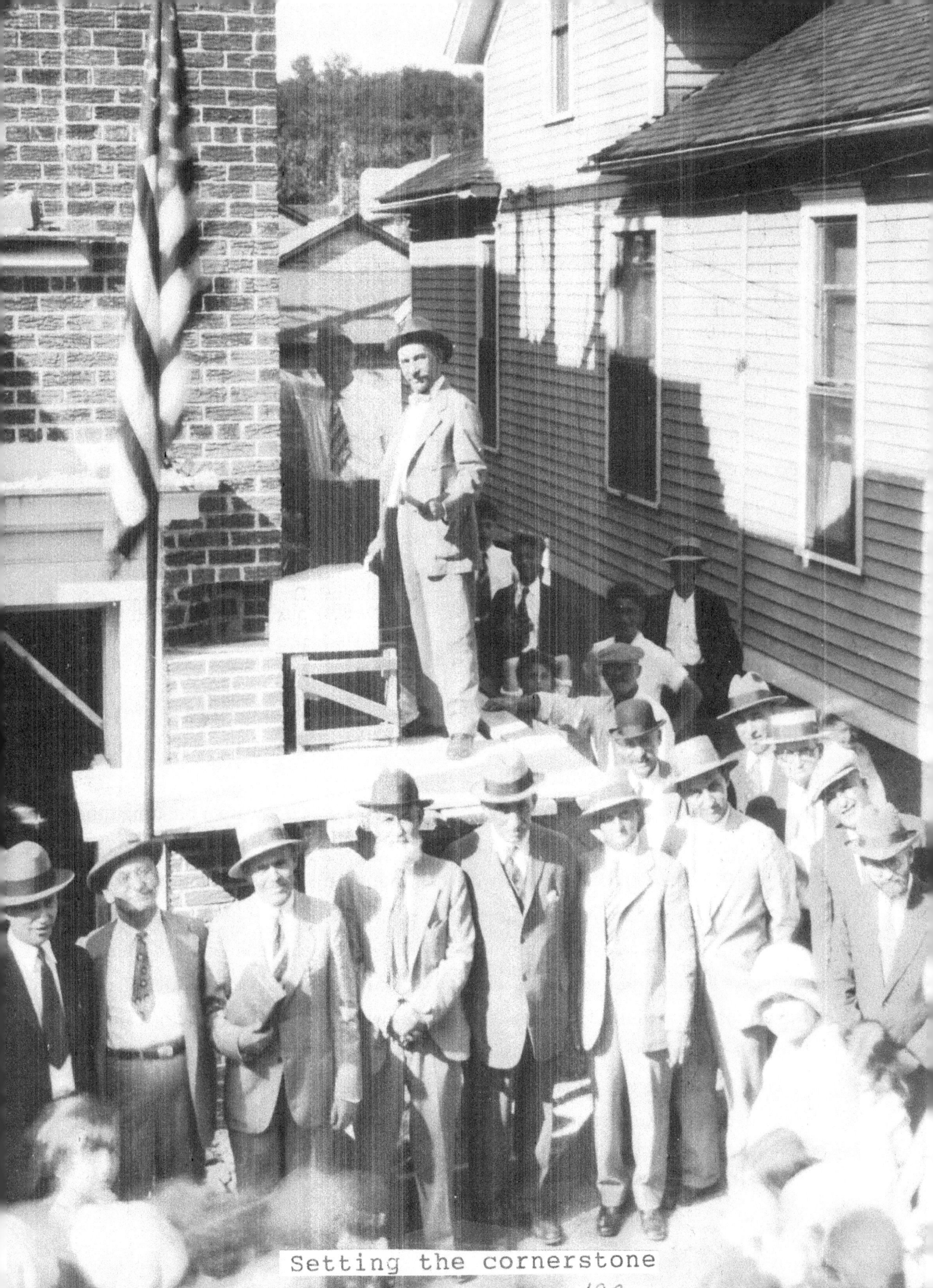

Setting the cornerstone

Over time, the congregation grew, yet traditional Orthodox would eventually dissolve. For instance, seating became integrated, no longer did men sit downstairs and women and children in the balcony. In November 1953, the congregation changed its official name to B'nai Israel. Come the early 1960s, the synagogue was expanded and remodeled by local architect, I.T. Carrithers, and by the mid-1960s, B'nai Israel's membership began to diminish. They lost Rabbi Karzan, its full-time rabbi, and the synagogue would see a succession of part-time rabbis and lay leaders, leaving room for modern Reconstructionism to emerge.

The synagogue's foundation was on shaky ground. By 1980, the threat of shuttering its doors prompted congregants to save the building, a theme which would permeate the synagogue's life for years thereafter. Over time, attempts to oxygenate the once-thriving hub of Jewish life continued. A small group of committed citizens have been reviving the building –– which is listed on the National Register of Historic Places –– and the congregation is seeing an increase in commitment, attendance and enthusiasm for the place that has been the Hebrew home of Jewish Council Bluffians for nearly 140 years.

FOR MANY YEARS, men of Council Bluffs dreamed of building or owning a building a property for Jewish charitable, philanthropic, benevolent, educational and religious activities. December 1, 1943 at the home of Leo Myerson, the group was told that Sam Meyerson and his son were pledging $10,000 toward a building fund for a Council Bluffs Jewish Community Center.

In 1946, the Council Bluffs Jewish community finished negotiations for the $15,000 purchase of the Pottawattamie County Red Cross chapter house on South 8th Street to be used as a Jewish Community Center which included men's and women's lounges, a library and rooms for social and club activities. On March 25, 1947, over 100 people attended the dedication. The first known activity to be held at the Council Bluffs Center was the Senior Hadassah Box Lunch Social on August 4, 1946.

In 1947, a lodge room at B'nai Israel Synagogue was furnished in memory of Lieutenant Irving Cohen, son of the venerable Harry and Anne Cohen. Irv attended Hebrew School at B'nai Israel, graduated from Abraham Lincoln High School and,

Dedication of Council Bluffs Synagogue. Simon Shyken seventh from left to right

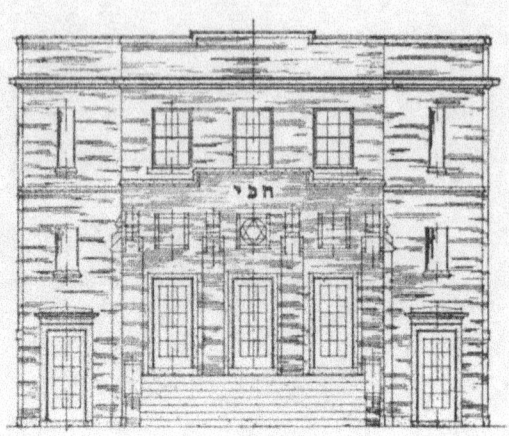

.....Program.....

Chebra B'nai Yisroel Synagogue

"Burning of Mortgage"

November 21, 1943

16 | COUNCIL BLUFFS HISTORY

in 1941, attended the University of Nebraska in Lincoln, pledging ZBT fraternity. His closest friend was Harold Bernstein; other buddies included Norman Smeerin, Stuart Simon, Bud Studna, Norman Rips and Irving Malashock.

In 1942, during his senior year of college, Cohen enlisted in the U.S. Army Air Corps. He trained at several flight schools in California, including Morton Air Academy. Cohen graduated in 1943 as a B-17 pilot and attended advanced school at Marpha, Texas, becoming a second lieutenant. In an article published by the Council Bluffs *Nonpareil* newspaper in October of 1944, Lieutenant Cohen was stationed with the Eighth Air Force in Europe. On November 25, 1944, while on his 15th bombing mission over Germany, the B-17 he was piloting was shot down.

Cohen's parents, family and friends held out hope for over a year that he was still alive. However, in a letter from the government, a presumption of death was dated November 26, 1945. Another letter followed. At the request of the President of the United States, Second Lieutenant Irving Cohen was awarded posthumously the Purple Heart for giving his life in defense of his country. He is buried at Ardennes American Cemetery in Neuville-EnCordroz, Belgium.

AZA #7, a Jewish boy's club, was one of the first AZA Chapters formed in Iowa. Organized in October 1924 under the leadership of Abe Katelman and his brother Louis, the first President was Lou Rosenthal, Vice President was Harold Cherniak and Abe Katelman served as Secretary. Fraternizing was one highlight of being part of the group, and every year The Chieftain Hotel -- Council Bluff's best -- hosted March Magic, a dance which drew dozens of bridge-crossers from Omaha's AZA chapters. Small-town swank at its finest.

1. First Synagogue in Council Bluffs, 1904
2. Burning of the mortgage. November 21, 1943
3. Jewish Community Center at 244 South 8th Street in Council Bluffs

In Recognition of the Sixth Anniversary of
the establishment of the State of Israel

In honor of Selma Gershun and
Samuel Meyerson —

HUGH McDONALD

*veteran Haganah fighter, brilliant economist
will be the principal speaker on
this occasion.*

Chairman:
Louis Bernstein

The

ISRAEL ANNIVERSARY CELEBRATION COMMITTEE

of Council Bluffs

Takes Pleasure

In Inviting You

To Attend

"SIX YEARS OF STATEHOOD"

A Dinner

Honoring

Samuel Meyerson   and   Mrs. Ben J. Gershun

in the

JEWISH COMMUNITY CENTER

ON WEDNESDAY, THE THIRTIETH

OF JUNE, NINETEEN-FIFTY-FOUR

AT SIX-THIRTY O'CLOCK IN THE EVENING

Reservations:
Mrs. Edward H. Tepperman
2-0149

AZA REGIONAL CHAMPS—Aza 7 of Council Bluffts won the regional AZA basketball championshi at Omaha Jewish Community Center last week, and qualified for district tournament play at Mir neapolis in March. The Bluffs crew downed AZA 4 of Des Moines 40-37 in a double overtime cham pionship game. Front row, left to right, Dick Shostak, Stanley Richards, Milt Brown, Larry Roffma Standing: Boomjug Telpner, Marvin Suvalsky, Buddy Roffman, Manager Sam Eveloff. Team mem bers not in picture are Jerry Passer and Joe Franks.—Nonpareil Photo.

4. Cohen Room in the Council Bluffs Jewish Community Center
5. "Six Years of Statehood" Program from Council Bluffs Jewish Community Center, 1954
6. Council Bluffs AZA Basketball Regional Champions, 1946-1947

BIKHOR CHOLIM & OAK HILL CEMETERY

A CANOPY OF leaves shrouds a sacred stretch of earth where Council Bluffs Jewish families and friends who once sat side-by-side in *shul* are together laid to rest. Meticulously maintained headstones read like a Who's Who of the community: Passer, Cohen and Krasne, to name a few. Coiffed grounds near Forest and Morningside Drives and the Kenmore/Keeline neighborhood echo with a symphony of chirps, offering a sound track of serenity. The cemetery has a story, like the children and grandchildren whose memories keep family lore alive.

"There's no such thing as an ending, just a place where you leave the story. It's your story now." -- Maggie Smith, The Second Best Marigold Hotel

The cemetery's history dates back to 1881, when 25 charter members formed the Orthodox Congregation of Bikhor Cholim, which in Hebrew refers to the mitzvah to visit and extend aid to the sick. According to a brochure written by Joan K. Marcus, William E. Ramsey and Betty Dineen Shrier, these early founders purchased a parcel of land then known as Holy Acres for a cemetery east of the city which was divided into two sections to be used by Reform families (Oak Hill) and Orthodox (Bikhor Cholim). That same year, the first grave, belonging to the Mayer family, was established; and developers included stand-out names like Katelman, Shyken, Sacks, Hoffman, Saltzman, Meyerson, Rosenfeld and Ungar.

72 years after its inception, Abe Katelman, who for years solely ran the Orthodox side, asked then-young attorney and former Council Bluffs mayor Maynard Telpner to help him reincorporate the cemetery with the state of Iowa, as timely changes were needed. It was 1953. The original articles of incorporation were written in a Yiddish version of English as the founders spoke English but with a Yiddish accent. When transposed on paper and read aloud, it was like hearing their grandparents speak.

"Abe was a one man cemetery association," said Maynard in a 2008 *Jewish Press* article. "He handled the affairs by himself because no one else wanted to help. It was always very important to him that the cemetery have proper supervision." The community produced a successful fundraiser to ensure the future operation of the cemetery. "We contacted every Jew that we could think of who had ever lived in Council Bluffs," Maynard said.

Back then, Jewish life was at its zenith. Family-owned businesses boomed, *shul* was a second home and women's volunteer organizations Hadassah and Sisterhood thrived -- a surprise to many now who were not aware there was even one Jew in Council Bluffs, let alone roughly 180 families during that time. Today, only five of the original members of the community still call it home: siblings Gail, Doug and Susan Krasne, and Mark Eveloff and Mike Gallner, boyhood best friends, neighbors and now cemetery board members. Mike, who in 1987 helped get non-profit status awarded, recalls Abe's fatherly role in Bikhor Cholim affairs.

"When there was a death in the community, Abe would come to Sam's Market, my grandfather Sam Sacks's store, to start the cemetery arrangements, especially when there wasn't a rabbi involved. When he died, my grandfather took over for him until he died in 1983. Abe and my grandfather Sam were liaisons between John O'Connor (the beloved cemetery manager and the grieving family and decided which funeral home would do the work, what kind of casket would be used, how they were clothed and they made sure they met all the religious requirements of the cemetery association." Visitors appreciate the cemetery on the surface: its serenity, hilltop views and ease of navigation. But some may not know the behind-the-scenes effort it took to

Bikhor Cholim Cemetery, Council Bluffs, Iowa

integrate, modernize and manage the community's burial ground. Bikhor Cholim/Oak Hill includes a mix of Orthodox and Reform families, but it wasn't always so. Both sides were always two separate entities and managed entirely differently in all aspects. Abe, then Sam Sacks and his son Kenny ran the Orthodox side, while Leo Ungar and his nephew Bob Kully ran the reform section. Years ago, "My uncle Leo invited John Goldner, his wife Kay Lynn, my wife Connie and myself to dinner and asked us to get involved," says Bob, a longtime cemetery president who has passed the torch to Patty Nogg, and whose mother Carolyn Rosenfeld is buried there.

For decades, Ted Seldin has been instrumental in cementing the cemetery's longevity. In 1986, taking a cue from Abe and Maynard, Ted led a fundraising campaign for Bikhor Cholim which exponentially raised the size of the perpetual care fund, assuring the annual maintenance to perpetuity. As a result, for instance, experts were hired to repair the fence, shore up the foundations of decaying monuments and reposition those that had been vandalized. In 2004, Ted again took the reins, recruiting Bob to help consolidate the long-separated Bikhor Cholim and Oak Hill.

"The thought of us merging was an interesting thing to do, the right thing to do for the future," says Bob, a financial advisor. "We started to do some work on it and realized what it was going to take. I thought it would be a simple process, but once I got into it…Out-of-date legal documents were re-written, we pooled all assets into one account and created one contract with John O'Connor to maintain both sides. We also re-wrote burial rules so that on the reform side, non-Jewish people could be buried there," says Bob, referring to the traditional Orthodox law which prohibits non-Jews from being buried in a Jewish cemetery.

*Noteworthy burial customs: According to Jewish law, an Orthodox Jew is to be buried as he or she was born: complete with all limbs and organs, unadorned and in a traditional grave in the ground so the body may return to the earth. Chevra Kadisha is a holy burial society which performs a traditional ritual known as "tahara," the Jewish practice of ritually washing a body with water (or rechitzah) and dressing it in a white linen shroud (tachrichim) prior to placing the body into a pine casket. As they pour water over a body, they recite prayers in honor of the deceased, imploring God to receive this person in love.

During the merger, Bob and Ted met with Harold Bernstein and John Goldner in Shelley Gallner's office in Council Bluffs. "Shelley became the attorney for the whole system and we brought everything forward to have it for the future," Bob says. Today, Scott Meyerson, Leo Meyerson's grandson, is the attorney for Bikhor Cholim/Oak Hill, keeping it in the Bluffs family.

"If we don't do it, whatever knowledge we have, the next has less," says Bob. "There's a responsibility for the future to have the burial and legal records as up-to-date and complete as possible. If we wouldn't have done it, to ask the next generation to resurrect records would be more difficult. Literally, Patty Nogg, Ted Seldin, Marty Ricks and I walked the entire cemetery to write down what we could get from every grave stone for up-to-date records."

Bob, Ted and Marty Ricks –– retired Executive Director of the Jewish Federation of Omaha Foundation –– take on the task of approving budgets and allocating and investing funds. Marty was recruited to help with management when the Telpners moved to Oregon and the Seldins began spending half the year in a warmer place. Says Marty: "I offered that the Jewish Federation Foundation would house all the records, so continuity was established. It keeps continuing," Marty laughs, noting it took two or three years to streamline all legal documents, some of which are computerized, while others are archived old-school style: on paper.

"They knew I had Iowa roots and Ted knew from his dad Ben, who came once a year to Missouri Valley where I grew up to obtain the Council Bluffs Jewish Federation campaign pledge from my parents. I always felt a closeness from the time I started working with wonderful people like Ted, Bob Kully, Dr. John Goldner, Rick Katelman, Sissy Silber, Patty Nogg…Not only will they be buried there, but they have parents and siblings there and truly care."

The group relies on a cadre of volunteers. Board of Directors include Patty Nogg (President), Bob Kully (Vice President), Sissy Silber (Secretary), Marty Ricks (Treasurer), Ted Seldin, John Goldner, Gail Kenkel, Judge Mark Eveloff, Joel Finkel, Elyse Gallner, Michael Gallner, Rick Katelman, John Katelman and Gail Krasne Kenkel. During the transition process, they also enlisted the help of John O'Connor.

Oak Hill Cemetery, Council Bluffs, Iowa

"John was an encyclopedia of knowledge about our cemetery," Bob says. "He remembers the details of every transaction he had with any family and everyone buried there as his father did before him. His records were either in his back pocket or in a manila folder. John is as conscientious and pleasant an individual as anyone could find. He's a real gentleman, a real solid person."

An Irish *mensch*.

"John's got a big heart," says Marty. "Between him and his dad, they've managed the place for over 80 years." The O'Connors emigrated from Ireland and moved to the Bluffs. John started digging graves with his father Denis for 75 cents an hour during summers off from Abraham Lincoln High School where his classmates included many Jewish kids whose family plots he takes care of today, like the Passers, Finkels, Katelmans, Eveloffs and Gallners. Around 1957, John took over, continuing the tradition of his father who began managing the cemetery nearly a quarter-century prior.

These days, there are only one or two funerals a year and John has witnessed the community morph from bustling to bare-boned. "A lot of people are gone or moved away, it isn't the Jewish community in Council Bluffs like it used to be." So what has been the impetus for the man who has devoted virtually his entire working life caring for Bikhor Cholim/Oak Hill families? "You do a service for the people you know and try to help them out when they lose loved ones," he says. "It's rewarding."

Sissy Katelman Silber, Abe Katelman's niece, secretary of the board and a den mother of sorts when it comes to caring for the cemetery says, "Nearly the whole Jewish community is there. If you want to discover the history of Jewish life in Council Bluffs, you can go up there and read the inscriptions on the stones: when they were born, when they died…If it's written in Yiddish, it usually tells you who their fathers were, 'Son of so-and-so.' To me, it's a very peaceful place and it always brings back memories for me. As many times as I've been there, I enjoy walking around and just reflecting on names and it makes me recall good times. It's very comforting. Very peaceful, very peaceful."

THE PEOPLES STORE

By Sue Millward

THE EARLY HISTORY of the Peoples Store is unclear due to a lack of records available, but the store was first evidenced in a painting of Council Bluffs by George Simons dated 1857. There is no official record of who owned and operated the store then, but in 1861 Henry and Simon Eiseman, two immigrant brothers from Germany, settled in Council Bluffs and established their dry-goods business here.

By 1889 they had the largest mercantile firm in Iowa or Nebraska and prided themselves by offering "reliable goods at low cost to their customers." In that year, the brothers moved their ever-growing business to 418 West Broadway (the corner of Broadway and Bryant Streets) into a three-story building that allowed for a larger store and more inventory.

In 1907, when Simon Eiseman retired, the Peoples Store came under the management of new owners -- the Krasne and Bernstein families. During the late 19th century, many eastern European families fled their Russian homelands to avoid conscription in the Russian Army. Conscription meant 25 years of service in the czar's forces. Often the recruits (some as young as 10 year-old boys) disappeared, never to return, or if they returned, their villages and families were destroyed. The Krasne and Bernstein families were among those who fled their homeland and settled in Iowa and Nebraska. Louis Krasne and his oldest sons came to America in 1888.

One of their cousins had preceded them and settled in Fremont, NE. As a result, Fremont became the destination for Louis and his sons when they landed in New York. They were met by the Hebrew Immigrant Aid Society, (HIAS), given $10 and put on a train to their destination. At the time of their arrival, Louis was 50 years old His sons were: Isaac, 20, Herman, 17 and Jacob, 16.

They began as peddlers with a horse and wagon, selling their wares, but the story has it that when the horse died in Fullerton, Nebraska, they traded the contents of the wagon for the General Store which soon became knows as "KRASNES." The rest of Louis' family came over in 1892 after the death of their mother. They all assumed English names and English became their spoken language. As some of the sons became adults, they expanded to open general stores in many small towns. In addition to Fullerton, Krasne stores were found in Aurora, Norfolk, Oakland and Albion, Nebraska.

Herman Krasne opened a store in Norfolk with his brother-in-law, Sam Rosenthal, and moved on to Pierce, Nebraska in 1909 before finally settling in Omaha. In 1907, the younger brothers, George and Frank Krasne, moved to Council Bluffs with their cousins Lou and Mose Bernstein.

The four brothers partnered to buy the Peoples Store and offered a small inventory of staple merchandise that met "the dependable demands of the people of the community." The warm personality of the brothers, their quiet smiles and friendly handshakes soon won the hearts of the people of Council Bluffs. They were merchants and well-respected by their customers and employees alike for their integrity and honesty. They all became valued citizens of Council Bluffs and served in civic activities of their hometown.

As their success grew, so did the need for a grander showplace. In 1922, they expanded their store to include two floors and a basement that combined to become 49,680 square feet of selling and warehouse space (see photo). The store could now offer more variety than ever before. The brothers and their extended families continued to manage the Peoples Store for over 60 years, passing the management over three generations.

By the late 1960s, business started to decline. It was a time of the development of large shopping centers across the country. When Council Bluffs' Urban Renewal Project became a reality in downtown, the Peoples Stores was on the site they desired. The Krasnes / Bernsteins reluctantly accepted the offer made by the city, and in 1972 the business was closed after 115 years.

The Peoples Store was unique because at its peak in the 1940s and '50s, the store supported ten different families:

1) Frank and George Krasne managed the Men's Department
2) Their brother Herman with his son Millard had Women's Shoes and the Toy Departments
3) Other brothers Jake, his son Lawrence and grandson Leslie, Ike and his son Albert (all Krasnes) owned and managed the Notions, Accessories and Home Furnishing Departments
4) The Bernstein brothers, Louis and Mose, with Lou's son Harold, operated the Grocery and Hardware Departments.

Each family was responsible for the purchasing, displaying, sales and accounting for their department.

In this time of retail history, every city had a major department store and that is what the Peoples Store was to the people of southwest Iowa. It was important not only in its size, but it also served as a major employer in the local community. In 1936, the Peoples Store employed over 100 people.

Although we cannot possibly list all of the people who worked for the store over the years, there are many key people who will be remembered for their part in making the Peoples Store part of Council Bluffs' historic legacy:

Thomas Shaw, Blanche Green, Irene Mann, Art Britten, O. H. Murdock, Chick Perliss, Mabel James, Dorothy Moore, Herman Meyerson, Hazel Wynn, Morris Arkin, Abe Krantz, Daisy Henry, Ed Fagan, Myrtle Wright, Lloyd Daggett, Mary Grimes, Bill Rudd and so many more.

Herman Krasne Isaac "Ike" Krasne Jacob "Jake" Krasne Mose Bernstein

Frank Krasne George Krasne Louis Bernstein

Clothing for Men, Women and Children; Toys, Groceries, Meats, F Hardware, Chinaware, Paint, Radios, Dry Goods, Furnishings, Shoes, Rugs and Floor Coverings All Under One Roof

The Growth of the Peoples Stor

In the past 29 years the Peoples Store has grown and expanded with Council Bluffs. In 1907 a small building with only twenty-foot front, known as the Peoples Store was purchased by two young men from Omaha, F. M. Kransne and George Krasne, the two youngest sons of L. Krasne of Fullerton, Neb. with just a handful of staple merchandise consisting of the dependable demands of the people of this community this little business ship started upon its climb to success. These two men soon became popular with the people. Their method of guaranteing satisfaction or your money back soon began to lay a concrete foundation of confidence. Louis Bernstein, a brother-in-law and his brother, Morris, equipped a grocery on the scanty balcony in the rear of the store. As the old saying goes, "With a chunk of cheese and a handful of crackers." The personality of these two boys was soon to make itself felt. A smile, a handshake, a kindly turn soon melted the hearts of the people. Steadily forward and in just a few years the senior Mr. L. Krasne retired from active business and his son, Jacob, took over the interests of F. M. Krasne, who with his brother, I. Krasne, returned to the home store at Fullerton. A new personality, a lovable character, soon had this institution going ahead by leaps and bounds. More room was needed and expansion was made and in 1917 Mr. Herman Krasne entered the firm, coming from Omaha. On and on, bigger and bigger until in 1922 the present fine building was erected, 138x120 feet, two floors and a basement, 49,680 square feet of selling and warehouse space augmented by three fine warehouses. Over an acre of floor space. At this time F. M. Krasne and his brother, I., came back from Fullerton and took over the clothing and ready-to-wear. Also four grand sons, Lawrence, Leo, Albert and Clyde Krasne entered the firm, making in all three generations. Bernstein brothers taking over the grocery and also the hardware in the basement. In 1924 their business grew to the point where the grocery was sold to Meyerson brothers. In 1935 Herman Meyerson with the help of his son-in-law, Leon Frankel and jovial Rudolph Walters, assumed control of the entire grocery and meat departments. Over 30 people are actually employed in this one department. The opposite picture portrays the enormity of the present pay roll and what this home owned, independent institution means to Council Bluffs commercially. With never faltering faith in this community these men reinvested their earnings in real estate, now owning a creditable number of business houses as well as a considerable interest in the Broadway theater and the Bennett building. Eleven members of this firm are every one taxpaying resident of this city, helping to support schools, churches and government tha Council Bluffs may be an ideal American city.

1967. Leah Krasne serving refreshments to customers on opening day of 110th Anniversary event

At Right..KRAZY DAY in July 1967. Bob Krasne (left) and (fromback to front) Johnny Bernstein Kay Bernstein, Bayla Faye and Pearl Krasne. Selling ice cream at corner of Bryant & Broadway

At Left...1962, Morris Arkin with Rozy & Marty Krasne taken at back door of Peoples Store.

SECOND GENERATION PROPRIETORS

ALBERT KRASNE...son of Ike Krasne operating the second floor clothing and ready to wear sections of Peoples Store for many years. Clyde, brother of Albert was also engaged in this operation for a period of time.

MILLARD KRASNE....son of Herman Krasne operating the shoe section for many years. Millard later took over operation of the second floor departments n Albert. Now with partner, son Robert continues to control all these portions.

LAWRENCE KRASNE...son of Jake Krasne operating the main floor area of Peoples Store, later including the grocery store section also. Now, son Leslie continues to operate this sector of the store minus the grocery which was eliminated.

LOUIS BERNSTEIN...one of the original modern Peoples Store operators continues to co-operate with son Harold who now conducts the hardware, appliance, housewares and sporting goods departments. Pictures are shown on other pages.

Peoples Department Store, 308-10 Broadway, taken Wednesday November 21, 1928, 3:00 p.m.
Courtesy of the Council Bluffs Public Library

Nonpareil photo taken in the summer of 1955. Sign at right end over the awning,
People's Grocery Food Mart operated by Leon Frankel and Herman Meyerson

Ad in the Council Bluffs Nonpareil, October 21, 1943

HADASSAH

By Oliver Pollak

JEWISH WOMEN EXPRESSED their faith and social consciousness by joining temple and synagogue sisterhoods and groups like Hadassah, National Council of Jewish Women, Pioneer Women and ORT. This reflected a serious commitment of time and effort to fundraising for charitable causes in America, Israel and the Diaspora. In large and small communities, these organizations were platforms and training grounds for leadership. The cookbook was one of many endeavors to bring their mission into the public eye, and provide a memento of food culture.

"Hadassah has in the past and will continue in the future to serve the needs of Humanity."

- Mrs. Oscar [Stella] Greenberg

What's Cooking in Hadassah, Council Bluffs Cookbook, 1954

BACK TO THE FUTURE

THE KOREAN WAR ended in 1953. President Eisenhower occupied the White House. The New York Giants swept the Cleveland Indians in the 1954 World Series. Unemployment hovered at 4.9%. Bayliss Park, adjacent to the 1888 Pottawattamie County Courthouse with a four-sided clock tower, echoes the town into which teenager Marty McFly, played by Michael J. Fox in the 1985 film, *Back to the Future*, landed. The Broadway viaduct over the railroad tracks would be completed in 1955.

The Jewish community of Council Bluffs dates from the 1850s. The Synagogue at 618 Mynster Street dates from 1904. The Jewish population, estimated at 1,000 in 1918, declined to 125 to 175 families by the early 1950s. The Jewish infrastructure included a B'nai B'rith lodge, Jewish Federation, and a kosher butcher. The Jewish Community Center, opened in 1946, closed in 1963.

World War II, the Holocaust and the creation of the State of Israel, were accompanied by Hadassah's American and Canadian membership increasing from 15,000 in 1925, to about 250,000 in 1948 with 977 chapters; and 300,000 in the 1950s. Hadassah also grew in political status.

Thirty Jewish women met on March 4, 1930 at the Hotel Chieftain on Pearl Street to organize a Hadassah chapter. Business meetings were accompanied by a speaker, skit or program and were held at the synagogue and Jewish Community Center.

Council Bluffs Hadassah hosted a two-day regional conference in May 1938 at the Hotel Chieftain. Delegates from Des Moines, Fort Dodge, Ottumwa, Sioux City, Tulsa, Oklahoma City, Wichita, Kansas City, St. Louis, St. Charles, St. Joseph, Denver, Lincoln and Omaha were given a tour of the Loess Hills. The Council Bluffs Mayor, President of the Chamber of Commerce, President of B'nai B'rith, and S. Shyken, the President of Chevra B'nai Yisroel Synagogue, greeted the women. Beth El Rabbi David Goldstein gave an invocation and spoke on "Our Zionist Heritage." Cantor Edgar directed the choir. Rabbi Monroe Levens of Des Moines spoke on "Soil and Soul."

Council Bluffs and Omaha, a few miles and a bridge apart, shared goals. Council Bluffs members probably used Omaha's 1928 *Hadassah Kosher Cook Book*, the first Hadassah cookbook. Council Bluffs members Mrs. Jennie (Harry) Priesman and Mrs. H. D. Marowitz contributed recipes to the 1928 book. Charitable cookbooks reveal the dining traditions, tastes, merchandising, necessities of life, housekeeping, leisure and entertainment activities and Hadassah supporters.

Council Bluffs Hadassah claimed 90 members in 1954 when two books were published; the *B'nai Israel Golden Book* which included a photograph of the 25 women Hadassah Executive Board, listed 244 adults and their 94 "Jewels," a common mid-twentieth century expression describing children. The second book was *What's Cooking in Hadassah?* Hadassah published a 44-page, unpaginated, stapled booklet in blue ink with no indication of the year of publication, copyright or printer. Like many charitable cookbooks, no library owns it. Charitable cookbooks raised money selling advertisements and the book.

Seated, left to right: Mesdames L. Frankel, S. Roffman, H. Marovitz, O. Greenberg, E. Tepperman, R. Selo. Standing, left to right: Mesdames H. Cherniss, M. Grossman, Miss Marcus, G. Braunstein, L. Binstein, L. Marcus, J. Scharf, J. Katelman, B. Gershun, L. Bernstein, M. Bobrick, G. Krasne, M. Goodman, J .J. Brown, L. Krasne, B. Telpner, V. Mashbein, S. Meyerson, A. Leibovitz. Missing from the picture: Mesdames H. Cohen, Phil Falken, D. Korb, H. Kubby, H. Krause, Al Krasne, S. Lee, L. Meyerson, R. Gordon, L. Krasne, A. Maltz, B. Passer, S. Sperling, I. Sternhill, S. Suvalsky, M. Wohlner.

Hadassah chapters raised money to support its medical mission in Israel through annual Linen Showers, sometimes held at the Lakeshore Country Club, rummage sales, selling trees for Israel and collecting the blue coin box to purchase linen supplies for hospitals in Israel. The 20 page program for "Willie," a 1950 theatrical, contained merchant advertisements. They volunteered at the Dr. Philip Sher Old Peoples' Home and the Veterans Hospital.

The first Iowa Jewish cookbook, the 100-page *Iowa City Chapter of Hadassah & Pioneer Women* cookbook, appeared between 1947 and 1951. In 1953, Beth El Jacob Synagogue in Des Moines, where Rabbi Isaac Nadoff served, produced a cookbook. Nadoff later led Omaha's Beth Israel. There are about 20 Iowa Jewish cookbooks including Hadassah in Marshalltown (1971), Cedar Rapids (1972) and Des Moines (1977).

Mrs. Oscar Greenberg was the president and Mrs. Ben Telpner edited the Cook Book. Mrs. Rose (Joe) Katelman, a founder, prepared the cover. The all-important 12-person Advertising Committee sold advertisement to merchants. Mrs. H. D. Marowitz and Mrs. Phillip Falken chaired the cook book endeavor.

The 1954 publication date is based on the introduction that noted it had been six years since the momentous founding of the State of Israel. An advertisement for a new 1955 Kelvinator refrigerator, like automobiles, probably anticipated the event by one year.

Mrs. Stella Greenberg's four paragraph, "A Message From Our President," referred to the creation of the State of Israel, the Israeli Declaration of Independence, and Hadassah's role in the health of the Middle East. Ethel Levenson in 1928 mentioned serving the health interests of Jews, Christians and Arabs. Mrs. Greenberg in 1954 did not.

ADVERTISEMENTS FOR LIVING A GOOD LIFE

COUNCIL BLUFFS: BROADWAY illustrated the street's vibrancy. Many Broadway merchants advertised in the cook book. Omaha advertisers Nebraska Furniture Mart, "The best for less," Smith Pontiac and Nogg Bros., indicates some metropolitan economic integration.

Advertisements indicate consumer patterns and economic life. Master Furniture & Appliance, owned by Marvin and Selwin Suvalsky, purchased four pages featuring the Norge gas range with infinitrol burners, and "Adjust-a-Lite" range lamp, RCA Victor Television with deep throat for $149.95 with "Golden Throat" fidelity sound!" Whirlpool washer and dryer, Universal vacuum with exclusive thread-picking nozzle and a Kelvinator refrigerator. The Music Shop at 331 W. Broadway promoted the Philco Phonorama radio.

Transportation was represented by car dealers, repair shops, auto supplies, Council Bluffs Transit Co. and Red Top Cab Co. IPALCO Iowa Power and Light Co. stood ready to give juice to all the consumer electronic products.

Mom and Pop grocery stores, bakeries, dairies and wholesalers were frequently solicited to support nonprofit and charitable groups such as churches, Boy Scouts, PTA and the like.

Many groceries were started with small loans from family, friends or loan societies. Council Bluffs included Gamble Robinson Fruit & Vegetable, Bobrick's, South Main Supermarket, Sixth Street Market, Wigwam Grocery, Owl Grocery (Nathan Richards), Nelson Grocery Co., Bruno Bros. Produce Co., F. J. Krumenacher, Jr., Meats and Groceries and Risney's Candy and Tobacco Co.

Meadow Gold Products and Roberts Milk advertised their dairy products. *Mom and Pop Grocery Stores* identified several Jewish-owned Council Bluffs grocery stores. Ideal Grocery's Max Cohn observed that "the 100 neighborhood grocery stores which once existed in Council Bluffs declined to a '"handful."' The Ideal Building sold in 1978. The small grocery store era ended in 1997 when Samuel I. Bubb closed Bubb's.

Shaver's Food Mart and Hinky Dinky Super Market, both on Broadway, also had Omaha locations. As grocery store square footage expanded into supermarkets the number of products on the shelves increased dramatically. Small stores were eclipsed by regional and national chains. Also on Broadway was Beno's "A better department store" had a long presence in downtown Council Bluffs. Three national chain variety stores advertised: S. S. Kresge Store, F. W. Woolworth and J. C. Penney Co.

Jewish advertisers included Midwest Auto Parts (Harry Kubby and Sherman Sperling), Master Furniture & Appliance (Suvalsky), Joe's Super Market (Joe Gotsdiner), Herman's Clothes Shop (Stanley Katelman), Peoples Department Store (George and Frank Krasne), Iowa Clothes Shop (Harry and Anne Cohen and Seymour Lee), Gershun Department Store (Joe and Maurice), Katelman Junk Co., Micklin Home Improvement with stores in Council Bluffs and Omaha, Richman Auto Parts (Morris Goodman), Kulesh Jewelry (Ben and Carolyn Cohen), Chris' Sportsman Shop, Continental Keller furniture, Canar Manufacturing Co. upholstered furniture and Sherman Bakery.

The services sector included home maintenance, repairs, improvement, upkeep, plumbers, electricians and labor-saving devices. Coal and oil suppliers offered to keep the household warm, dry and comfortable. Laundries and cleaners offered to lighten the household burden. Jahn Radio Co. Television Repairs & Service fixed radios with tubes.

Personal and home aesthetics were served by three cleaners, two flower and beauty shops, one photographer and one veterinarian. Seven insurance agents, eight real estate agents and five banks and savings and loan associations offered their services.

Council Bluffs, a railroad center, catered to farmers and railwaymen. Two jewelry stores offered special timekeeping requirements: Kulesh (Official Railroad Time Inspectors Since 1911) and Warford (Official RR Time Inspectors). Baird, Lucey, Ben Klein, Sessions and Iowa Jewelry served local needs. Larry Roffman,

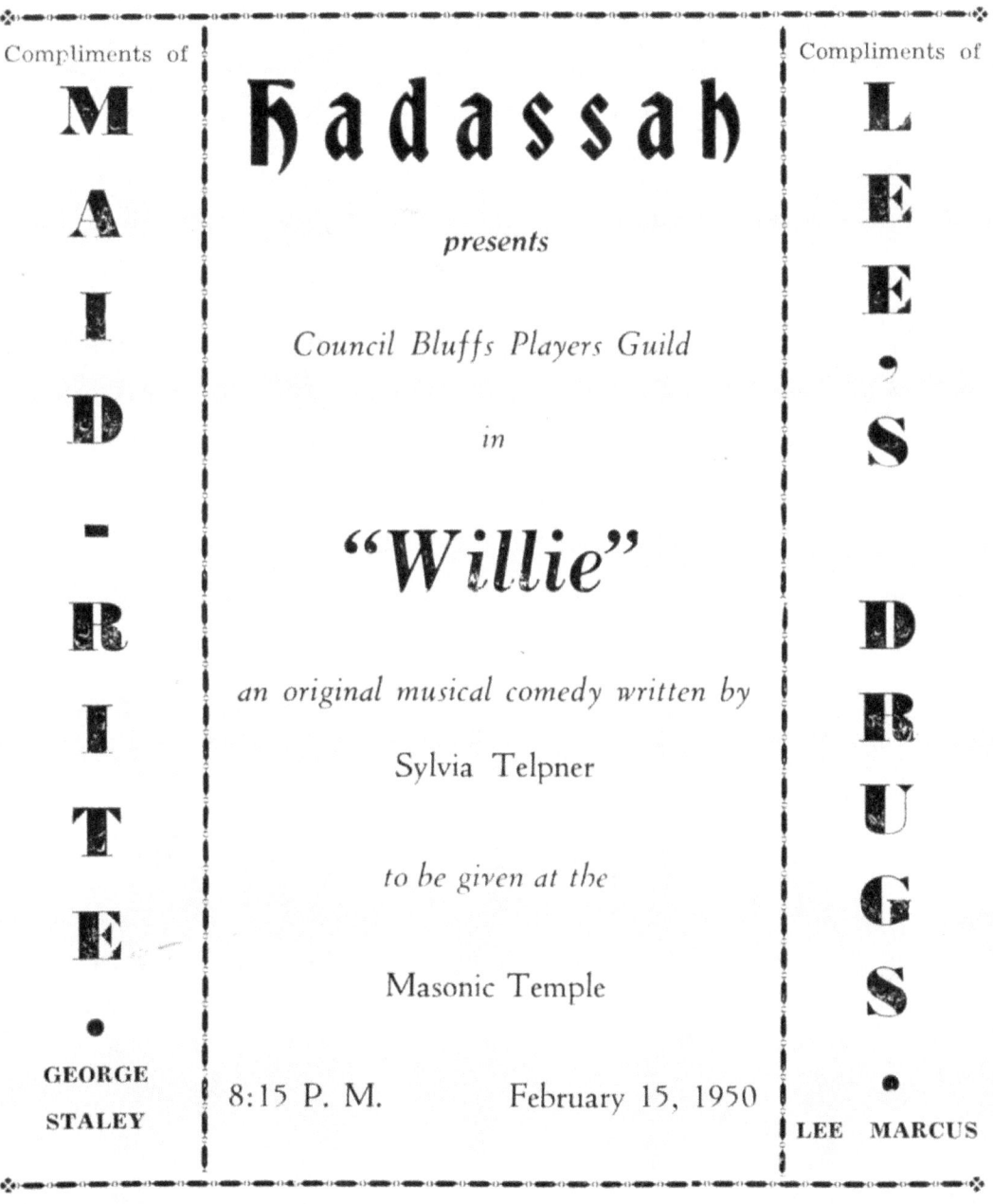

whose father Sam had a grocery store, stated, "Our biggest accounts were the railroad workers from the Burlington, Chicago Western and Union Pacific." Younkerman Seed Co., founded in 1891, and Earl May, supplied farmers and gardeners. Ainsworth Printing, Emarines and Farmer-Labor Press advertised, perhaps they printed Bar and Bat Mitzvah and wedding invitations.

Forty-eight doctors were grouped together on four pages with perfunctory greetings of support: "Compliments of," "Best wishes from," and "Good luck." There were drug stores: Joe's Service Drug Store, Taffe Drug Company, Lane Bros. Pharmacy, Frank Street Pharmacy, Keleher Pharmacy and Clark Drug Co., as well as Cogley Clinic, Maico Council Bluffs Company (hearing aids) and Shipley Optical Dispensary, at least five of which were on Broadway. Henry Meyer Mortuary and Sheely & Lane, Monuments and Markers Broadway supplied end of life arrangements.

Hotels and restaurants provided residents and visitors hospitality. The eight story, 300-room Hotel Chieftain and The Ogden, "Comfortable since 1869," were the leading establishments. Club 64 promoted itself as "The Midwest's Finest Steak House,." Ambassador Lounge, Maid-Rite Loose Meat Sandwich (an Iowa institution), Wimpy's Tavern, Johnnie's Café, Lane's Café and Nesbitt's Twin City Bottling, makers of Orange Crush, all advertised. Only the Council Bluffs Wholesale Beer Distributors ad referred to alcohol. The state of Iowa ran retail liquor sales, grocery stores sold only beer. No recipes called for alcohol.

Hadassah

GREETINGS AND SALUTATIONS

Numerous supporters purchased one-inch greeting blocks. Like the doctors, they expressed "Best wishes" and "Compliments of" to Hadassah. Among the Jewish salutations were:

Julius Barron	Lee Morris
Max Cohn	Joe Passer
Sam Eveloff	Louis Passer
Phillip Falken	S. Roffman
D. Fox	Sam Sacks
Richard Gordon	Charles Saltzman
Abe Katelman	Sam Saltzman
Lou Katelman	Dr R. A. Selo
Edna Kline	S. Shyken
Milton M. Krasne	J. Siegel
Toby Krasne	George Steinberg
Herman Krause	Max Steinberg
Mr. & Mrs. Leo Meyerson	Nathan Steinberg
Meyer Meyerson	Eddie H. Tepperman
Sam Meyerson	M. Wohlner

RECIPES

The immigrant, traditional European Jewish and Kosher dishes with varying spellings and humorous typos, were generally homemade. There were 46 Jewish recipes and 69 from a wider culinary culture. Ninety-six recipes were signed, and nineteen anonymous and unattributed.

Jewish fare included old-fashioned meat *kreplach*, *pitcha* (jellied calves feet), sweet and sour meat (*esseck fleish*), stuffed *miltz* (spleen), stuffed *kishke*, noodle pudding (*kugel*), lung, Lima bean *tsimis*, *flomen tsimis*, liver and rice ring, cabbage rolls, borscht, Hungarian Goulash, egg *kichlich* (cookie), *kashe*, *taiglech* (dough cooked in honey), *blintzs*, potato kugel, gefilte fish, pickled herring with sour cream and two recipes for poppy seed cookies and one for poppy seed cake.

Jewish holidays included matzo balls, Passover burnt sugar cake, two more Passover cake recipes, matzo pudding, a dish for Yom Kippur, *hamantaschen*, *mandel brot* and *mandel bread*, honey cake and potato *latkes*. Mrs. Cele (Max) Moscovitz furnished a recipe for bagels. There may have been some playful competition; Mrs. Maynard Telpner provided a recipe for pizza and Mrs. Ben Telpner proffered Easy Pizza which used English muffins.

The dishes were very 1950s: caesar salad, skillet burger balls, Spanish grill, chicken creole, Italian spaghetti, Hawaiian chicken salad (Hawaii became a state in 1959), three dishes with pineapples, tuna and Chinese noodles and chop suey.

RECIPE CONTRIBUTORS

FORTY-SEVEN INDIVIDUALS signed their recipes. President Greenberg submitted the most. With the exception of two single women, all the contributors were identified as "Mrs." followed by their husband's first name. Many of these women were kin by blood or marriage. For example, the Shapiros were related to the Telpner and Meiches family. Many of them were members and officers of B'nai Israel, Sisterhood, the *Golden Book* committee and B'nai B'rith (The number following the name indicates the number of recipes contributed):

Bella Alper
C. H. Amick
Harry L. Cherniss
Harry Cohen 2
Lillian Cohen
R. Cohen
Doris Cohn 2-Ideal Grocery-Max
Harold Finkel 2
Leon Frankel
Lena Gotsdiner
Dave Greenberg
Oscar Greenberg 9
Stella Greenberg 2
E. Hertzman
Jack Kahane
J. Katelman
George Krasne
Lawrence Krasne
Lloyd Krasne –Bubb's- Edythe
Harry Kubby
A. Leibowitz 6
Milton Loss
Harry Matas
Herbert Meiches 3

Cele (Max) Moskovitz
Chick Perlis
Ernest Priesman 4
Harry Priesman
Mrs. Jennie Priesman
Justen Priesman
Allan Pullmer
Ruben Ratner 2
Ida Robinson 2
Sam Roffman
Ella Scharf 3
Irene Selo
Audrey R. (Morris J.) Shapiro 7
J. Shukett
Sherman Sperling
Mable Stewart 3
Harold Stieman 2
Max Stieman 2
George Steinberg 3
Ben Telpner 5
Gene Telpner 4
Sally Telpner
Joe Wiesenthal

At least 15 of the 47 contributors have memorial plaques at B'nai Israel.

CONCLUSION

MRS. BEN TELPNER, the editor, concluded: "The publication of this first issue of Hadassah Cook Book was made possible by your interest and desire to assist in helping an independent and economically sound democracy in the Middle East." She signed it, "Happy Eating." It proved to be the first and last cookbooks; democracy in the Middle East is still problematic.

The Council Bluffs Jewish community dwindled. The last full-time rabbi, David Korb, left in 1969. Part time, short term seminary students and lay leadership kept the door open. Jewish children acquired education and went into the professions. The population gravitated to Omaha, Kansas City, Chicago, Denver and Los Angeles.

Hadassah, 72-years-old, held its final meeting presided over by the President, Mrs. Sally (Maynard) Telpner and Vice President, Mrs. Edythe (Lloyd) Krasne at the Lakeshore Country Club on May 29, 2002. Council Bluffs Hadassah dissolved. The cookbook is a remnant of a once-vital community.

End of An Era, The Daily Nonpareil, 2002

End of an era

Jewish group to fold after 72 years

TIM JOHNSON
Staff Writer

After 72 years of operation, the Council Bluffs Chapter of Hadassah is disbanding.

The group, part of the Women's Zionist Organization of America, will have its final meeting Thursday at noon at Lakeshore Country Club, vice president Edythe Krasne said. Members will then become part of the organization's Omaha Chapter.

Officers are disappointed that the chapter is folding but feel the time has come, President Sally Telpner said.

"The problem is, there's only three or four of us left that do it all," she said. "It's just gotten to be too much for four people."

Hadassah is the only Jewish organization left in Council Bluffs, except for the B'nai Israel Synagogue, Krasne said.

Besides Telpner and Krasne, active members include Lee Eveloff, who has served as treasurer for 22 years, and Recording Secretary Flora Telpner. Ida Perlis, another key person, moved away last month. This summer, Telpner and her husband, Maynard, will move to Oregon to be closer to their children and grandchildren.

Although the chapter technically has 22 members, many have moved away – some to Omaha, Telpner said.

"The other ones don't even come to the meetings much," she said.

"It's disheartening when we have to ask our non-Jewish friends and our relatives from Omaha to come to our meetings," Krasne said.

Hadassah International is an organization for Jewish women that helps support health, education, growth and social action and advocacy programs and publishes a magazine and religious materials. The group raises funds for the Hadassah Medical Organization, Hadassah College of Technology and Hadassah Career Counseling Institute, all in Jerusalem; development projects in Israel, international disaster relief, youth programs, English and Hebrew tutoring and other programs.

The Council Bluffs Chapter was organized in 1930 by Rose Katelman, Betty Sternhill and Jennie Marowitz, Krasne said. Meetings were held at the Chieftain Hotel and later at the B'nai Israel Synagogue.

The group held linen shows, fun nights and other fund-raisers and later published an advertising book, she said. That was eventually replaced by a fund-raising letter.

"The linen show is, we give money for the hospital for all the baby clothes and gowns – everything that's linen in the hospital," she said.

"They used to make them here in Council Bluffs at meetings, but it got to be too much to ship it," Telpner said.

Fun nights offered food, skits and other entertainment, Krasne said.

"We used to always serve kosher hot dogs and chips, and we had a lot of fun," she said.

Sylvia Telpner used to write and direct skits, which people paid to see.

"One time many, many years ago, we formed a choir, and we performed for one of the Hadassah conventions that was held at the Chieftain Hotel, Krasne said.

The concert provided more comic relief than divine inspiration, she said.

"That was the only performance of the choir," she said. "It was not very good."

For many years, the chapter sold advertisements for an ad book published annually, Telpner said. That was eventually replaced with a fund-raising letter.

"Businesses have been very supportive," she said.

Staff photo/Tim Johnson
Vice President Edythe Krasne and President Sally Telpner of the Council Bluffs Chapter of Hadassah display a Hadassah banner. The local chapter will hold its last meeting Thursday.

In recent years, the chapter has prepared a table for the Table for All Seasons benefit for the women's organization at First Congregational Church, Krasne said.

"They help us out," she said. "They always send us a check every year to thank us."

Over the years, the chapter's numbers have dwindled, Telpner said. Meetings were reduced to two a year.

"We lost our woman power," she said. "They started getting older."

Younger generations of the families already here have moved away, and few Jewish families have moved to the city, Krasne said.

"We've been able to keep going here because of the wonderful community of Council Bluffs," Telpner said.

"Council Bluffs has always been very good to the Jewish people," Krasne said.

The final meeting will feature a movie clip of a musical performed at a chapter fundraiser in approximately 1950 in the former Danish Hall at Fourth Street and West Broadway, Krasne said. The drama was written and directed by Sylvia Telpner and choreographed by Joan Leavitt.

"It's a clip of the dress rehearsal," she said.

Those interested may make reservations by calling Telpner at 322-5607 or Krasne at 323-9172.

Irving Cohen in uniform, 1944

SECOND LIEUTENANT IRVING COHEN

Irving Cohen was a man of valor. The son of Harry and Anne Cohen was a Council Bluffs boy who risked, and lost, his life in battle. Like most of his fellow Jewish contemporaries, Irving attended Hebrew School at B'nai Israel. After his death, B'nai Brith dedicated The Irving Cohen Lodge, a room located downstairs in the *shul* where a photograph of Second Lieutenant Cohen is displayed to the left of the lectern, offering congregants and Friday night service-goers a reminder of the hero who was once an integral part of the Jewish community.

A graduate of Abraham Lincoln High School, in 1941, Irving attended the University of Nebraska in Lincoln where he pledged ZBT fraternity. There, he befriended Harold Bernstein –– his best buddy and surrogate brother who still recalls Irving with great affection –– Norman Smeerin, Stuart Simon, Bud Studna, Norman Rips and Irving Malashock.

During his senior year of college, Irving enlisted in the U.S. Army Air Corps. He trained at several flight schools in California, including Morton Air Academy, graduated as a B-17 pilot and attended advanced school at Marpha, Texas, becoming a Second Lieutenant. In October of 1944, Second Lieutenant Cohen was stationed with the Eighth Air Force in Europe. One month later, on November 25, while on his 15th bombing mission over Germany, the B-17 he was piloting was shot down.

For over one year, his parents friends and family held out hope Irving was alive. Yet a letter from the U.S. government would arrive, stating a presumption of death dated November 26, 1945. A second letter followed: at the request of President Truman, Second Lieutenant Irving Cohen was awarded posthumously the Purple Heart for giving his life in defense of his country. His grave site is at Ardennes American Cemetery in Neuville-en-Condroz, Belgium.

THE SELDIN FAMILY

The Seldins' immigration story echoes those of Eastern European Jews who braved uncertainty for a better life. In 1913, Ben I. Seldin emigrated at the age of 16 to America from *Mozer*, Russia, somewhere near *Minsk* and *Pinsk* along a river. "His older brother Eli had come to Omaha ahead of him, working at the Union Pacific yards in Omaha for 25 cents an hour and provided money to bring his brother to the U.S.," says Ted. "My father was one of the Jews who didn't immigrate through Ellis Island, but instead through Galveston, TX. He never talked a lot about the old country except I understand my grandfather was a merchant there in the *shtetl*."

Originally, Ben – whose last name in Russia was *Zeldin* – arrived in Omaha on Easter in 1913 during one of the great tornadoes of the time. "Someone from the *shtetl* had a relative who owned a grocery store which was later known as Rosen's Frank Street Market at Frank Street and Broadway in east Council Bluffs. At first, to the best of my knowledge, my father lived behind the store with a job of delivering groceries by horse and wagon in the area, including along a creek which became Forest Drive."

The teenage Russian immigrant became an American businessman as others had, earning his way from the bottom up, learning English in night school at Boyle's College at 8th and Broadway in Council Bluffs.

At the start of World War I, Ben enlisted in the Army where he served at Fort Omaha, home of the Balloon Corps, and thereby attained his citizenship. While in the Army, he met Bertha Jacobson, an émigré from Loon, Sweden whom he married after discharge. The family eventually included four children: Ruth, married to Bernard Raskin; Norma, married to Stanley Silverman; Millard, married to Beverly; and Ted, whose wife is Sarah.

Initially, after Army service, like many Jewish immigrants, Ben had a small grocery store on Broadway in Council Bluffs. However, in 1923, he became an independent life insurance agent and started selling small debit policies for Metropolitan Life, with premiums of 25 cents a week. Later, he became an agent for John Hancock Insurance Company and continued growing his agency from life insurance to all types of insurance. When making calls in small nearby towns, he would also solicit contributions for the Council Bluffs Jewish Federation.

"I would ride with him to places like the Missouri Valley, Glenwood, Walnut and Hamburg. Marty Ricks, who grew up in the Missouri Valley, once told me, 'Did you know your father sold my father two insurance policies which provided funds for me to go to college?'"

In the late 1930s, Ben obtained his Iowa real estate license and began selling homes and commercial real estate in Council Bluffs. "There had been no new home construction during WWII because all materials were going towards the war effort. In the early '40s, he realized there would be a need for housing for returning G.I.'s," Ted says.

In 1945, Ben began home building by constructing a prefabricated home as a method to get available materials for construction. When Millard was discharged from the Navy in 45 or 46, he joined his father in the home building and development business in Council Bluffs and Omaha while obtaining his business degree at the University of Iowa. Stan Silverman, after returning from Navy duty, began doing part-time accounting and later joined the firm full-time.

The first three Seldin children were born in the '20s, and Ted in 1931. All four grew up in Council Bluffs and graduated from Abraham Lincoln High School. According to Ted, Ben and Bertha encouraged their children to get the maximum education. As Ben was building his insurance agency, the family lived in various houses in the Bluffs. Ted was born at 611 Oakland Drive in the shadow of the Lincoln Monument. Nearby were the family homes of Sam Meyerson, Richard Gordon, and the Sam Sacks family. Sam and Ida Sacks's son Ken and Ted played together as youngsters and became close friends over the years. When Ken Sacks became an attorney, he would represent the Seldin family firm.

In 1944, Ben and Bertha bought a home at 510 Forest Drive -- in the neighborhood which had been Ben's goal while delivering groceries in the area -- and later built two new homes on Forest Drive. In 1949, they built a home next to Leo Meyerson's family on that street. Other families on Forest Drive included the Ben Gershun family, the Sam Roffman family and Dr. Isaac ("Ike") Sternhill, the highly-respected doctor in Council Bluffs.

"When anybody didn't feel well, he was there," Ted says . "During house calls, he would patiently listen and talk, which was a great comfort. The city of Council Bluffs honored him by naming a park after him, Sternhill Park on north Eighth Street."

Back in the '30s and '40s, B'nai Israel synagogue flourished. As a homemaker, Bertha Seldin participated in Hadassah and *shul* activities. Ben, like other active male congregants including Simon Shyken and Abe Katelman, took his turn as President. In the early years, families were located in close proximity to the synagogue and in traditional fashion of the time, would walk together to and from *shul*, but that later changed. When the Hebrew School expanded, Ben supervised the construction of the educational wing which still stands.

Encouraged by their parents, Council Bluffs kids attended *cheder*, *shul* and Sunday School where the boys were sometimes less than angelic in class. Through the years, there was a succession of rabbis and Hebrew school teachers. Some of Ted's classmates included Marvin Suvalsky, Don Nogg, Sam Fried, Stanley Davidson, Larry Roffman, Leslie Krasne and Ken Sacks. Like the rest of the community, Ted's family would attend services on High Holidays. When he was Bar Mitzvahed in 1944, Ted recalls in his speech, he expressed concern for the safety of his brother and all who were serving in the military at the time, including Millard who was in the Navy, Stan Silverman, sister Norma's husband and sister Ruth's husband Bernie Raskin who served in the Army in Europe.

"The community had a strong commitment to Jewish activities and it carried over to all of us," Ted says. In the '40s, the Council Bluffs Jewish Federation purchased a large house on South 8th Street which became the Jewish Community Center where B'nai B'rith and other groups would gather. The younger generation joined AZA #7, a B'nai B'rith Youth group which participated in various events and athletic competitions at the Omaha JCC and across Iowa.

Over time, contemporaries of Ted who were also AZA #7 members included Leslie Krasne, Ken Sacks, Larry and Bud Roffman, "Boonjug" Telpner, Sam Fried, Stanley Davidson and his brother Gilbert, Marvin Suvalsky, Stanley Richards, Milton Brown, Milton Gordon, Bud Katelman, Jerry Passer and David Bear. In the '40s, they participated in Omaha JCC sporting events such as softball and basketball.

"Our softball team played in the Omaha JCC league at Elmwood Park on Sunday mornings. Leslie Krasne's family owned a big Pierce Arrow automobile. On Sunday morning, Les would start in east Council Bluffs, picking up the rest of the members as he headed west to Elmwood Park, arriving just in time for our 9:30 deadline to play AZA #1 and other teams. If we didn't get there on time we forfeited. We had all nine of us in that Pierce Arrow, so we didn't have to forfeit."

Ben Seldin was highly involved in both the Jewish and business communities, like dozens of other Jewish families who owned and operated businesses which earned respect in the Jewish and larger community. "The community supported the Jewish retail stores," says Ted. "The Morris Passer family each owned grocery stores, one of which was on North 8th Street just down the street from where I was born. As a kid, I would go there and if I had a penny, I'd buy candy."

Downtown were Sam Sacks's and Sam Roffman's grocery stores. Richard Gordon's grocery store was on North 8th Street, while Phil Sacks' grocery was located at 20th and Broadway. On the south side were Sam Bubb's and Lou Passer's grocery stores. In west Council Bluffs were grocery stores owned by the Davidsones, the Frieds, the Gotsdiners, the Cohens and Joe Passer.

Ted recalls other Jewish-owned businesses which had a loyal following within the greater community. The Peoples Store was a sprawling department store owned by the Krasne and Bernstein families where customers shopped for everything from hardware to suits to toys. Iowa Clothes Men's Shop was owned by Harry and Ann Cohen. "Harry and his wife Anne were highly respected and were very helpful to customers when they had recessionary problems," Ted says.

Other downtown Council Bluffs businesses on Broadway included Goodman Auto Parts and Kubby's Auto Parts (West Broadway); Harry Kutler's Open Front Bargain Center; Continental Keller furniture company, located across from The

Peoples Store; Lena and Morris Grossman's general store; Herman Kraus's The Bargain Spot; and two jewelry stores, Brodkey's and the Kuleshes.'

"Lou and Rose Katelman had a hardware store. When Lou passed away, Rose worked for years with her daughter Sissy. If anybody needed a special item of hardware, they could find it with Rose and Sissy."

Jewish politicians included Joe Katelman, a partner in Katelman Brothers scrap metal business. Joe was first a councilman, then mayor of Council Bluffs. "He had a very strong influence and a strong personality. The city's swimming pool in south Council Bluffs, Katelman Pool, is named after him," Ted says. Maynard Telpner, a well-known, long-time practicing attorney was also a city councilman and later became mayor. Attorney Ken Sacks won recognition as the first Jewish attorney elected County Attorney in Pottawatamie, Iowa -- the same day Kennedy was elected. There were also "very capable attorneys" like Ben Kubby, who originally practiced law in the Bluffs and, upon moving to Des Moines, became a magistrate in the Des Moines Court system. Both Ben and Millard Seldin served on the Council Bluffs City Planning Commission.

The major entertainment of the time, of course, was listening to the radio. "Sunday night programs included Jack Benny, Bob Hope and Fibber McGee and Molly. Phil Harris and his band, 'Band of Renown,' played big band music. When I was old enough I'd listen to Nebraska football games on KFAB. The first time I watched TV was as a freshman at the University of Iowa in '49 or '50, on a black-and-white small screen."

Upon graduating in May, 1955 with degrees in economics and a JD in Law, Ted passed the bar exam in June. In July, he immediately went on active duty in the Air Force, serving as assistant Judge Advocate at the 163rd Troop Carrier Wing, during which time he was admitted to the U.S. Court of Military Appeals

In 1956, Ted married Sarah Nadler from Waterloo, Iowa and later the couple had two daughters, Stephanie and Beth. In 1957, upon separation from the military, Ted joined the family business. The Seldin firm built several hundred single-family homes in Council Bluffs and in West Omaha as it developed Westwood communities between 120th to 132nd and Center. In 1966, the firm built and managed the first

Howard Johnson's west of the Mississippi at 35th and Broadway. Subsequently, the firm built and operated hotels in Omaha, Des Moines and Wichita. They have built over 4,000 houses in Council Bluffs, Omaha and nearby communities and now manage apartments across eight states.

Because the Seldin family had a strong sense of Judaism, they were active members of the Jewish communities in Council Bluffs and Omaha. In the 80s, Ken Sacks and Ted were asked by Abe Katelman, who at that time managed the Council Bluff's Bikur Cholim/Oakhill Cemetery, to aid him in continuing management of the cemetery. Ken updated the non-profit corporation status and re-organized its records. Subsequently, Bob Kully and Ted met and addressed the need for two separate cemetery associations. Ultimately, the Orthodox and Reform associations were merged with the burial rules remaining the same for each section.

"In order to ensure the adequacy of the perpetual care fund, Patty Nogg's mother Betty and other Council Bluffs women compiled a mailing list of families interred at the cemetery and created a letter-writing campaign to raise money for the fund to ensure it was properly maintained. Under Iowa law, if a cemetery is not properly maintained with a perpetual care fund, it can become a municipal cemetery, which the Jewish community would not allow. Now we have a good operating perpetual care fund. When viewing the cemetery, one finds much of the history of Council Bluffs Jewery."

The Council Bluffs' Jewish community reflected the larger story of America's Jewish immigrants who upended their lives for a promising future in a foreign land. Over time, this western Iowa Jewish community gained the respect of each other and the greater community. "Members of the Jewish community had an impact on Council Bluffs." Now? Memories linger, time passes, generations give way to the next. It was realized it was important to record history.

Says Ted: "It's a matter of preserving history while there are those here to tell their stories."

7. Photo of Ted Seldin's family, 1979. Ted and Sarah with daughters, Stephanie (left) and Beth

8. Ted Seldin

DOUG AND GAIL KRASNE

Joey: Gail, Doug, let's start with an easy question. When were you born?

Gail: September 21st, 1951.

Doug: And I'm June 6th, 1953.

Joey: Your baby brother!

Gail: He's still getting counseling about that.

Doug: The biggest part of my early childhood was getting the crap scratched out of me by Gail! And when she had no fingernails and they put tape over them, she still scratched me! It was awful!

Gail: He was so annoying.

Doug: No I wasn't!

Gail: Yes you were.

Doug: Susan, our sister, left me in a baby carriage when I was just a baby in the driveway in the summer to go play next door with her friend, because Mom was inside doing God only knows what, but not having anything [sniffs] to do with me! [laughs]. Gail would get up in the morning when she was five, make herself a peanut butter sandwich, put it in a paper bag and say, "I'm going up the hill to play!" And I'd run out after her going "Me too!" She would go 22 steps and then lose me! I had to learn my way around the neighborhood at a young age or I'd need bread crumbs in my pocket! She'd make me crazy if I wanted to follow her, so I'd go find somebody and I'd play.

Gail: The neighborhood, Kenmore and Keeline on the East End of Council Bluffs, was full of kids. A lot of Jewish people.

Doug: There was a place my daughter lives built by Ben Seldin, a Jewish man who built most of those houses. There were tons of post-WWII families who moved into that little valley there because then the veterans came back, got married, had kids and needed houses. And we had a lot of industrialization for the war, so we turned our industrial capacity towards building houses.

Dad grew up in Council Bluffs. His Mom died when he was eight of appendicitis (she got it, it burst, the doctor was on vacation and the infection killed her. Her name was Blanche). So Dad's father Harry was left with three boys and two grocery stores, and didn't know what to do with himself.

Joey: His dad started grocery stores?

Doug: Yes, but not the one Dad was in; that was my mother's father. They were all in the grocery business. And then Grandpa in the Depression overreached, got into trouble, lost his stores and ultimately ended up buying one in Audubon, IA.

Joey: What was Grandpa's store in the Bluffs?

Doug: I think it was the Peoples Store originally, because the one in Audubon was The Peoples Store.

Gail: He went out long before the Peoples Store, which was the department store, came about.

Joey: How are you related?

Doug: Dad's great-grandfather was brother to The Peoples Store. Krasnes Grandpa moved to Audubon and Dad was in his teens. He went there for a while and then he came back to live with Aunt Esther, my grandpa Bubb's sister, and Uncle Max and finished high school here.

The community was very strong back then. First there was the Jewish community, and then there was the grocery, retail and wholesale business within the Jewish community. The Jewish community was strong because, as many immigrants have to deal with, particularly ones who aren't assimilated as easily because they're different, they bonded. Then there's this subset of grocers. Retailers were the same way -- the Iowa Clothes people and the Peoples Store people and Mrs. B at Nebraska Furniture Mart -- they had a tendency to be close as well.

So Dad comes back from the war and what happens? The Jewish community Uncle Max Cohn talks to some people, Grandpa Bubb talks to some people, other people who know the family talk to some people and before you know it Dad has a job with the food wholesalers. He's doing this, making money, and now Susan comes along; then Grandpa came to him one day and said, "I'm getting older, want to come into the store with me?" Who wouldn't? He knew Grandpa, the nicest guy in the world. This is gonna be great!

Gail: And they had a very strong, blue-collar neighborhood. Many of those constituents were railroad families with a steady income. You knew a stream of people would be going through. People were loyal to the neighborhood communities.

Doug: Dad was wrapped up in the store, and God love him; he would go down there at 7:30 every morning, close at 6:30 every night and get home at 7. I worked there starting at 10, so I saw what went on. It was the Lloyd Krasne Social Club.

Joey: How observant was your family?

Gail: The older folks were Orthodox: Esther and Max Cohn, and the grandparents Bubb. For the holidays they went to B'nai Israel in Council Bluffs. We had large, extended family gatherings for the high holidays and Passover. Seders were so long I was ready to knock my plate off the table! "For the love of God, can't we have something to eat?!"

Doug: The *seder* was the only time during the year I got to stay up past 10 because it ran so damned long! We didn't begin eating dinner till nine or 10! I'm a five-year-old kid going, "You've got to be kidding! I'm starving here, guys! Give me a matzah or something!" We had a long *Haggadah* and they did it in Hebrew!

Gail: When they were gone and it was our family, Dad did the Maxwell House coffee 10 minute *seder*. So we went from hours and hours to, "OK, they were oppressed, people were pissed, they had a battle, we won! Eat some matzah, some gefilte fish a boiled egg, now EAT!"

Doug: When the older generation beyond Mom and Dad started to die, that's when we went to Dad's version of Haggadah Lite. And it really was. It was all about getting to the matzo ball soup! Don't screw with me, I want to eat!

Gail: Four questions! Why? Why? Why? Why?

Doug: Dad led it like a band leader as he got older! "All right Gail, take it away!" But he'd skip a bunch if he was hungry that year.

Gail: "We're going to leave pages 13 and 14 out and go to page 50!"

Joey: So when they all passed away, you guys took the reins.

Doug: It's become very different. Our grandparents and Esther and Max Cohn were the anchors. Nobody argued. If they said they were having dinner for the high holidays, you didn't say, "Crap, we were going to go out with friends." You showed up. When Esther and Max got older and Grandma and Grandpa got older and passed away, the connecting glue wasn't there anymore.

The further you get from the old country and the mores...and part of it is modern society. I don't think it's all, "Gee, we don't care as much about family as our parents did." I think it's that nobody moved away from the family when my dad's generation grew up and we are much more mobile as a society now.

Joey: Absolutely. So tell me, what was Hebrew School and your Bar and Bat Mitzvahs like?

Gail: The laypeople taught! Friends of our parents! Frieda Suvalsky, Benny Schneider, Helen Finkel, Joel's mother. Betty Lee, Patty Nogg's mom. I think the rabbis in today's universe realize that we don't have robust members of Jewish families that belong to the synagogues, and they have to do a really stellar job of connecting with these kids and making what they learn in religious school relevant. You know, give them that feeling of, "I'm going to be a Jew in my life. I'm going to practice, contribute."

Doug: My Bar Mitzvah service was at B'nai Israel, but there was no rabbi. My rabbi was from Beth El, because I went over to him. I had a tape player that was this big reel-to-reel, the size of this damn table. I'd listen to it over and over at 40 Kenmore where we grew up, night after night, with a pair of headphones listening to that rabbi sing my *Haftarah* portion because although we knew some Hebrew, we were not fluent.

Gail: And being Orthodox, everything was in Hebrew.

Doug: There was a rabbi when we were small.

Gail: Rabbi Korb, then Rabbi Karzan.

Doug: That was it. I thought he was there because we didn't have enough money to pay him. There weren't enough people left.

Gail: When you look at this robust group when we were growing up, by the time we got to middle school, I'd say we were down to a third of the numbers. They moved to Omaha or went away. In Omaha you had a choice of Conservative, Orthodox and Reform.

Doug: And multiple synagogues.

Gail: They had a true program where we had a smaller community.

Doug: Mom and Dad didn't have any, what I would say, super-religious, deep-seated feelings. They weren't like Esther and Max or that generation. They were Jewish, but I think they were more Jewish by birth than they were by practicing.

Gail: Although the social organizations, like B'nai B'rith, Dad was President and Mom was President of Hadassah.

Doug: Multiple times.

Joey: Why do you think that was?

Doug: Community.

Gail: A lot of Judaism is social interaction. It's the religious faith, but it's also that social connection.

Doug: Judaism is clearly a religion, but even more so in my mind, it's a culture. The things I knew about my parents and grandparents and our relatives, and the sense of community we had as a kid, it's very hard to recapture that. We were a small group of people living amongst a much larger, secular society who were all different than us.

I remember going with my grandfather and my uncle Max to *minyans* when I was five in the basement of the old B'nai Israel synagogue. What child willingly goes there? I remember the collegial atmosphere of those men their age. The *davening*, the *tallits* over your head and the *tefillin* on your arm…I always wondered how any of those guys were doing the same thing because it never sounded like it. It was like they were all in their own little world and they'd say, "I'll go talk to God the way I want to, you do it on your own terms."

There would be this constant hum, and then I remember how after it was over there were handshakes and hugs amongst this group of older men. I could never completely get my arms around it. And of course, I'd go to Forbes Bakery with Grandpa and Uncle Max in Max's big Buick.

Gail: That was a bakery in Omaha.

Doug: Grandpa and Uncle Max would buy bagels, challah and rye bread, and then they'd buy pastrami, corned beef and tongue. Then we'd go back to Esther's house and everybody would come. Dad would come back from the store because he worked Sunday mornings, and we'd all sit down and eat. But I didn't need to because I was with Grandpa and Max and they'd eat a bag of warm bagels between them on the way home!

I will tell you the real reason I went to *minyans*, not because I wanted to see these guys with *tallits* on their head who looked like Casper the Friendly Ghost! I mean, it was interesting, but I can still close my eyes and smell the fresh bagels cooking and the corned beef and pastrami and chopped liver in the meat market. I can hear the old Eastern European Jewish women come in no taller than my grandma at 4'10 and scare the absolute crap out of the butchers by pointing at them going, *"I vant ze corned beef! I don't vant ze FATTY MEAT on ze top, I vant ze good stuff on ze bottom. GIVE ME THAT NOW!"*

It was like a floor show! I absolutely adored it. I couldn't wait because there were women I started to recognize in there and it was going to be a show! I guarantee you they made the butcher show them each layer as they sliced it! And if you put any fat on it, "THROW THAT CRAP AWAY! YOU GIVE ME THE LEAN ONE!" And they'd make them go in and go to the middle! Sometimes they had to cut a corned beef in half to get to the thick layer without the fat.

Joey: A cardiologist's nightmare. So what was Mom's cooking like?

Doug: Mom didn't like to cook. To her, spaghetti was Chef Boyardee and that was fancy.

Gail: And we had a schedule! Monday was fried chicken, Tuesday was pot roast…

Doug: No seasoning. Never any sauce. If she made Chinese…

Gail: Flick, into the pan.

Doug: Chung King canned noodles! She'd boil Uncle Ben's minute rice, have Dad bring home sirloin that she'd fry in a pan with nothing, pour the rice and the meat and noodles together and dribble soy sauce on it! I thought, "Why does everybody think Chinese food is so good? It's bland!"

Joey: For a Jewish kid not to know good Chinese food?!

Doug: Well, my dad didn't like that stuff. We went to steak houses. Period. We ate at the 64 Club off Highway 6. It was run by an Italian guy everybody knew was connected to the mafia.

Joey: Oy! How did growing up Jewish in Council Bluff influence you?

Gail: The roots were an anchor. No matter how you practice in your adult life, the rich memories…

Doug: And the sense of morals.

Gail: And the family gatherings at Esther and Max's, Grandma and Grandpa's and the cast of characters from the Old Country with their accents.

Doug: They all had them!

Joey: Where were they from?

Gail: Russia/Lithuanian area.

Doug: At Gail's son Eddie's graduation at Ithaca College, Ben Stein did the commencement address. He said, "When you're done with this, don't worry about finding your job or your career. Go find your parents and your grandparents and hug and kiss them because you stand on their shoulders." I think what my grandparents did in coming over here, not speaking the language, they were kids when they came here. Everything that we're able to do: my ability to complain about my situation or my government, my ability to start businesses, to raise my kids.

Everything I have, no matter what my dad or mom did or didn't do, is completely dependent on those people. We don't think about that often enough, and it's not just them. It's this extended family Gail and I had growing up. The people who weren't related to us at all, like the Cohens, Harry and Annie Cohen. These people were like our grandparents. They lived up the hill -- two nicest people I've ever met in my life.

Gail: Harry would stick his false teeth out.

Doug: In *schul*!

Gail: I'd get hysterical and then I'd get in trouble for laughing!

Doug: He'd get us in trouble for doing it and then he'd turn around and grin at us! But he was so adorable! So we're the benefactors, and I told this to our kids: none of us is responsible for all the successes we have, or for everything we're able to do or the lives we live. We are at some level, but at a great level everyone else who came before us is responsible. And all these people cared about us.

Not even just Jewish people. We had a whole range of people in our neighborhood who watched out for us and were nice to us and helped us and cared. And if there's anything that growing up in our family, and growing up Jewish meant was that feeling of extended community. I feel like we've lost that to some extent and I don't think just Jews experience it, but Italians, French and Germans. We just don't pay enough attention to our families and we forget what came before us.

Gail: But I also think we were a focused nuclear group during that era. The immigrants settled in that cluster of love and support for each other and we're a global society today.

Joey: It was all about family because it had to be.

Doug: That was the only way you could be sure you wouldn't starve to death!

Joey: And your neighborhood?

Gail: When we were all little we lived in the same neighborhood, Kenmore.

Doug: Kenmore and Keeline were two streets next to each other that were the two big Jewish enclaves in Council Bluffs. Patty Nogg's parents and grandparents lived on the same street. So Patty and Judy and her brother Pete grew up there.

Gail: There had to be 10 Jewish families on these two streets.

Doug: The mayor, Joe Katelman, all three Suvalskys…

Gail: Mashbeins…

Doug: Finkels, Cohns…

Gail: The Bubbs.

Doug: Krasnes, Max Cohn, Benny Schneider, the Bernsteins…

Gail: And one of Mom's Mahjongg buddies, Stella Greenberg.

Doug: There were two or three primary enclaves where you'd see a fair number of Jews: Kenmore/Keeline and Forest Drive. That area had a lot, like Maynard and Sally Telpner and the Colicks.

Gail: And the Perlisses.

Doug: Eddie and Vera Tepperman. Then on Oakland was the Eveloffs, the Gallners…The Roffmans lived off North 8th. People tended to be in a relatively concentrated part of town and my guess is when they first came, Jewish people were not well thought of in certain circles. So I think the norm would be, "Gosh, this person lives here and our cousin married them. When we get out of an apartment and into a house we can try to be in their neighborhood."

The truth of the matter was, we had an enormously supportive community. Number one, they watched out for us; number two, they made sure we didn't mess up. I thought of most of the people in that neighborhood as almost being surrogate parents or cousins. I felt like any one of those families, like the Lees, opened up their backyard and treated…

Gail: Treated us like family.

Doug: Patty Nogg's grandfather was everyone's grandfather. There wasn't anybody he didn't treat as if they weren't his grandchild. It was so fun to grow up in that environment. If I wanted cookies, I could go up the street and go to anybody's house. Annie Cohn would give us cookies, Esther made us *mandlebreit* all the time. I was at the Finkel's house all the time!

Gail: And I would have to say, too, our success was their success. If there was a child who got an award in school then the whole group was, "Oh, isn't this wonderful?"

Doug: At the weekly mahjongg game, when you made National Honors Society they'd be like, "Oh my God, we saw in the paper! Douglas, that's so wonderful!" My cheeks were purple from being pinched from the age of about three months till I was 19. So many of them emigrated here and had the Eastern European accents. I got such a kick out of listening to these ladies!

Joey: Lots of Yiddish.

Gail: Lots of Yiddish! "Gail, don't *dray* your mother such a *kup*!" "Don't drive her so crazy!" "*Hock* me a *chineck*!" was another. "Drive me crazy." We thought it was hysterical! They were very deadly serious about it!

Doug: There were multiple groups of women who had Mahjongg games. Council Bluffs was like the King of Mahjongg Land.

Gail: "Three crack." "Two bam." And the noise of the tiles clicking.

Doug: These women were all 4'6" and could barely see over the tables! On the other side the men all played poker. There were a group of Meyersons: Herman, Sam and another one.

Gail: And together they were five feet tall!

Doug: Herman would sit on a New York phone book so he could see through the steering wheel! He drove a Cadillac and lived next door.

Gail: His bad driving was legendary.

Doug: He hit the light pole every time he backed out of the driveway!

Joey: [Laughs] Were there other characters?

Doug: There was a doctor in town named Ike Sternhill.

Gail: He had cigar breath.

Joey: [Laughs] That's healthy.

Gail: He always had a stogie in his mouth and we always had to get our shots from him!

Doug: He had a bristle brush mustache. You'd could've cleaned bottles with it!

Gail: He looked like Groucho Marx. We'd walk in and he'd say, "How's my little Gail today?" You'd be sitting on the table and he'd come up and do an Eskimo nose rub with you!

Doug: Sweetest man in the world. His wife's name was Betty. He made house calls. He was the doc for every Jewish family in Council Bluffs. He delivered babies, he took care of flus and colds and whatever it was other than broken bones. There was a group of them that played cards together: Grandpa Bubb, Al Fox, the Meyersons and Doc Sternhill.

Gail: Here's the table, and here are the men, and all you can see are their eyes and their cards!

Doug: Grandpa Bubb was 5'3.

Gail: And shrinking!

Doug: Herman Meyerson was 4'10.

Gail: And shrinking!

Doug: I used to go up there as a little kid and spend the night so I could watch them play cards! My grandparents Bubb lived up the hill and I would go up and they called me little Sammy because my grandpa's name was Sam. He had red hair, I had red hair and I was little Sammy. I was three or four. To most people you'd think I'd be a nuisance, but they used to bring out the divan, an old footstool, Grandma would pop popcorn in one of those old speckled pots, poured butter and salt on it and I'd have a bowl of popcorn and this big divan in front of me listening to these guys *kibbitz* about playing poker. I remember from a young age, Herman Meyerson would lean into Al Fox, who I think was his brother-in-law, and say…

Gail: "Al, what have I got?" Every single time!

Doug: He couldn't figure his cards out!

Gail: "What do I do?"

Doug: "Should I bet, Al?" And Al's still playing! I remember thinking, "How does this work?"

Joey: [Laughs] What a unique experience for you to be one of the guys at four-years-old!

Doug: We grew up cross-culturally. We lived with Eastern European Jewish culture, our grandparents and their kids. We were very lucky. I view our generation as the first to became truly secular from day one. You know, our parents were born to very near-term immigrants. My dad was born in 1917, Grandpa came over in like 1892.

There was a period of time there, 20-plus years that elapsed, but that's the blink of an eye, and those communities were still very insulated when Dad was little. It was a very Jewish community. Every Sunday, my grandmother Cohns' family had command performances and the whole stinking group showed up. Sometimes it would be extended family, cousins, in-laws…Dad would say they were just a ball.

Gail: I would say as an educator in today's world, we teach multi-culturally and we talk about, "Tell me about what you do in your culture." Or if you're Hispanic, "Tell me about this holiday," and you talk about it. I remember specifically growing up as a little girl, they did not want to discuss the old country and they did not want to talk about old country customs or celebrate their knowledge of another language. They wanted to be Americans. Period. And they didn't want any references to Lithuania. I would think in today's world you'd hear the family members reminiscing about what they recall of their life in their other country. But zero. Nothing.

Doug: Until we got much older, and they got much older and were very far removed from it, even then, our grandparents' generation never really talked about much. It was the stories that our parents could relate that they had heard from grandparents and parents. So it's really secondhand. It got lost.

Gail: And you miss the sharpness of the memories and stories that you could've had had they been more open. But I think that they were fearful of what a community would say about…

Doug: They didn't want to be outsiders.

Gail: And at that time in the '40s and '50s, you could easily be ostracized if you were different from the norm.

Joey: Especially in Council Bluffs, Iowa.

Gail: There was anti-Semitism going on. The Jews didn't feel they were welcome. So they felt they'd just zip their lips and be Americans.

Doug: And they had accents. That's part of it. In a lineup you couldn't pick what I am and where my family came from. It could be Germany, England, Italy, Russia… The reality is, they were stereotyped because if they walked in, opened their mouths, people knew they were from Eastern Europe.

Joey: Thank God for your family and the love you all had for each other.

Doug: I still have the birthday card Dad gave me two years before he died which he wrote. Not Mom; he wrote it. And second of all, he told me how proud he was of me and how much he loved me. It still sits on my dresser. I can't get rid of it.

Gail: On the back it says, "But not as much as Gail."

Doug: No, it would've said, "Not as much as who?"

9. Bubb's Grocery located at 1911 South 12th Street, 1920s
10. Edythe and Lloyd Krasne in 1943
11. Edythe and Lloyd at Bubb's Grocery, 930 S. 10th Street

Susan, Gail, Doug and Edythe Krasne at Hannukah

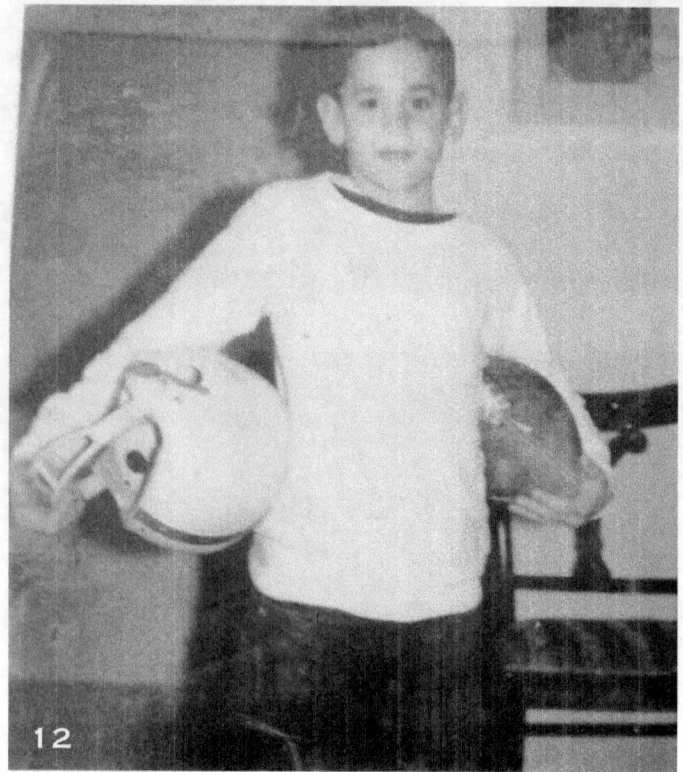

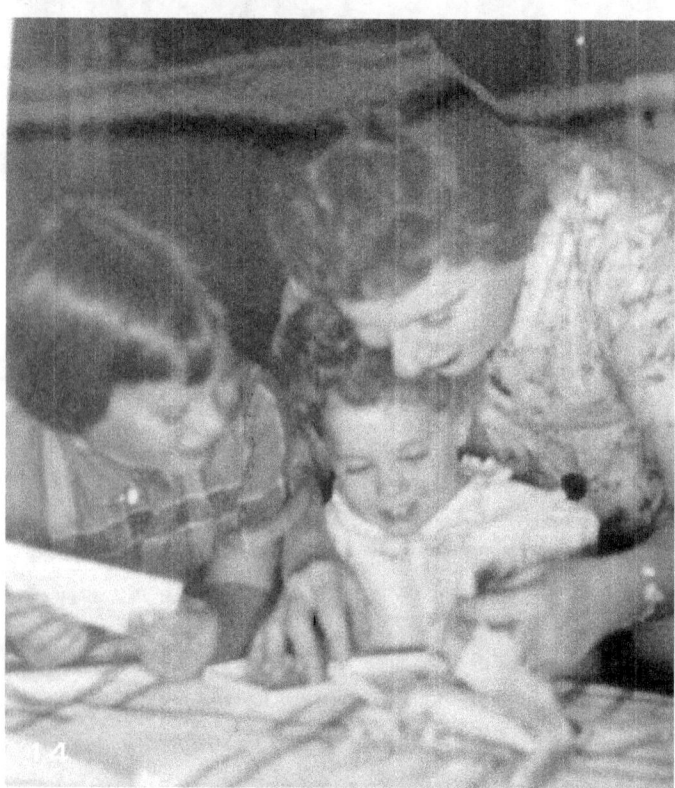

12. Doug on his way to an NFL career... if NFL meant "not for long"
13. Doug practicing his golf swing while I practice piano
14. Susan pushing Gail in the stroller
15. Skippy Cohn, Gail, and her mother

16. Gail's birthday party in the basement. Robin Mashbein (left) and Rhonda Suvalsky (right)
17. My dad took this picture of his kids brushing their teeth
18. Our beloved Grandma & Grandpa Bubb at their Mynster Street Apartment
19. This is a Jewish holiday food-fest. My grandma Bubb is on the far right

20. This is our beloved Kenmore neighborhood gang on the first day of school. (Pictured left to right Doug, Sherry Galvanti, Susan, Kathy Hannan, Jimmy Brown, Jane Hannan and Gail.

21. Gail Krasne, cheerleader

22. Doug in his geeky teenage years

Lloyd Krasne

REBECCA BLOOM

My parents, Jerome and Freda Bleicher, had farmland in Iowa by the Missouri River. It was called "bottom land" because it was in the Missouri River flood plain. My dad was a gentleman farmer and the people who lived and farmed the bottom land, Wayne and Mary Hoefeldt, were like my surrogate farm family. As a kid, I'd go to their place, sleep over, hang out and ride dad's horses which came from Esther K. Newman camp. When the camp dissolved, Dad was like "Ok, I'll take them."

What's interesting about the Hoefeldts is they did everything. They were like the homebody people, like typical farm folks. Her life was centered around the home: she cooked, washed and cleaned. She could drive -- probably to buy more food. She could fill a table full of food at lunch. In winter, they'd trap rabbits. They were survivalists, that was the norm back then. They had a different skill set than you and I have.

And they had Boston Terriers. I remember one named Scamp, great name for a small dog, isn't it? Smart dogs, they went everywhere with them. They'd lie in the truck, in the garden, followed them everywhere. They had dogs in lieu of children. Big, heavy people. Big people like to eat their own cooking a little too much. He was big but toned because he was out working. She baked pies…delicious pies…delicious everything.

Wayne was like the big, happy uncle and didn't mind me tagging along with him. We gardened, we walked, he had an orchard, a big strawberry patch…It was fun! I learned by osmosis. He and Mary canned more meat and veggies than you can imagine. And they jarred whole chickens! They had all this stuff in their basement next to the ringer washer and you'd go down there and go, "What's that?!" It was amazing. They lived off the land.

My dad was a surgeon who worked in several hospitals: Lutheran, St. Joe's and Doctors Hospital in Omaha. He also had a clinic where I went to work starting at around 12. My brothers and are I were gophers: "Go do this, that, stuff envelopes, take this message to this secretary, billing…" At that age, I got paid a pittance, but when I got into high school, I received a salary and helped in the lab. During that time I met a Jewish woman, the clinic's chief med tech who has become a lifelong friend.

My life with my dad evolved around both the farm and working at his clinic in South O, the Prairie Clinic at 26th and J. He'd have Wednesday and Sunday off and we'd go to the farm, to Wayne and Mary's place, to help out. I'd climb around in the orchard and helped wherever I was needed. My dad was big on having a side-kick, he liked just having somebody to bum around with. Dad didn't do any of the field work, didn't get on a combine and harvest the corn, but he had horses and rental properties.

It wasn't your average upbringing.

My dad had a lot of skills; he could repair anything. The well water system was broken? He'd climb down into the well pit and fix the thing. When you're a farmer you have to know that stuff. He loved to tinker; he was a tinker-er. Not only loved it, but knew what he was doing most of the time. I don't even know where he got those skills, but he passed them along to my brothers. My oldest brother Norm can fix anything. He owns apartment buildings and does a lot of troubleshooting. My brothers had a lot of training and due diligence with Dad.

He was kind of tough on the outside, but a marshmallow on the inside. He was serious, but when he got started laughing everybody laughed. They'd be like, "Oh my God, Jerome is laughing!" He was really smart. At night, at the kitchen table, he would ask you questions about chemistry or "Spell this word." Kind of a BOOM-BOOM-BOOM education, even at the dinner table. Education was very prized. Too esoteric for the rest of the world, my dad was.

On his approachable side, he had a way with people. He could walk up to anybody -- that was the doctor in him -- and strike up a conversation about *kolaches* (a Central European pastry). Since so many immigrants were in South O, he talked and schmoozed with those people. He learned Polish for "How are you?" "*Yak shemash*." They would bring him all kinds of food, gifts, tchotchkes, hand-knit socks…He was well-loved as a doctor by his patients and he was of that age where he made house calls. If a kid was too sick to bring to the clinic or a patient couldn't get a cab, he'd make a house call. He was very generous with his time and his person. He had a very giving spirit with a lot of different people, not just family.

The big change came when I was in 7th grade. We had lived two houses down from Warren Buffet in Omaha, but we moved to Green Hill Farm in the Bluffs in 1970. One of the reasons Dad wanted to move was because he was tired of being called into the E.R. at all hours and needed a calm place with peace and quiet. Also, I think, when doctors deal with traumatic situations, they need a refuge.

We were isolated because the farm was between the Bluffs and Glenwood, Iowa. If I wanted to call a friend, it was a toll call from Iowa into Nebraska and cost too much. Chatty teenager years? Forget that. Kids I had grown up with since kindergarten I couldn't call up and chat with because my parents were always, "Get off the phone!"

Cleaning and cooking, I remember lots of cleaning and cooking. We were all obligated to pitch in: clear the table, do dishes, yard work…It was expected, it was not an option.

Farming runs in my family. My grandfather Robert came to this country in 1906 from Poland. He and my grandmother Sue had Jerome in 1921. He worked for the railroad so they moved to Omaha and he eventually worked in insurance. When he died in 1956, Dad took his inheritance and started buying farmland.

I was born in 1958, July 25th, and by the time I was 12 Dad had three different farms on the Iowa side: Green Hill, Pony Creek and The Bottom Farm: Wayne and Mary's place. He was just a really hard-working person, like me. I think, "Could I go work inside now?" At my farm, Bloomsorganic in Crescent, Iowa, (20 miles northeast of Omaha) I move around a lot which is what he enjoyed about it, too. You get exercise without being in a gym and you have things to take care of. I think that's the biggie, things to do physically and the quiet. When he was in the field, he didn't have a cell phone like we do now.

Characteristics of the Bleichers are: work hard, work with your hands and a curiosity to problem-solve on your own two feet. I learned from Dad to have *chutzpah* and jump in and be a do-er. My brothers Jon, a radiologist, and Joel, a plastic surgeon, are both gentleman farmers on the southeast side of Council Bluffs. Both are doctors who live on and own their farms. My brother Bob lives near Lincoln, in Eagle, NE. He's a pulmonologist, a partial owner of a hospice house and owns a tree nursery, Eagle Nursery. One of the ways our father influenced us is around farm ownership and getting your hands dirty, pride and enjoying the fruits of your labor. Not everybody gets to eat homegrown food.

I have six brothers: Norm, Joel, Paul, Dan, Bob and Jon. I'm the baby. Interestingly, my mom was the youngest of seven and had six brothers as well. They were around some when I was a little kid -- you know boys, they're very independent, they were off doing boy things. But as a girl with all boys, it was a struggle. People think you are so spoiled by all those brothers and they protect you. They were rough and tumble with me, they didn't pussyfoot around because I was a girl. I was a tomboy. How else could I survive?

The Bleichers also have strong personalities; they're highly opinionated. You have to have enough *chutzpah* to get involved with big projects. You think owning a home is big? No, owning a farm is like 100 times bigger.

My mom was smart and funny. She stayed home, cooked and took care of the kids. She allowed my dad to shine in his work and agreed to move to the farm. When I was a teen, she went back to school to become a part-time LPN at Lutheran Hospital in Omaha. She was the daughter of bakers on South 24th Street in Omaha in the early 1900s.

We had a blast. I was the only daughter, so we would shop, go to lunch, all that girl stuff. We had a fun time just being girls. She would cook really traditional foods at home because Dad was a meat and potatoes kind of guy. My mom was really picky about what she bought at the grocery store, only certain canned goods and cuts of meat. We went to three or four different stores, one to buy veggies, one to buy meats…It was fun! Shopping took hours. We had to go to three stores and stop and have lunch in between.

My dad would drag me to the hospital to see his patients after surgery. It was always pretty gory. It was a way to see his world and appreciate what he did for a living. How many kids get to go to work with their parent? It has made me more compassionate about medicine and caring for sick people. We lived in his world because he wanted us to help. We helped at the clinic, we helped at the farm, we cheered people up…He helped people get well by speaking the truth and being straight-forward about their condition. He was extremely real and did not mince words. He gave his patients tough love.

Dad was a Renaissance man. He appreciated art, music, was a history buff and he could fix stuff. He loved heavy iron! Norm said when Dad was 80 and trying to repair the CAT (the Caterpillar tractor), he attempted to take a heavy plate off the bottom of the CAT and said, "Oh well, no big deal, if I die that way, fine."

It's weird when I look back to the time when they moved me to the farm. Being around farming when I moved as a teen, I didn't like it. But I went to art school, raised children and when an opportunity came I purchased my own land and was always interested in preserving the environment. I'm a child of the 1960s. Betty Friedan, you know? The whole women's and environmental movements.

Once we moved to Iowa, Dad started to get involved in the synagogue. When he saw that pitiful old B'nai Israel, he helped in a more physical way, especially after he retired in 1991. He was more of a caretaker and a lay leader over at B'nai. He ran Friday night services when nobody else would. I think what my dad liked about B'nai was, he felt he was needed there and could play an active role. He was an active guy. "Sure!" Pitch right in, clean, make it a *haimasha* place. He was involved in the planning, everything from financial support to programming and physically helping get the building into a reasonable condition so it was safe.

There were very few people at B'nai Israel, no rabbi, no clerics, all lay leaders. Although there were visiting rabbis at High Holidays. My parents went every Friday night; it was like their social hour. Mom was involved with cooking for the *onegs*, doing the little Jewish mother thing. Dad ran the show, along with a core group, some my parents' age and some younger who shouldered the place together, like Alan and Sandra Kurland, Marty Rosenberg, Rod and Linda Sadofsky, Sam and Lee Eveloff, Eddie and Vera Tepperman, Rose Katelman…Dad would invite speakers, lead the service, or stand up and talk about some book he read.

Dad voted with his feet. He helped keep the doors open just by being present. He saw a need for more people, their presence and involvement.

My husband Brent and I got involved when we had children: Alex, who was born in 1986, and Eli in 1988. Brent suggested we hire part-time Reconstructionist student rabbi once a month -- they were all women. Marti Nerenstone, a lay leader, bridged the gap with the young and old and was willing to move the synagogue activities to the Unitarian Church in West O.

The first annual *Tu BuShvat* was attended by 50 people. People from Storm Lake Iowa, people from all over, even non-members came. *Tu BuShvat* is the New Year of the trees, when the almond trees are blooming in Israel. I was all about that. Marti led the congregation in song and my husband and I thought, "Hey, we have young children, they need to be creatively involved in their Jewish lives." It was fun to sing and dance and eat and learn through doing.

I integrated the farm and art with B'nai. I have a B.A. in Art Education from Creighton and an M.A. in Art History from the University of Idaho. So, I started as an artist, then I had an opportunity to own my own farm and be a farmer, plus I taught religious school where we did art projects around the various holidays. It evolved into this more environmentally-sound lifestyle.

My folks, who passed away in 2003 within 21 days of each other, loved their grandchildren as much or more than us! They were always pleased to see their progress whether it was in the Jewish realm or as human beings. They generously left money for all 15 of the grandchildren for college education. They were humble and lived simply for the betterment of their children and grandchildren.

They treated everybody like family. This one fix-it guy was trying to detox from alcoholism; my dad gave him an opportunity to work and helped him dry out. He was the kind of doctor with more of a purpose than your average doctor. He poured himself into people.

Throughout my life, they employed people in their home to help them as they aged and always treated them very nicely. Dad always had a helper or three around who were also people he knew through the clinic, some were even patients. I think it's a Jewish thing, a hospitality thing. It's important to welcome people into your home and treat them like your family.

Rebecca Bloom at Council Bluffs Synagogue

23. Jerome and Freda Sherman Bleicher
24. Jerome E. Bleicher

MICHAEL GALLNER

STROLLING HOME FROM *shul* on Rosh Hashana circa 1962, Mike and his grandpa Sam Sacks shared a moment B'nai Israel-goers might have found befuddling. The Sacks' (and synagogue) patriarch, as usual, had run the service in his signature rousing style, punctuated by a bang on the bima and shouts towards the chatter-filled balcony. "*Tshah! Tshah!*" he'd yell in Yiddish. "Quiet! Quiet!" Afterwards, the crowd *kibbitzed*, then dispersed. Now, it was just a boy and his grandpa.

Sam: "Did you like the way I made the high notes, Mikey?"

Mikey: "You mean the low notes, Pop?"

The Russian immigrant who commanded an audience and respect as a lay leader sought affection, maybe confirmation. "I always told him, 'Pop, you were great!'" Mike says. "He was an amateur cantor in the purest meaning of the word amateur: for love. Pop was good, he hit the notes correctly and knew the tunes but he didn't know the terminology. I was in music at school and sang in chorus in 8th and 9th grades, so he respected my opinion. He didn't have the greatest voice in the world, it certainly wasn't Richard Tucker (one of the world's greatest operatic tenors who recorded Jewish liturgical songs), but he could bring it home."

At home, 520 Oakland Avenue where Mike and his younger brothers Shelley and Gary grew up, mom Esther and Grandma Ida Sacks bustled about the kitchen, preparing a traditional holiday meal for 20. "Mom would make her blueberry *lokshen kugel*. It was sweet and it was rich and it was good." Leafing through "Council Cooks," a cookbook compiled by the Omaha section of the National Council of Jewish Women published in 1973, he reads the recipe instructions. "'Spoon blueberry pie filling over the top and bake for another 15 minutes, and that made it blueberry,'" he laughs.

Seders, Rosh Hashanah and breakfasts at home and at Sam and Ida's house on Roosevelt Avenue are recipes for nostalgia. "The family included cousins Larry and Sivi Roffman, Buddy and Judy Roffman, Harvey Roffman, Norman Roffman, Aunt Ruth Shapiro, Uncle Kenny, Aunt Velma and Susan Jo and Karen Sacks. My grandfather, assisted by my Uncle Ken, led the *seder*. I enjoyed searching for the *afikomen*, even though I knew it would be in a hi-fi cabinet or under my grandfather's plate. He always acted like he was very clever, but he really just wanted to move the ceremony along."

On Sundays, Mike's dad David, whose only day off work was then, would take Shelley or him to Adler's Bakery and Roffman's Delicatessen (owned by Esther's first cousin, Normand Roffman) to buy bagels, lox, whitefish, sable, cream cheese, challah, rye bread, corned beef, tongue, or pastrami and treats for the week to come. "Within an hour of our anticipated return, my mother's kitchen would fill with the aroma of frying yellow onions for the onions and scrambled eggs," he says.

In early November, 2016, Mike experienced the *bracha*, the blessing, of tasting his mother's onions and eggs again, only this time the dish was prepared by Gary. In his kitchen in Phoenix, his brother stood stove side, slowly sautéing the onions on low. "They tasted just like our mom's," Mike says. "She used to feed it to the vultures –– hungry boys who hovered over the stove –– to be devoured quickly, while hot."

Cousins gathered around the dining table swapping stories while Gary and his husband Steve Hildebrand's sons, Schnauzers Sweeney Dogg and Hubbell, campaigned for scraps. Seated were sisters Susan (Gelb) and Karen Sacks –– whose father Kenny, a respected Council Bluffs attorney, won an election to be Pottawattamie County Attorney in 1960 and was at one time president of the Iowa Trial Lawyers Association –– along with Susan's husband Steve Gelb, Sam Talpalatsky and his wife Liz and Raia Windmiller and her husband Manny who had driven from San Diego to celebrate Gary and Steve's debut of "Love Is Here To Stay: A Gershwin Cabaret," a show they co-wrote and produced.

Particularly characteristic of the Jewish Council Bluffs community's *menchness* is the story of siblings Sam and Raia who, with their parents Luba and Mark, fled

Cold War Russia in 1975 with the aid of Sam Sacks and Shirley Goldstein, the humble heroine who helped sparked a movement to free and relocate Soviet Jews.

Sam Sacks's own immigrant story is cinematic in its depiction of a young man's struggle from persecution to redemption. "Pop grew up in Kiev, I believe in the *shtetl*. He was conscripted to the White Army during the Revolution where he fought for the Czar against the Bolsheviks. Pop deserted and crossed the border into Europe, then traveled to Argentina where his older sister had migrated and became a street peddler. One night, Pop was beaten, robbed and left for dead. Before he left Russia, his parents had given him the address of Roffman cousins in Omaha. He lost it. In his unconsciousness, the address entered his dreams. He wrote for their help to reach America and when he arrived, or perhaps before, he was told of their 27-year-old maiden daughter Ida, and an arranged marriage occurred in 1923. They had two children: Esther, born in 1928 and Kenneth in 1931."

Like the myriad Jewish families who owned grocery stores in Council Bluffs, Sam Sacks too got a piece of the pie. But before launching his own business in the mid 1920s, he worked for the Kulakofskys at Central Market in downtown Omaha. After a few years, young Sam asked his boss's permission to open his own store across the river, which he did: Sam's Market at 10th and Broadway. "That store was very successful during the Depression and the war. My grandfather and grandmother worked hard and made a lot of money for the time," says Mike.

Then, in 1954, construction of the Broadway viaduct prompted the city to exercise its right to eminent domain and bought out Sam. He would soon launch a new store at 215 South Main Street re-named –– never one to mince words –– Sam's New Supermarket. "My grandfather acted as a security officer and bookkeeper after my father came to the business in 1948. My father was a butcher, stocker, inventory manager, cashier, bookkeeper and delivery man during his time at Sam's, which had a full-service meat market where pre-cut meats were displayed in cabinets, but a butcher could prepare special cuts to order. Our grade of beef was choice, and not prime, but the customers really seemed to like the service," says Mike, who at 15, started as a stock boy and sacker, then earned his stripes as cashier, delivery boy, butcher (he still has the scar on his finger for proof) and ultimately assistant manager.

"I'd drive to the Omaha Stockyards on weekends. I packed several fore-quarters of beef in the trunk of our Oldsmobile because we had run out of chuck roasts that had been delivered in bulk on the previous Thursday. I would also drive to the warehouse where Mrs. B's is now located if we ran out of an advertised item. I learned a lot about the poverty in which some people lived in the west and south end of Council Bluffs and even close to the store. It was pretty rough, a very good lesson in compassion and empathy. I've never felt better than any of the people I served, whether it was in retail or in my profession as a lawyer, and that held true for both my brothers, too."

Mike learned another truth. Working side-by-side with his Pop, he witnessed another side of the devout, doting elder who *kvelled* over his grandchildren. "We were the center of his world. He was so kind and he'd call us endearing Yiddish words like *heiss*. I still don't know what this means. But he had two different personalities: the personality I loved was, at the store, supplanted by this old-time merchant who didn't trust or like anybody who wasn't Jewish because of the persecution he experienced as a boy in Russia."

By contrast, living in Council Bluffs on Roosevelt Avenue was easy street for his children, Esther and Kenny, who grew up surrounded by Jewish kids. Kenny's best buddy was Milton Gordon, while Esther's close friend was his sister Ethyl. Her other neighborhood pals included Eleanor Passer, Phyllis Wolhlner, Owen Meyerson and Yale Gotsdiner.

The beloved Bluffs girl graduated from North Eighth Street Elementary, Bloomer Junior High, Abraham Lincoln High School and attended Temple University where she would meet her future husband David Gallner, a fellow student from Bridgeton, New Jersey.

"My mother wanted to be a journalist, but she was too much in love with my father to not get married and move back to Council Bluffs," Mike says. On August 31, 1947, they tied the knot in the penthouse ballroom of Omaha's then-in-vogue Blackstone Hotel, the same location as their surprise 25th Anniversary party.

Esther Gallner was a woman you'd want in your fox hole. "She was so well-liked and so supportive of everything we all did, including my dad. She was a great companion to him. He was in the theater and would perform at Chanticleer and the Omaha Playhouse. She went with him to rehearsals, to shows, to cast parties… And my mother had a great circle of friends, most of whom she knew through Jewish women's organizations like Hadassah, B'nai Israel Sisterhood and the National Council of Jewish Women. Alice Mashbein was her 'phone friend.' They spoke almost every day because they both had illness and didn't leave the house too much during the last 10 or 15 years of my mother's life," says Mike, referring to Esther's diabetes and kidney disease which caused her premature death at 47.

His mother's culinary prowess earned her rave reviews. Take her stuffed breast of veal ("Oh, God, incredible"), cheesecake ("With a buttery graham cracker crust, it was something") or her vegetable beef soup ("Phenomenal") served with lima beans, parsnips and chuck roast -- from, where else? -- Sam's. "She could really cook things up."

Sometimes she'd take the night off. Yom Kippur, 1961, fell on the last day of the regular baseball season before the World Series. "Roger Maris was chasing Babe Ruth's single season home run record. Our mom went to Christy Creme and picked up our break-the-fast dinner: two cheeseburgers, french fries and a large chocolate malt. Each!"

When her boys were young, Esther would lull them to sleep with this local favorite:

> *"Council Bluffs by the river*
> *How you make my liver shiver*
> *With your big tall bluffs and your old Missouri River*
> *How I love you with my heart and I love you with my liver*
> *Council Bluffs by the river…"*

Mike's Wonder Years-esque early boyhood was marked by biking, baseball and buddies. Not long after his birth on May 16, 1948, he befriended Mark Eveloff whom he met when the Gallners first lived on Military Avenue and the Eveloffs lived on Frank Street. The two toddled together in diapers (see blackmail photograph), eventually lived 10 houses apart on Oakland Avenue, and through their Bloomer Junior High years, " We did everything together. When we went to the movies, Aunt Lee gave

Mark $1.10 for admission, pop, popcorn and a box of animal crackers." Often the pair would grab their baseball gear and bike to Robert's Park or the diamond on 8th Street by what is now Sternhill Park, topped with a pop at Passer's grocery. Mark was like a brother to me."

Starting at 10, Mike played for the Royal Rockets in the city cub league. "My dad sponsored the team; my uniform said, 'Sam's New Supermarket, Inc.,'" he laughs. "It was such a small store but they put the 'Inc.' on it." And while he loved to shoot hoops and toss around a football, at 12, Mike became acquainted with his first love: golf. He'd log long hours at The Elks Club (now Council Bluffs Country Club) alongside the roughly dozen Jewish families out of 300 members including the Eveloffs, the Lees, the Schneiders, the Selos, the Finkels, the Perlises, the Sidney Cohens and the Ben Cohens. He lettered for the Abraham Lincoln Lynx golf team.

During the '50s and '60s, B'nai Israel was the nucleus of Jewish life. For the Gallner boys, having a grandfather who acted as rabbi-in-residence when there wasn't a full-time rabbi (which was often) upped the ante. "My brothers and I had to attend all five morning hours on both days of Rosh Hashanah and most of the all-day services of Yom Kippur. Pop knew all the daily prayers, could lay *tefillin*, conduct *seder* service and wanted to perform for the community. If we were Catholic, he would have been a Deacon."

Come holiday and Torah services, "Les Krasne would circle the sanctuary to ensure people would say their *aliyahs*. Then, when one man read from the Torah, another would follow along and correct him. It was always two old men. When my grandfather was a Torah reader, the corrector loved to chime in –– loudly –– and say if he screwed up," Mike laughs.

Before B'nai Israel was renovated in the mid-'60s, the Orthodox set-up was this: bima in the middle, ark on the east wall, pews on all sides. "So traditional. I remember seeing *The Jazz Singer* with Al Jolson and thinking, 'God, that's what our synagogue looked like.'" On one pew stretching from the ark to the east wall was where the older, "more pious" men sat, like Lou Katelman, Saul Suvalsky and Simon Shyken, Sam Sacks's co-leader whom he greatly admired and called, "Shyken."

In Mike's mid-teens, he and his brothers were obligated to sit in the front row with Sam Sacks from 8 a.m. until 1 p.m. on Rosh Hashana, both days. "It was like, 'When does it end?' When they did a mourner's service, for instance at You Kippur, we'd go outside for a long time then. My grandfather would send somebody out to get us. 'Your grandfather's looking for you,' and I was like, 'Oh gosh, c'mon.'"

So…what did Mike and his cronies do during those breaks? "We would look in cars and if the doors were open, we'd take cigarettes," he laughs.

Still, the rebel had a cause: Bar Mitzvah study with Rabbi Korb. "He had a bit of a temper, if you didn't do a good job he'd scream at you. But he was a good man. We prepared for the Friday night service by reading some prayers in English, some in Hebrew and I think we did the *Kiddush*. We didn't read from the *Torah* but from the *Haftorah* and the *Maftir*. Everything had a precise tune, like the concluding hymn in the *Haftorah*, '*Adon Olam*…'"

For Michel Gershen Ben Dovid's April 29, 1961 Bar Mitzvah, a dual service with Steve Perlis, he wore a black suit from Herman's. Custom-made. Such an indulgence for the son of a butcher? "It was probably because I was fat," he laughs. The day fell on Gary's 7th birthday. "We had at least a dozen relatives from Chicago, Philadelphia and New Jersey who came and he was upset because nobody was observing his birthday. So some of the relatives bought him some presents. It was so sweet. I feel badly he didn't get to have his birthday."

Roughly 200 guests, including a dozen of David's east coast relatives who traveled by car, train and plane ("It was exciting to meet them and see how they loved their Dovid") indulged in the fruits of Esther's efforts. "She prepared food for months in advance. The main dish was Lobster Thermidor, which was, indeed, *traif*."

In strict Tevya fashion, Sam Sacks's wish for his grandson was to remain connected to his faith, maintain a Jewish identity, carry on his legacy. Tradition. Come the Sunday after Mike's Bar Mitzvah, his Pop attempted to strike a deal. "He said, 'Mikey, I will give you a dime for every time you recite your *Haftorah*,' and I thought, 'That's easy.' If I did it ten times, a dollar was a dollar back then. But I never did it again."

Mike did, however, continue to attend Sunday school, this time taught by Freda Suvalsky and dad David. "He wasn't that religious, but he did it in service to Pop. He'd teach us about current events; it was like sociology for him. He liked being the head of the class, talking to people and having them respond, the Socratic way. I considered that a sacrifice because he had little, if any, time to himself. He worked 72 hours a week. We enjoyed having him and I respected what he was trying to do."

According to Jewish law, Mike was now a man. So on Saturday mornings at five-to-nine, he was awakened by a Russian rooster. (Ring ring…) "We need a minyan Mikey, come down, please?" And he'd think, 'Jeezy Joe, can't a guy catch a few more winks?' Of course, he complied -- who dared contest their grandpa? -- but maybe manhood wasn't so swell after all. "With adulthood came responsibility," says Mike who, because he is a Levite on his father's side, would get called to the *Torah* after Harry Cohen, if he was there, to say blessings before and after the reading of the *Torah*.

By high school, Mike's Jewish life had lost its luster. Call him *meshuggana*, but far more fun than making a *minyan* was grabbing a prime spot in the front row at Ewald's Drive-In to survey the scene, hanging out at teen nightclub Sandy's Escape until midnight or spinning Pat Boone records at Richard Selo's house down the block on Oakland.

Also by that time, Mike had become acutely aware of his minority status at school and in the community. Out of 425 students in A.L.'s class of '66, the handful of Jewish kids were Mark Eveloff, Richard Selo, Jan Schneider, Richie Lee, Judy Cole, Deborah Mezey and Steve Perlis. That said, "Bill Hughes, who wasn't Jewish, was friendly with Richard, Steve, Mark and me, and those friendships continue to this day. It didn't matter about religion at all, Bill didn't see religious distinction."

The principal, however, did. Mr. W.W. Owen. "We called him 'Dub-Dub.' I was acquainted with him because during my senior year I got in trouble a few times. Let's just say I used an old room pass that didn't belong to me. Mr. Owen brought me into his private office and mentioned several names of 'terrific Jewish students' who had been in school during his tenure and then proceeded to tell me he never had trouble with anyone of my 'race' other than me. I felt like he was a fool. I'm a member of a religion, you're not very bright to have referred to me as part of a race. It stayed with me but it didn't hurt me because I considered the source."

Sadly, it wasn't Mike's first exposure to discrimination. During one of Joe Katelman's City Council campaigns a few years prior, "Aunt Lee gave Mark and me a bunch of handbills to pass out in front of Sam Katelman's Penny's building. More than one time I handed a bill to somebody and they tossed it on the ground and said, 'I ain't votin' for that Jew.' It hurt, but I had enough savvy to know intelligent people didn't talk that way."

Antithetical to these cutting comments was life with Russian immigrant grandparents who brought old-world wisdom, culture and *chutzpah* to the table. While Sam was out of the house acting as *shul* lay leader, Ida was busy being a professional Jewish grandma. Quiet, loving and kind, she'd don her apron and whip up a batch of chopped liver, sugar and cinnamon dusted strudel or homemade horseradish, ripening the roots in a cardboard box in her crawl space. Ida would entertain 20-plus guests on the holidays at her home on Elmwood drive. Some Sundays, she'd even entertain the butcher.

"She didn't drive, so my dad would take her to Shukert's meats in Omaha near 50th and William where she'd always order chuck roasts, hamburger and rib steaks. Mr. Shukert would cut the meat, bring it to her for her inspection, and she'd say, "That's not lean enough; I *vant* it lean!" He'd respond simply, 'Yes, Mrs. Sacks, I know you want it lean, it's as lean as I can make it."

Over time, older generations died out leaving the younger set to survive on memories, stories and gratitude. "It's a blessing to have your grandparents as long as you do," Mike says. Though the years, though he maintained relationships with friends not of his faith, he would gravitate towards Jews. "I find I have most commonality with people of my own faith and culture." By the time he graduated from the University of Iowa, Creighton Law School and the University of Kansas where he earned a Masters degree in Tax Law, religion had left his life. The young attorney's focus was virtually threefold: building his career, his family –– he has two grown children Virginia and Jordan –– and his golf CV. To date, he has hit every continent except Asia and Antarctica and plays in an annual tournament dubbed, "The Kiddush Kup."

Moving to a new synagogue. Herman Meyerson, Saul Suvalsky, Rabbi Karzan, Sam Sacks, Joe Katelman and Ken Sacks, 1963

But in 1987, Mike's past would call, prompting him to re-engage with the Council Bluffs Jewish community. "I became involved with Bikur Cholim/Oakhill cemetery at the behest of Ted Seldin when he saw a need to increase the cemetery's endowment. He asked that I, as an attorney, file for Chapter 501(3)(c) non-profit status for the cemetery. I contributed to the fund-raising effort and was pleased to know my family's final resting place would be maintained forever, due to our success."

Three more decades would pass before Mike rediscovered his roots in an even more meaningful way, this time at Patty Nogg's annual cemetery Memorial service.

"I had not attended until Shelley became sick in 2013," he says. "I felt like I was filling in for him in order to represent and honor our family." When Shelley passed away, he was buried in Bikur Cholim cemetery alongside parents Esther and David, which further kindled Mike's desire to belong to the community. He would join the Bikur Cholim/Oakhill cemetery board and helped recruit his niece Elyse, Shelley's daughter. "We're in the process of taking on younger members so the board can be preserved."

Curiously, Sam and Ida Sacks are interred at Golden Hill cemetery in North Omaha where, apparently, her parents and several brothers are buried. "It seems ironic that this couple, Sam and Ida, would be together in Omaha when his love of Council Bluffs Judaism was so much a part of his life."

For over 40 years, Mike has practiced law in his hometown, offering him the opportunity to witness Council Bluffs morph from black-and-white to color to high-def. "Everywhere I drive and walk, I see reminders of our past; vacant lots, empty buildings…Where I bank now used to be Herman's clothing store. I recall Katelman's Hardware, Marcus Clothes, Marcus Department Store, Union Mercantile, The Bargain Spot, White Front Market, Kaypers, Master Appliance, Sixth Street Market, Iowa Clothes, the Peoples Store, Peoples True Value Hardware, Avenue B Grocery, Bubb's Grocery, Dr. Isaac Sternhill's home on Forest Drive…"

Minus a two-decade stint in Omaha, Mike has always lived within less than a mile radius of yesterday's landmarks, like the former JCC on South 8th Street and B'nai Israel, which is located the same distance from his home now as it was when he lived on Oakland Avenue. From Mike's home office on Bluff Street –– in the former

Abraham Lincoln Field House which has been converted into apartments retaining original details like soaring ceilings, basketball court floors and now-stationary bleachers –- Mike can see the building which housed Sam's New Supermarket.

Fall of 2016, over half-a-century after his stroll home from *shul* with his Pop, Mike joined B'nai Israel. "I felt it was time, it was time to come home further." He realized during Rosh Hashanah services, "I hadn't been in that synagogue since Sam Eveloff's funeral in 2002. Before that, I can't even remember." On Yom Kippur, dressed in a black suit (off-the-rack he's far more svelte these days), Mike was invited along with several congregants to carry a *Torah* from the ark to the *bima* which he cradled during *Kol Nidre*, his ancestors' spirits lingering like *Shabbos* candle smoke.

"I thought about my family's names on the wall: my parents, my grandfather Michael whom I'm named after, my father's sister Aunt Jeanette Friedenberg, Velma and Kenny Sacks, numerous Roffmans…" Mike's aperture is widening, offering a porthole to his past, a clear view of the man who found his place in the Council Bluffs Jewish community. Who was Sam Sacks? "He was like millions of other immigrants. All he wanted was to be a patriarch. He wanted to retain the flavor of his youth," Mike says. "Now, I am like the patriarch my grandfather sought to be."

Outside Sam Roffman's store at 620 W. Broadway in Council Bluffs

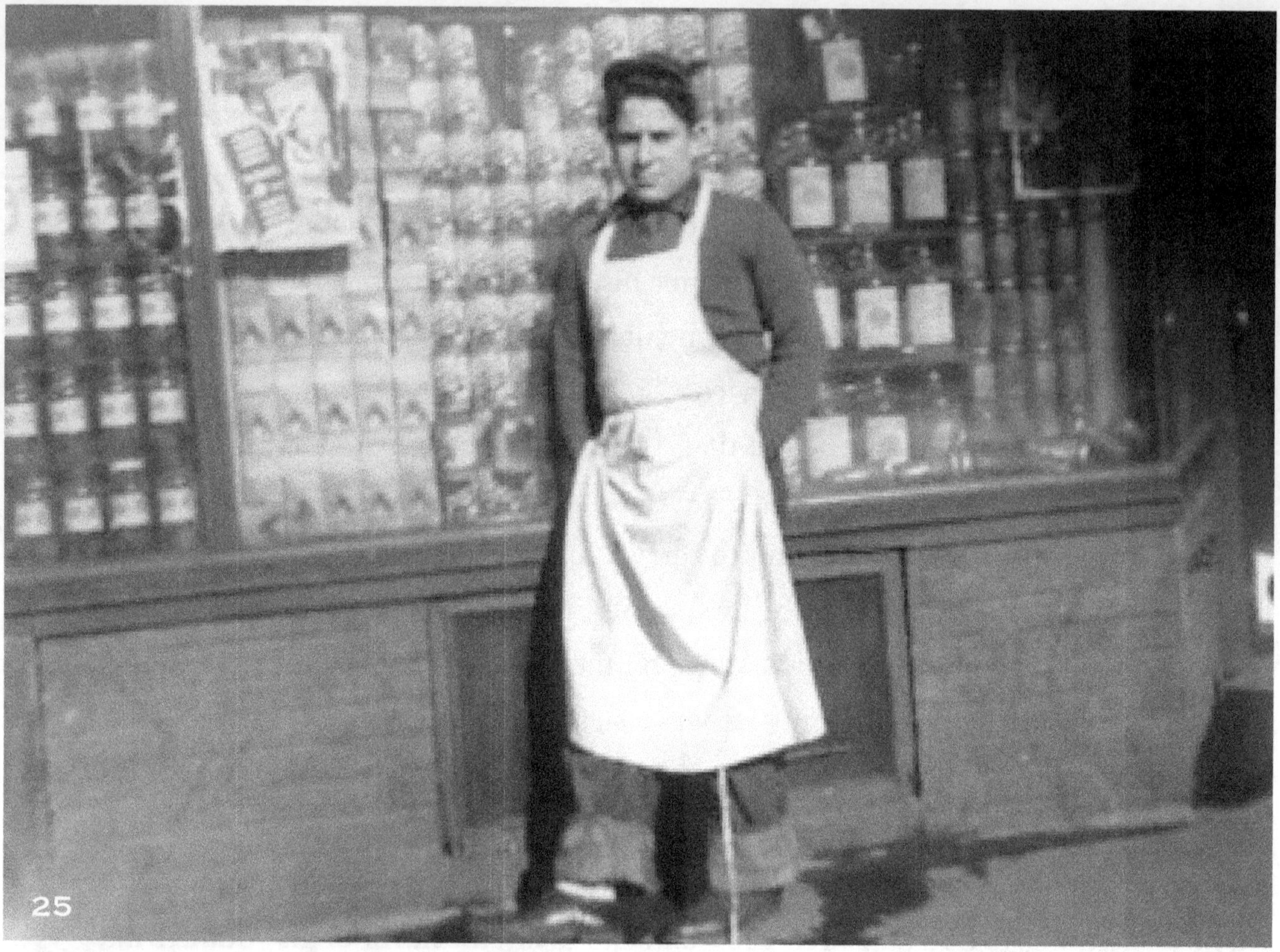
25

26

27

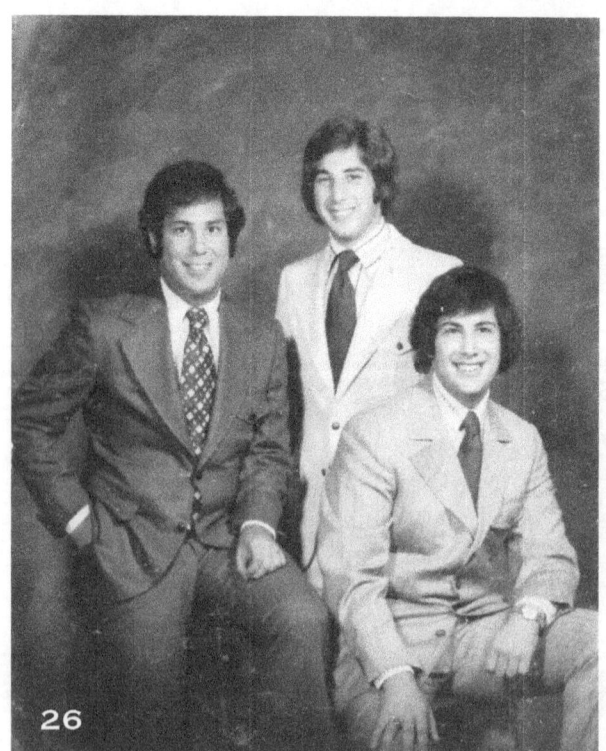

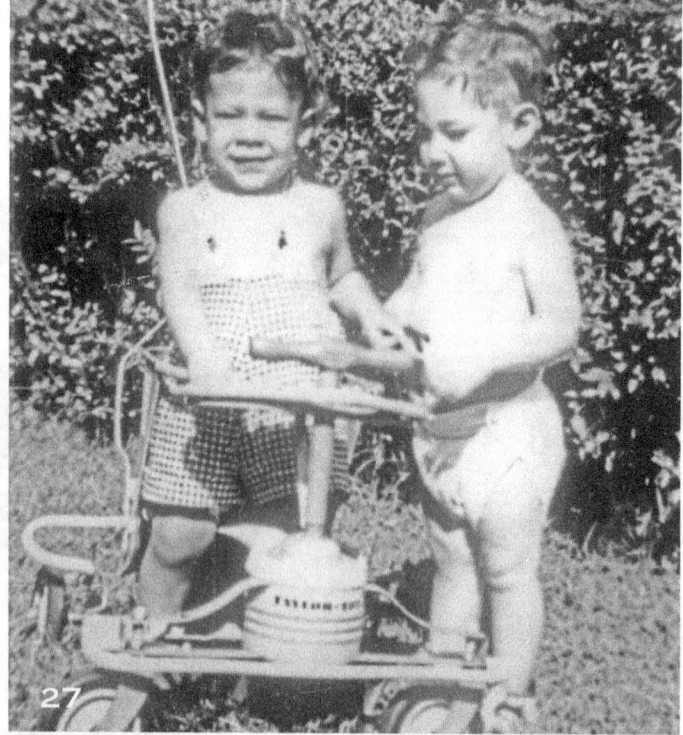

25. Larry Roffman in front of Union Mercantile in Council Bluffs
26. Shelly, Mike and Gary Gallner
27. Mark Eveloff and Mike Gallner

Wedding of David Gallner and Esther Sacks Gallner, August, 1947
Left to right: Celia Gallner, David Gallner, Esther Sacks Gallner, Sam Sacks and Ida Roffman Sacks

SOL KUTLER
1927 - 2017

Joey: So Sol, how did your family get to Council Bluffs?

Sol: Well, when the Jews from Russia and Poland came to the U.S. in 1910, they came in through Galveston, Texas because many Jews had been coming through New York. HIAS, the organization that took care of immigrants, arranged for the Jews to come through Galveston. My parents were from Kiev Gaberne in a town called Pavolitch (which is no longer in existence in the Ukraine as it was completely destroyed by the Nazis when they came into that area). So in 1910, my dad came through Galveston.

My dad was born in 1889. His name was Harry Kutler, but his Russian name was spelled *Kotlyer*. In the United States, Cutler is always spelled with a C, so this differentiated our family. HIAS originally sent him to St. Joe, Missouri where he worked. He did not speak the language and he barely had money to exist.

At one time, he worked in a meatpacking plant, but later worked as a carpenter for the railroad. In 1913, he went back to Russia to marry my mother Sarah and brought her to Council Bluffs. They opened a restaurant on Broadway between 7th and 8th Streets where they worked for a few years.

Before moving a little further down the block to 732 West Broadway, he opened a clothing store: The Open Front Bargain Center. The uniqueness of the store was that the front could be opened up entirely, customers did not have to go through a door, they just walked by, took one step and were in the store.

Joey: Neat! Tell me about growing up Jewish in Council Bluffs.

Sol: Well, I was born May 24, 1927. My Hebrew name is *Bitzalel* (he was the architect of the first Temple in Israel). My parents were Orthodox, we walked to *shul* -- the way we pronounced it is "*shiel*", which is the Russian pronunciation -- and we were very observant during the holidays. For instance, we wouldn't turn on a light at Yom Kippur and we would fast.

My parents were observant, I was not. Although when you're living there you had better be observant! You do what your parents want you to do. I was a good boy, so when I was asked, "Do you believe in God?" Of course, otherwise I'd be a bad boy! And I went to *cheder*. I really didn't care to go but made the best of it. However, I did look forward to playing touch football in front of the synagogue before class. We played with a stocking cap.

Joey: How'd you rig a stocking cap?

Sol: We'd roll it up! Some of the boys in my class were Marvin Richards, Jack Brown, Herbie Tepperman, Mickey Roffman and Millard Seldin. By the way, Marvin Richards and Eddie Cherniss made up a song about Council Bluffs [Sings with verve]:

Council Bluffs, Council Bluffs, how you made me shiver/with your nice clean streets and your muddy Missouri River/Oh, how I love you with my heart and I love you with my liver/Council Bluffs -- by the river.

And the Omaha kids would sing, "In the river." [Laughs] In *shul*, the older men were like good uncles or grandfathers who had an old-world way about them. They'd come over and pull your ear, always nice and friendly. Conversations were going on all the time, nobody was listening, only talking, and the kids would run through the synagogue. In desperation, the president of the *shul*, Sam Shyken would pound the lectern and in Yiddish would shout: "*Zy shtill!*" or "*Law zein shah!*" "C'mon, be quiet!"

Joey: [Laughs] Sounds like you guys were all family in a way. Your friend's grandpa could smack you on the arm?

Sol: And pinch your cheek! It hurt! And they'd talk Yiddish. "*Klainer!*" A *klainer*'s a small person. "Mr. *Klainer*" -- either cute, nice, or terrible. It's all the same! Yiddish played a big part in our growing up; it was used often in the synagogue. Even my brother, at his Bar Mitzvah, gave two speeches: one in English and one in Yiddish. If someone was getting up on the *bima* to talk, like Mr. Shyken, who seemed to be there forever, they'd speak in Yiddish.

In fact, when the synagogue was first formed, all the rules and regulations were originally written in Yiddish! They talked in an accent and were practically all immigrants. We were the up-and-coming American generation. And, of course, the women sat up top and the men down below, and we'd go up and see our mothers and they'd all *kvell* over us.

Nobody liked to go to Hebrew school. I don't know any one that ever liked to go! We would drive the teachers crazy. We'd go outside the door and yell: "Who's a bum? He's a bum! Rosenblum!" And we'd run away. Rosenblum only lasted one year! Then we had Cooper. He thought that he would mollify us by sending me to the grocery a block away and get bananas for the kids. I don't know if he thought we were all monkeys! [Laughs]

One time, the rabbi picked up Mickey Roffman and threw him out the door, but he was holding on to the desk at the same time, so the whole desk and Mickey flew out the door! And we had one teacher who used to hit our hands with a stick! We had a new rabbi every year, except Rabbi Cassel; he did my Bar Mitzvah. I liked Sunday school because they taught history: the Temple, the Babylonians, the Romans. I love, love history.

Joey: How religious was your family?

Sol: They weren't ultra-Orthodox. I think if they had to travel on Saturday that wasn't a problem, but we kept kosher and observed all the holidays to the Nth degree. My dad was a businessman who was open every day of the week. He opened at 7 a.m. and closed at 10 at night. If someone knocked on the door after 10 -- we lived above the store -- my dad opened up, too. It was a different lifestyle and work ethic in those days.

If my dad had to eat lunch or something, I'd come down and watch the store even as a kid, at eight or nine. If someone came in the store, we had a buzzer which would ring upstairs and my dad would come down and take care of the customer.

Joey: So as a Jew in Council Bluffs you were a huge minority.

Sol: A huge minority, but there were a lot of Jews, considering the size of the town and our congregation was very vibrant and strong.

Joey: Did you only spend time with Jews or did you have friends who were not Jewish?

Sol: My parents particularly wanted us to stay with the Jews. If I dated a *shiksa*, my mother would have killed me.

Joey: [Laughs]. Tell me about your Bar Mitzvah.

Sol: My Bar Mitzvah was at the *shul*. Interestingly, I had one relative who was very religious and walked all the way from about 19th and Burt in Omaha on Saturday morning. Forty years later, I was going through some old things when we were moving and I found a card. "Congratulations on your Bar Mitzvah!" It had five dollars in it which was the norm for gifts from my family in those days.

After the ceremony, I invited five or six guys to the Strand Theater. When the movie was over we went to Martin's drugstore. Martin was one of the Jewish people who had a store on the corner of 5th and Broadway. We all had malts and sodas, and that was my party. At that time, this was the way we usually celebrated our Bar Mitzvahs. We had a lot of family in Omaha. My mother's sister *Malka* who came from Russia to Council Bluffs or Omaha, could speak no English, got off the streetcar, had no one's address and just started walking around until she found a relative.

Joey: Did she?!

Sol: She did! My dad literally brought these relatives over from Russia. He had smuggled about 100 relatives and friends out of Communist Russia in 1921. It took him a year and cost him his fortune. And he came back to find that his seven-year-old son Morris had died while he was gone. They called him "*fahter*," which means uncle; they used it as an affectionate term and out of respect.

Joey: Is "*fahter*" Yiddish?

Sol: Yes. And "*meema*" is Aunt, so my mother was *Meema*, and I called my aunt and her sisters *Meema* Zelda, *Meema* Ruchel, *Meema* Malka, *Meema* Leah, and *Meema* Esther.

Joey: Love those names! So what do you remember about the holidays?

Sol: I still remember coming home from *shul* on Yom Kippur and going to bed without turning on the lights, so we were totally in the dark. Now, I do remember the holiday –– I think it's between Rosh Hashanah and Yom Kippur –– where they wave a chicken over your head!

Joey: You pulling my leg?

Sol: No, I'm serious. I don't know if it was to wash away your sins and things like that, but my mom would take a chicken and rotate it over my head. It was called *shlugging kapoorus*. You sling whatever *kapoorus* is, I'm not sure. But you're slinging… You're doing something with this chicken! And it's a live chicken!

Joey: I'd like to interview the chicken.

Sol: [Laughs] Then they changed it so you could do it with money.

Joey: What were your thoughts about the chicken?

Sol: I hope the chicken doesn't poop on me! My mom would do that to me! I'd lie in the bed in the morning, and then here she comes with the chicken!

Joey: Great way to wake up. You should have checked into a hotel before then [laughs]. So, how did growing up Jewish in Council Bluffs affect who you are?

Sol: It had a great effect, the time and place. We grew up during the Depression and World War II. Those were great equalizers. So there was no great distinction or difference among the Jews in status. It was almost like one big family. We knew all the little solipsisms, their mistakes, their accents and their wisdom from what they'd been through. It transferred, it came to you. You had a much broader general type of upbringing than say, a gentile in Omaha or Council Bluffs.

Joey: Did you experience anti-Semitism?

Sol: Anti-Semitism was fairly prevalent throughout the United States. People like Father Coughlin on the radio, and Henry Ford who published a newspaper, were openly anti-Semitic. Personally, I experienced it just among my peers. When I was six-years-old, some kid started calling me a dirty Jew. I got in a fight with him and I won the fight [laughs]. But when I told my mother of that experience, she said I should not fight, that I should run away. I was a good kid and I listened to my mother, but it was bad advice [smiles].

Because shortly thereafter, there was a gang of kids who started tormenting me with their insults and instead of me standing up to them, I would run away and they would chase me. My life in the neighborhood was not a happy one under those circumstances because many times I was afraid to even go to the corner grocery store.

So after a number of years, as I got older, I learned how to fight from my cousin who had been a professional boxer. On one occasion, I was sent by my mother to the grocery store and coming toward me was the leader of the gang, an ugly kid [laughs] who comes right up into my face and I said, 'Get your snotty-nosed face out of my way or I'm going to take this milk bottle and break it over your head.' He moved away and never bothered me again.

Shortly thereafter, I met another member of the gang as I was again going to the grocery store and he called me a dirty Jew. I grabbed him by his shirt, pushed him up against the wall of the store and told him, 'You give me any more trouble and I'll knock the shit out of you.' [laughs]. I never had any trouble after that.

I learned a good lesson: you just don't take it. You don't run away, you don't take it. As anti-Semitic guys are after you, you have to stand up to them. Most of the time, bullies are cowards. If they know they can terrorize you, they will.

Joey: Wow, Sol, that's a book unto itself! Tell me about the Jewish stores.

Sol: My dad's store was on Broadway between 7th and 8th Street. In that block was Abraham Snead's drugstore, Diamond's kosher market, Kushner's grocery (which was eventually replaced by Leo Meyerson's Radio Company), Max Cohen's pawn shop, Ruben Brown's slock shop [laughs], Kramer's Department Store and Katelman's store.

That was just in one block. From 8th to 9th Street was Roffman's grocery, Perlis's cleaners, Brown's pawn shop and Sacks's grocery. Going the other way up Broadway, you came to Richards' Owl Grocery, Krauss's Bargain Spot, Grossman's Department Store, Abraham Snead's Liberty Theater and Harry Cohen's clothing store, The Iowa Clothes Shop, next to Martin's drug store.

Further up the street I remember Stan Katelman's shoe store, The Peoples Store, Suvalsky's appliance store and Ben Seldin's real estate company was just off Broadway.

Joey: And after you left the Bluffs, what was life like?

Sol: After dental school, I went into the Air Force in 1949 and was stationed in Savannah, GA. On the first day, I went to a function at the JCC and asked, "Who's the nicest, most popular Jewish girl in Savannah?" They told me it was Cherie Hirsch, she had just been the regional AZA sweetheart of Georgia and South Carolina. I met her the next day, married her the next year and brought her back to Council Bluffs. We went to the synagogue and everybody said, "Solly's got a Georgia peach!" Everybody's *kvelling* for Solly.

By the way, my name is not really Sol, it's really *Tsalee*. The grandfather I'm named after said, "If you name someone after me, don't give him a Russian name like *Ivan* or *Stephan*. It's got to be *Tsalee*." Don't Anglicize it. But I had to pass a test to get into kindergarten because I was only four-and-a-half years old. It would have questions like, "If you're going to school and it starts raining, what do you do?" Well, you go back and get a raincoat! Then they showed me money: pennies, nickels, dimes, quarters and half dollars. From my dad's store, I knew how to open the register, so I knew money.

Joey: At four?

Sol: Yeah! I got it every time and they said, "You can start school." I'm in school and I am registered as *Tsalee* Kutler. In Kindergarten, you have to write your name on the board, so I got up and wrote it: *T-S-A-L-E-E*. And the kids would start laughing, so I told my folks, "I'm not going through my life with people laughing at my name, we have to have a family conference." So we got together, my mom, my dad and my brother Ben, and my brother says, "Well, how about Sol?" Now, I knew there was a baseball player called Solly Hemus, so I said, "OK, it's gonna be Sol." It was an endearing name to my mother who used to say, "*Tsala-llah de bist a doll-alallah*."

28. Esther and Harry Kutler
29. Ben Kutler and Sam Karchomsky

30. Sarah Kutler, 1915
31. Sarah Kutler and Family, Kiev, Russia
32. Morris Kutler with Booky and Lil Kushner
33. Harry, Sarah, Ben and Sol

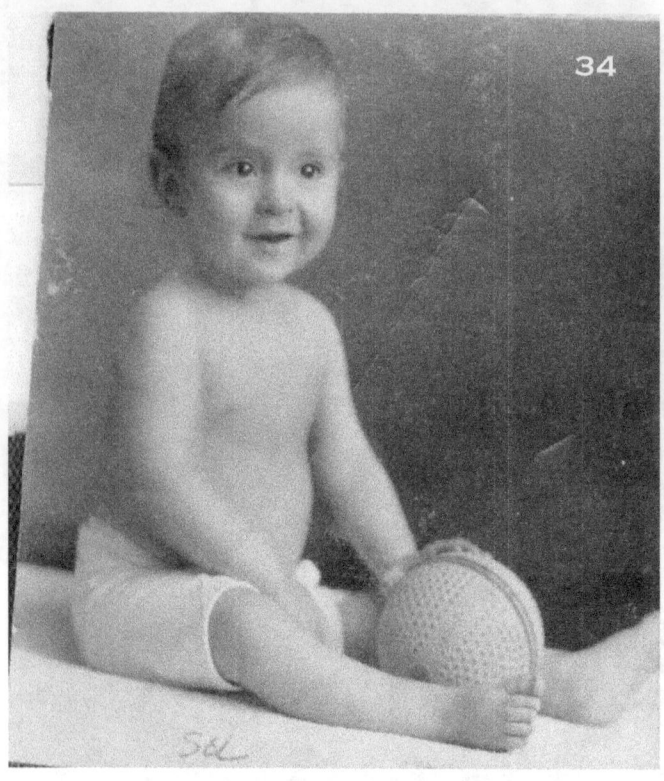

34. Sol at one year old
35. Sol at six years old
36. Class picture. Sol is in the third row up, fourth from the left, Washington School in 1938

37. Sol and Cherie's engagement, 1950
38. Ben Kutler with wife, Harriet and mother, Sarah
39. Sol's friends at Peony Park, 1954
40. Kutler's Cousins club
41. Sol Kutler induction to Abraham Lincoln High School Alumni Hall of Fame, 2000

קענטס. זשורנאל, יילונג, אויגוסט 7, 1949

אַ גאלעדי פ

סאל קאטלער, זוהן פון הערי און מרס.
קאטלער פון קאונסיל בלאפס. אַ שטאט
אין אייאווא סטעיט, וועלכער האט גע-
ענדיגט אויף דענטיסט אין קרעיטאן דענ-
טאל קאלעדזש, אמאהא, צו 21 יאהר.
דר. קאטלער איז געווען דער אינגסטער
"גרעדיועיט" אין דער געשיכטע פון
יענעם קאלעדזש.

A DENTIST AT TWENTY-ONE is Dr.
Sol Kutler (above), son of Mr. and Mrs.
Harry Kutler of 732 West Broadway,
Council Bluffs, Iowa, who received his
D.D.S. degree from Creighton Dental
College, Omaha. He was youngest
graduate in the history of that school.

Dr. Sol Kutler to Duty in Air Forces

Dr. Sol Kutler, 22, 732 West Broadway, will leave Wednesday for duty as a first lieutenant in the U. S. air forces dental corps at Chathan air base, Savannah, Ga.

Kutler

Dr. Kutler was graduated from Creighton Dental college in June. At 21 he is the youngest student ever to complete the six-year course. He is a member of Phi Epsilon Pi.

He was graduated from Abraham Lincoln high school June 19, 1944.

He was commissioned in the air force Nov. 1.

Bargain Center Sold By Kutler

8-11-55

The business and merchandise of the Open Front Bargain Center at 732 W. Broadway has been sold, owner Harry Kutler announced Wednesday.

It was purchased by the Leader Store in Omaha. Price was not disclosed.

Kutler, who operated the business for 39 years, is retiring. He said he plans to rent out the two-story building.

Kutler

Kutler came to Council Bluffs from Russia in 1913 when he was 21.

Kutler and his wife, the late Mrs. Sarah Kutler, operated a restaurant in the same block for three years after he first arrived here.

Mrs. Kutler died last year.

Death Takes Harry Kutler

Funeral services for Omahan Harry Kutler, longtime owner of a clothing store in Council Bluffs, will be at 11 a.m. Wednesday in the Jewish Funeral Chapel, 1912 Cuming Street.

Kutler, 85, of 1112 Mayfield Avenue, died Monday in an Omaha hospital. He had been ill with cancer for several months, his son Dr. Benton Kutler said.

Kutler owned and operated the Open Front Bargain Center at 732 West Broadway in the Bluffs for 45 years, retiring in 1957.

He came to the United States from Russia in 1910 and worked in a packinghouse in St. Joseph, Mo., and for the Burlington Railroad out of Omaha before going into business for himself in Council Bluffs.

He also is survived by his widow, Anna, another son, Dr. Sol Kutler, Omaha, and eight grandchildren.

Burial will be in Golden Hill Cemetery.

Thank you for your commitment to community service. Through your generosity and hard work, you have shown that the tradition of neighbor helping neighbor is alive and well in our country. Your efforts profoundly influence the life of your community and they are a shining example for us all. Barbara joins me in saluting you and sending you our best wishes. God bless you.

Gy Bush

Life of service, hallmark of Dr. Sol Kutler

One of the metropolitan area's best known dentists, Dr. Sol Kutler, has roots in Council Bluffs that run back to the early 1900's. His father, Harry "Shorty" Kutler owned and operated the Open Front Bargain Center at 732 West Broadway for over 30 years. Dr. Kutler is an Abraham Lincoln graduate, class of 1944.

Dr. Kutler, best known as the creator of the American Denture Clinic, has devoted a large share of his life to volunteer dentistry in third world countries. How did he get involved in this? One reason, he says, is the example set by his father. In 1918, shortly after the Bolshevik revolution occurred in Russia, Harry Kutler returned to Europe and spent a year, and his life savings, smuggling people out of Russia. That selfless act in the face of such danger was a lesson that made a strong impression on young Sol. He recounts a story of a time when someone was expressing admiration of this feat to Harry, asking him why he did it. Harry's reply was a simple, "I knew it was the right thing to do." That largely explains why Dr. Kutler has done so much for so many.

Dr. Kutler got his start in humanitarian work with Direct Relief an agency located in Santa Barbara, California that arranges for medical help to be given to underdeveloped countries. However, the participating physicians are required to pay their own travel expense.

His first stop was Haiti. His 19 yea-old son accompanied him They stayed for six weeks, living with the people in the slums, amid overpowering filth and poverty.

Since that first sojourn, Dr. Kutler has traveled to Africa four times, Vietnam, Hong Kong, Philippines, Belize, and the Negev Desert. The conditions are usually very crude. A typical office is a samsonite chair, with a coffee can for a spittoon. Sometimes indoors, sometimes out, sometimes with electricity sometimes without. A typical stay was six weeks.

Dr. Kutler has "a day full" of stories and anecdotes about his travels. On his trip to the Negev Desert, he had the opportunity to meet Ariel Sharon and Itzak Shamir. In Belize, he treated several prisoners, finishing up by flashlight! On his last day, as he was preparing to leave, the prisoners arrived by truck, and presented him with a model ship they had custom-built as a thank you to him.

Dr. Kutler has received numerous awards for his volunteerism, including Rotary International's Humanitarian of the Year. One that got away was the Rotary's World Understanding Award. He didn't feel too bad though for as he put it, " I got beat out by Pope John Paul III". Dr. Kutler has a unique perspective on the honors he has received. "Many people would shy away from the attention, or take an 'aw shucks' approach. However, I think I have an obligation to use these awards and the position they have given me to inspire others to service." And inspire others is exactly what he has done. To date, Dr. Kutler has organized several teams of doctors and dentists to go overseas. He was responsible for getting a heart surgeon to Kenya who performed that country's first bypasss operation. Also, an American Ear, Nose, Throat doctor has established free clinics in Kenya as a direct result of Dr. Kutler's influence. Although the three dentists practicing with him allow for more time off, Dr. Kutler still continues his service to others, and probably always will. One of Council Bluffs' finest native sons, Dr. Sol Kutler.

***

The fundamental secret of science is that seeking truth is more important than truth itself.
—Friedrich Nietzsche

Proclamation by Governor Ben Nelson making "a Place Like Nebraska" the Official Ballad of Nebraska

Sol with Governor Ben Nelson

PAUL SHYKEN

My grandfather Simon Shyken came here via St. Louis from a town in the Ukraine called *Lechervitz*. He couldn't speak the language, had no formal education and was 21 years old. He was married and they had a daughter. However, he left his wife and daughter behind in *Lechervitz* with the intent of coming to the U.S. and later bringing them to join him. It was the early 1900s when he arrived in the U.S., and he peddled junk, whatever he could get to buy and sell to make a couple cents.

He and a friend, also originally from *Lechervitz*, traveled to Council Bluffs to visit a friend from the old country, Mr. Saltzman. I remember hearing the story of how when they were traveling by train to Council Bluffs, they put their *tefillin* on in the morning; and everyone on the train looked at them like they were from Mars!

In Council Bluffs, Mr. Saltzman had a hay and feed store and he offered my grandfather a job. He jumped at it because it would give him a steady income so that he could save up enough money to bring my grandmother and their daughter, my aunt, to the U.S. It would also allow him the chance to leave St. Louis, where as a Jewish peddler he was often beaten and harassed.

My grandparents with their one daughter, my aunt, settled in Council Bluffs. My grandfather met a man named Getsy Whitebrook and they became close friends. Getsy then offered him a job in his hay and feed store for more money, which my grandfather could not resist. I guess my grandfather and Mr. Saltzman were not so happy with each other, or maybe Mr. Saltzman was not so happy with my grandfather! But they eventually made up.

My grandfather and my grandmother Bertha bought a house and had more children: first was my aunt Fanny, who was the oldest born in Russia, then my aunt Rose, then my father Sam and finally my aunt Ruth. My grandfather was very proud, and he was a shrewd businessman. After a while, he had accumulated enough money and bought a junkyard. He called it Shyken Junk. Wisely, he got all of the utility companies in Council Bluffs as his accounts and things prospered for him because utility companies were constantly repairing and changing their infrastructure. My grandfather was able to benefit and would buy their old work and outdated metals.

While he was in the junk business, he was also buying real estate. Junk dealers would buy junk, but they couldn't sell it to the foundries. The only way they could get it to the foundries was through a broker, so my grandfather sold his scrap to a broker in Omaha, Aaron Ferer and Sons; I think they're still in business. Mr. Ferer took a liking to my grandfather, so he'd lend my grandfather money and my grandfather would pay him back with scrap. Over the years, my grandfather was able to accumulate quite a few pieces of real estate in Council Bluffs using the money loaned to him by Mr. Ferer.

When the Depression struck, his scrap business was pretty much worthless. Therefore, he took one of his buildings at 33 South Main Street and decided to buy and sell used furniture in that building. He was very good at that. Meanwhile, he kept buying junk for next to nothing and he accumulated a lot of junk in his junkyard, but he was unable to sell anything. He only bought and kept selling furniture. He prospered in his furniture business, and then war broke out in Europe.

In wartime, the price of junk skyrocketed! He sold the junk, got rid of the furniture store, retired around 59-years-old and devoted his time to the synagogue and his real estate. He did very well.

My grandfather was very patriotic. In his home office he had a picture of FDR and he had an American flag. FDR was a hero to the Jewish immigrants. Life was so good in the U.S. compared to life in Russia. When they moved to a new house, I noticed the FDR picture was gone but the flag was still there. I asked my cousins about that and they said, "Yes, we remember it was gone but nobody ever asked any questions." Well, I think I now know why it was gone once it came out about FDR's treatment of the Jews during the Holocaust. That ended it. But he didn't talk about it, at least not when I was around.

One of the first things I knew about the Holocaust -- I couldn't have been more than three or four-years-old, but I remember it as if it were yesterday -- my grandfather's father was killed in the Holocaust when he was 96 or 97. He had been taken out to the forest along with the whole family who was still left in *Lechervitz*, and they were all shot and killed. I've got a book that has all the *yahrtzeits* of his family. I remember my grandfather sitting *shiva* and I remember him crying, he was so broken up. It was not only his father, but his brothers, sisters and their families who were all killed. They probably never thought anything could happen in *Lechervitz*, and they were content and wanted to stay there. And they did but, unfortunately, they all perished.

B'nai Israel was very dear to him. At that time, it was not uncommon for younger people in Orthodox synagogues to be more Yankee, more American, and they wanted to do away with the separation of men and women and they wanted microphones. There was a group that wanted to make B'nai Israel more traditional, and my grandfather was very much against it. He wanted it to stay an Orthodox synagogue, and he was able to prevail for many years.

He was fair with the people on the other side of the issue, but he went so far as to seek council from an Iowa Supreme Court Justice. He got an interpretation saying that B'nai Israel is incorporated as an Orthodox synagogue, and per the articles of incorporation, the building's owned by the Orthodox synagogue and it can't be changed. My grandfather had the money, acquaintances and wherewithal to keep going with it. As long as he lived, the synagogue remained Orthodox. After he died, it changed and became a synagogue with mixed seating.

My grandfather had no education, but there was a piece of a letterhead that I found in his office that always impressed me once I learned about it. I wondered "Why did he keep it?" Apparently, a doctor in Council Bluffs named Dr. Matt Tinley was under consideration for Vice President of the U.S. either under the FDR or Truman administration. He had appointed/selected my grandfather to be on his advisory committee while a candidate for Vice President. My grandfather was on an advisory committee for a U.S. Vice Presidential candidate! To come from a little town in Ukraine with no education and he was on a letterhead of a potential vice presidential candidate as one of his advisors! I was amazed!

He was influential in the city and really active in the synagogue. That was his true love, I think. When he died, the funeral was in the synagogue, and my father and my aunts did not want that, nor did my grandmother, because an Orthodox synagogue will usually never take a body into the sanctuary unless it was someone like the rabbi. Even today in an Orthodox synagogue, one should not ever take a body in because according to Jewish law, one becomes impure if they come in contact with a dead body.

But people who were on the opposite side of the mixed versus separate seating issue wanted his funeral in the synagogue because they still respected him, regardless of their differences. They made an exception and I don't think they ever had a funeral in the building after that, but my grandfather was held in high regard by a lot of the people.

He was very charismatic and very fair with people. And his relationship to his wife...one of my cousins said, "They didn't have a marriage, they had a love affair." And he was so giving. I was at a *shiva* house just a few years ago making a condolence call and a lady came up to me and introduced herself. I knew who she was, but I didn't really know her well. She didn't live in Omaha anymore, but I knew her brother when I was in high school, and she said, "I'm going to tell you a story you've never heard."

Many years ago when her mother was a small child, her mother became ill and her mother's parents took her to the doctor. This was in the Depression and their family had no money, so they had to pay the doctor by trading something. This woman's grandmother gave the doctor her *Shabbos* candlesticks for treating her young child. That's all she had of any value.

Many years later, the doctor's wife decided to sell some things, so she called someone to buy them. A man came and he looked at what she had to sell and said, "I'll give you a fair price for the items, but I want to know from where these candlesticks came." The doctor's wife found out and told the man. The man said, "I'll give you a fair price for the candlesticks, but you must promise to return the candlesticks to the person from whom they came." The purchaser of the candlesticks included one more condition, "You're not to tell the lady why you're giving them back. Just give them back." So the doctor's wife gave them back. The lady at the *shiva* house continues the story. When the doctor's wife gave my grandmother back the candlesticks, my grandmother said, "I can't take them, I want to know why I'm getting them back." So the doctor's wife told the mother how it came to be that she was returning the candlesticks.

The lady telling me the story says, "I have those candlesticks now and I light them every Friday night and say a prayer." She asked me, "Do you know who it was that said the candlesticks must be returned?" I had an idea who it was already, and then she says, "It was your grandfather."

He did a lot of those things; and when people would fall on hard times in Council Bluffs, he'd get people together and help them out. For example, at my grandmother's funeral, there was a man who was crying and I had no idea who he was, I'd never seen him before. I asked my father who it was and he just kind of brushed it off, so I kept asking him, "Why was he crying? Who was he?" My father said, "I'll tell you the story but promise me you won't ever mention the name."

He said that the man sold insurance, and in those days, when one sold insurance the agent would collect the premiums and send the money to the insurance company. The man had to feed his family and had to use some of the premium collections. My grandfather and other people took care of the bill that he owed the insurance company. That must have been why he was crying. I don't know why I get choked up about it but…he was grateful that my grandmother's family saved him. My grandfather never talked about this, ever.

When he came to America, they Americanized his name. It was not Shyken, it was "*Cheitnitz*." When it came time for my grandfather to get his citizenship papers, he had to go before the judge. He needed witnesses, so he took two of his friends who lived in Council Bluffs. He went before the judge and the judge says, "What is your name?" My grandfather didn't know what they were talking about! The friend who understands English, translates in Yiddish and says, "Tell them your name, *Shia*." My grandfather responded, "*Shia*." The judge spells it, "S-H-Y-K-E-N." Shyken, that's your name."

My grandparents were very observant. They called it '*Shomer Mitzvah*' and '*Shomer Shabbos*.' *Shomer*, translated literally, means someone who watches the *mitzvah* or the commandments, someone who's observant. I remember reading a book by Rabbi Feldman in Atlanta, and he said, "Some people are observant, some people are religious, some people are both." I think my grandfather would have fit the bill; he was both.

My grandmother was a wonderful cook; there was nothing she wouldn't do for my grandfather. But there was nothing he wouldn't do for her. Nothing. He was always buying her clothes; he couldn't give her enough, and she never wanted more! She was a very simple, plain woman. He lavished everything on her!

There were frequent guests at my grandparents' house. My grandfather was at the synagogue every morning and most evenings, but always the mornings -- and, of course, on *Shabbos*. One of his guests was from Las Vegas and when he was in Council Bluffs, he was invited to their house. The reason that this man was in Council Bluffs was due to the dog racing. Council Bluffs had dog racing in the '30s and early '40s. Meyer Lansky came to oversee the dog track but he also always came to the synagogue. Like everybody else, he was at my grandparent's too! I remember saying to my dad once, "Do you think *Zayda* really knew who he was…" Dad said, "I don't know; he never talked about it." Meyer Lansky always donated money to the synagogue each time he was in Council Bluffs. My dad said Meyer Lansky was a very generous man to the synagogue, which is interesting.

Another interesting thing about Council Bluffs is that before the Interstate, people would have to take Highway 6 to come from Chicago or travel east to west. Highway 6 was kind of a torturous road near Council Bluffs, and it was nicknamed "Suicide Six" because there were a lot of accidents on that road. It was not uncommon to end up in the hospital because of a car accident. If somebody injured was Jewish, observant and observed dietary laws, there were no kosher provisions to provide anyone in the hospital. So, as a kosher home, my grandmother would cook and my grandfather would bring the food up to them in the hospital. I remember someone said they used to call my grandfather Dr. Shyken because he always used to walk down the hospital halls!

I was 17 when he died, so I got to spend a lot of time with him while growing up. The last time I saw my grandfather was on a Wednesday, and then he died on a Friday. On that Wednesday, my mother picked me up from school to take me to visit him at the hospital. He was at Clarkson at the time, and he was pretty sick. It was hard for him to talk, but we talked a little bit. I eventually had to leave him, and we both knew we weren't going to see each other again. I kissed him goodbye and he took my hand and held it to his face and he said in Yiddish, "Go the right way, my child." "*Gey der rechtgen veg mein kint.*"

It's well over 50 years ago and I still remember walking down the hospital hallway after leaving his room. "What did he tell me? What did he want me to do?" And even to this day I think about it from time to time because he was certainly a knowledgeable person in spite of having no education. You see his handwritten words and it's from someone who didn't even know how to write when he came to this country! And I've often thought about that. It's a good memory to have.

He also said, "Remember from where you came." "*Fergest nicht fon ver dee kimnt.*" People have to remember from where they came. You don't know where you're going if you don't remember from where you came. I think it also speaks volumes in the sense that, if I think about from where I came, I, too, came from the *shtetl* in Europe. I'm no better or different than they were. I've had all kinds of privileges that have given me wonderful opportunities; but that's where I came from and I shouldn't think I'm better.

They were wonderful people even though they had nothing. If you try to keep that in perspective, treat other people like you want to be treated, just remember that because you may have done well financially, or achieved some status or title, they don't mean anything if you want respect. I don't believe respect comes from a title. You have to earn that respect. He did, and he didn't have a title; but he earned respect because of who he was.

I remember at Beth Israel once, they were reading in the *Torah* portion about the blessing that the *Kohanim* give to people. Today, they recite this blessing on Jewish holidays; in some places, they do it every day. God tells the *Kohanim* to bless the people, to bless the Jews. He says to Abraham, "Be a blessing to others." I think about that, "How are you a blessing to others?" By the way you act. People teach all kinds of things, but the most important part is how you behave. If you're not an example, it doesn't matter what you teach. People aren't going to respect you, and my grandfather exemplified that in every way.

לפ"ק לעטלוויץ

Skyken family in Europe

42. Simon, Bertha, Bess, Sam, Pacey and Keva Shyken
43. Shyken house & scrap business
44. Inside of synagogue before remodeling

MARCIA TEPPERMAN KUSHNER

IF BOOKWORM VERA Silberman read love stories -- "I read morning, noon, and night," she said -- none were likely more *bashert* than her own. Vera, Marcia Kushner's mother, was a reticent gal living on the Lower East Side who preferred to spend time with characters in her books rather than with friends. Her mother Augusta grew increasingly concerned, but Vera wouldn't have any part of it. Yet, at 15, she ran into Bertha, an old kindergarten pal on the street and relented, accepting a dinner invitation to her mother's delight. "Grandma practically pushed her out of the house," says Marcia.

That moment marked Vera's venture out of her comfort zone and into the arms of a man who would swiftly change her life. At dinner, a charming 20-year-old gent named Eddie Tepperman sat beside her and inquired about school and her interests. "Eddie was very much a people person," said Vera, whose subsequent courtship with her beau included tennis dates, plays and movies. In 1924, they married in a traditional Orthodox wedding ceremony, a union which lasted over 70 years. "They adored each other," says Marcia.

After their two children arrived – son Herbert, born September 15, 1925 and Marcia, March 4, 1929, President Hoover's inauguration day – so did rough financial times. "The Depression hit hard," says Marcia, whose father owned a restaurant on the Rockaway Beach boardwalk which burned down. His sister Sophie and her husband Dave Kaplan who lived in Missouri Valley, Iowa, felt their grocery store could support two families, so his brother-in-law in New York gave him a little old Chevy he couldn't afford to keep, and Vera, Eddie, Herb and Marcia beelined for the midwest.

Soon after their move in 1931, however, they realized the store could not, in fact, support both families, so the Teppermans relocated to Omaha, traded the Chevy for a truck, and rented a room in the home of a Jewish family, the parents of Nate Gimple.

"Dad went peddling fruit; then a store came up to rent in Council Bluffs, a building owned by Ernie, Leo and Nate Nogg's parents. It was at 16th and Broadway, a little mom-and-pop grocery store called Teppy's Cash Market. Up the street on 15th and Broadway was Steinberg's grocery. They ran a really nice store. They were our competition. Very, very nice Jewish people.

"My parents hoped they would do a cash-and-carry business and sell groceries cheaper, but they had people on the books and it was the Depression. People had no money. Most were on Relief and WPA," says Marcia, who remembers Eddie always had a pencil behind his ear used to list prices on a paper sack.

The vintage corner building included a four-room apartment upstairs where the family lived. Soon, in 1938, son David would be born. "It was small; but as a kid, it didn't seem that small to me. We had a very antique bathroom with a wood-framed tub. We often bathed in a tin tub near an oil space heater in the kitchen. A hole in the floor allowed heat to rise from the store, which was part of the construction because there was no central heating. My brother and I looked down at people, we wanted to drop things on them. That wasn't allowed, but who could resist?" she laughs.

The building's interior mirrored the neighborhood. "It was a very, very poor, mixed neighborhood. There were a few black families. Living in a mixed neighborhood made me comfortable with blacks which wasn't everyone's experience. It was very valuable to have a sense of comfort around people with black skin in tiny Council Bluffs."

Since Council Bluffs blue laws dictated they had to close the store one day a weekend, being Jewish, Teppy's was closed on Saturday and open on Sunday. "It wasn't a religious, but a business decision," says Marcia. "I was bored out of my gourd on Saturdays when my mother was rapt listening to the Metropolitan Opera on the radio while reading whatever book in which she was absorbed.

"My family was very culturally-minded. We had a phonograph machine and we played only classical music records. And we always went to the library. My mother didn't drive, but you could always find her walking to the library carrying tons of books. Yale Gotsdiner said he spent hours there looking for sources for a debate and always saw my mom there. She stuck me in the children's room while she browsed the stacks. We walked home with piles of books."

Starting around eight-years-old, Marcia took piano lessons at Beck School of Music, an elegant, white-framed house across from Bayliss Park. When her teacher Jack, a protégé of the owner Mrs. Beck, was drafted, he recommended Marcia to Mrs. Beck. "I was scared! I wasn't a good music reader and didn't practice a lot, but I had musical sense. Once a year, we had a recital. It was the horror of my life. My mother came (Dad didn't because he couldn't leave the store) and after the performances, we went to Martin's drug store owned by Jews. They made the best hot fudge sundae!"

Eddie or "Teppy" as folks called him, worked diligently to keep the family afloat. Hard-pressed to make a decent living in the little store, Teppy thought outside the cardboard box: sell fresh produce at a stand next to the store and import truckloads of watermelons which he sold to other merchants. Still, Marcia says, "We couldn't generate enough capital to make the next move to a better store; we could not get out of the hole."

But with the onset of World War II in Europe, the U.S. went into high gear to build up a defense industry. Once Teppy got wind defense plants were under construction in Wahoo and Mead, NE and they needed carpenters, he swapped his apron for a tool belt. "My parents felt it was a handsome wage. He was handy and got the notion he would pass himself off as a carpenter while Mom and Herb at about 16 ran the store. Dad bought used tools to look like he had been doing it for ages. They asked for his social security number, yet he didn't have one because in those days, unless you worked for someone, you didn't have one. For months, he went off and worked and wasn't even home every week."

One fellow Jew would help reunite the family. In January, 1942, Nate Gimple, whose parents opened their home to the Teppermans upon their arrival in Omaha, spotted a tiny grocery store for sale in the Drake Court Apartments, an upscale building that stretched from 17th to 20th Streets between Leavenworth and St. Mary's across the river. A relief, as Dad would be home full time and could potentially make a good living. But for Marcia, then in eighth grade, the timing was treacherous.

"Miss Wild was a teacher at Eighth Street School, everyone loved her, and I couldn't wait to have her. But my parents decided to move. I was so distraught. The principal, darling Miss Hannigan, seeing my distress, offered to keep my Council

Bluffs address on my attendance sheet so I could finish out the year without paying out-of-state tuition. So, I got up early and took the streetcar which ran from downtown Omaha across the bridge to Eighth Street in the Bluffs."

For the next few years, Eddie and Vera ran the Drake Court Grocery Store. Yet, when an opportunity arose to take over the White Front Market, a fine grocery in Council Bluffs that served the carriage trade, they grabbed it, packed up and set up shop. *Baruch Hashem*! "Blessed God!" back to the Bluffs, where business was so good, the family would build a home up on the Bluffs on 5th Avenue.

For a grocery of the White Front Market's size, it was unusual that Eddie would be elected as state president of the Iowa Retail Food Dealer's Association. "That was a very big deal," Marcia says. "Seldom did a small, independent grocer become a powerhouse." The IRFDA had a history of being politically active, and during Eddie's tenure, they lobbied bills that supported their industry. "My dad really reveled in that.

"He could hold an audience; he was a powerful public speaker, very bright. They recognized him as a natural leader of their organization." Apparently, Eddie was not the only man who could hold an audience. In 1958, upon his election to the Iowa Retail Food Dealer's Association, their local chapter, the Council Bluffs Grocer's Association held a dinner in his honor. Who would they hire for entertainment?

Henny Youngman.

The Teppermans' Jewish life started soon after they arrived in Council Bluffs. "Being affiliated was a new thought to my family, but we knew it was important to be part of the community and we joined the synagogue. My mother never went to Hebrew school and my father learned Hebrew in the old country. We were very much out of the social swim of the Jewish community. We were poor, at the bottom of the rung in the Jewish community," Marcia laughs.

It was through Hadassah that Vera linked up with Jewish women. One in particular set her mind and heart afire. "Frieda Suvalsky was a powerhouse, an extremely bright woman who was behind Hadassah. She saw in my mother a very interesting woman and took her and our family under her wing. She was very crazy about me; I was kind of her daughter." Marcia would eventually join Young Judea and credits her parents for giving her "a very positive sense of being Jewish."

Since there were no girls exactly Marcia's age in the community, she hated going to Hebrew school. "I had no girlfriends there; there were younger and older girls. Marsha Gordon was a bit younger and her sister Ethel and Esther Sacks were a little older. My parents didn't think it was a big deal for a girl to not learn Hebrew at that time, but I attended Hebrew School sporadically."

Still, at nine, Marcia wowed her family after hearing Herb practice for his Bar Mitzvah. "I picked up the opening chant of the *brochah*. They thought I was very clever." The September, 1938 service took place about a week after baby brother David's *bris*, allowing her maternal grandparents to be there for the double *simcha*.

Vera had an equitable temperament. But don't be fooled. "She was no wimp," says Marcia. With the advent of World War II, and word of concentration camp atrocities, her mother and father became stalwarts for Jewish causes.

"My parents went to meetings with out-of-town speakers and were attempting to raise funds to get Jews out of Germany. When my brother David was born in 1938, my mom wanted to give him the most Jewish name as a sign of being proud of being Jewish. The day France fell to the Germans, she wept all day long. 'The Jews of France are doomed!' she said. It was scary for me. We had a little weekly newspaper at Sunday school that showed children in Europe wearing yellow bands on their coats. We are all very upset. When I was about 12, a Jewish girl from Harlan, Iowa visited our family. We went to a movie together and when we came out, someone was calling, 'Extra, Extra! Pearl Harbor has been bombed.' I walked home to my family's house. We were all so upset."

After the war, Vera's political activism gained momentum. The introvert from the Lower East Side went full throttle as she became involved in Israel Bonds and the League of Women Voters, participated in the Iowa caucuses, joined AIPAC (American Israel Public Affairs Committee) and even traveled to Washington to attend one of the organization's national meetings. She was president of the Sisterhood, president of Hadassah "forever," says Marcia and, with Frieda, repeatedly lobbied their senators and congressmen to support the recognition of Israel.

Eddie, too, was unstoppable. President of four organizations -- the Jewish Welfare Federation, the Irving Cohen Lodge of B'nai B'rith and B'nai Israel, where he also served as the first Men's Club president -- at the 13th annual father and son banquet of the lodge held at *shul*, Lloyd Krasne presented him with the annual Herman Krause memorial award, given to an outstanding member of the lodge. Ben Schneider served as banquet chairman, Maynard Telpner was master of ceremonies. Even St. Louis Cardinals pitcher Bob Gibson spoke. To boot, three congregants spoke on behalf of each generation: Ben Seldin (grandfathers), David Gallner (fathers) and Keith Tepperman (sons).

On April 16, 1972, Vera and Eddie received the Ben J. Gershon Memorial Trophy at the annual dinner-meeting of the Council Bluffs Jewish Federation at B'nai Israel. According to an article in the *Jewish Press*, "The annual award is made to individuals who have made notable contributions to community efforts for service and humanitarian causes." (Note: Previous winners of the Ben J. Gershon Memorial Trophy included Sam Meyerson, Harry Cohen, Ben Seldin, Joe Katelman, Abe Katelman, Sam Sacks, Sam Saltzman, Mr. and Mrs. Saul Suvalsky, Louis Bernstein and Dr. Isaac Sternhill.)

During an era when a woman's place was in the kitchen, Eddie was the exception. The chief cook at *shul*, mainly for fundraisers for the Federation or B'nai B'rith, his artistic presentations may have rivaled his recipes which proved to be incentive enough for folks to cross the river. "When friends in Omaha heard he was cooking, they came," says Marcia. Dad's signatures? Cornish game hen, blintzes and "Eddie's *kugel*."

During services, the sanctuary scene was Norman Rockwell, Jewish style: kids racing in and out and the women upstairs talking so loud Sam Sacks would bang his prayer book on the bima. "*Tshah, Tshah!*" he'd shout. "Be still!" Sometimes Marcia would climb downstairs and sit with her dad. "He could chant a really good *Haftarah*, even into his 90s."

Edward, whose Hebrew name was *Yitzach*, was born in 1899 in *Bessarabia*, a slice of land between Russia and Roumania. His dad *Hersch*, who came to America first, learned English and worked in his brother-in-law's laundry business until he saved enough money to bring the family over.

Eddie, 14, and his sister Sophie, 16, left Europe in June, 1913 and traveled with a group illegally across the border of *Bessarabia*. "They tore a paper bill in half and left half with their mother *Raisa* or Rose," says Marcia. "When they got across the border, a guy who took the group brought the other half back to their mother to prove they made it across border. Two kids, 16 and 14, had never been out of the area of *Bessarabia*. They traveled to Amsterdam where they stayed for a few days at a Jewish woman's house who put up immigrants waiting to board boats to New York City."

During the Teppermans' early days in Council Bluffs when funds were scarce, tearing a paper bill in half would have been the ultimate in *chutzpah*. But no matter how high their house sat, or how low their bank account got, money was never their priority. Instead, they survived on love, joy and community. At Marcia and her husband Shel's 50th wedding anniversary, Jack Brown, Herbert's best friend, wrote a tribute to the Teppermans, his surrogate family.

"Everyone worked hard, but there was a kind of bonhomie (including with customers in the grocery store) that pervaded the atmosphere. Eddie brought a kind of ebullience and verve and wonderful, radiating smile to everything he did. There was a totally natural, unpretentious sense of style about the Teppermans and the Silbermans, and a strong sense of integrity that was built into the character of every member of the family."

Perhaps brother Herbert said it best. In his speech at Eddie and Vera's 50th anniversary party in 1974, he said: "If hard times ever come to you and you haven't got much money, you can take lessons from my father and mother on how to raise a family without any money and without being poor."

45. Tepperman's White Front Market on South Main Street
46. Ed Tepperman being honored

47. Ed cooking at Council Bluffs Synagogue
48. Vera & Ed Tepperman in their kitchen

JANIE FOX KULAKOFSKY

Joey: So Janie, what is your link to Council Bluffs?

Janie: My grandparents, Sarah Saltzman Fox and Dave Fox, lived in Council Bluffs and both the Saltzmans and Foxes had businesses there. The Foxes were in the auto parts business; the Saltzman side was in the coal business.

Council Bluffs Auto Parts was located at 138 West Broadway. My father Jack was in business with Dave and my father's brother Uncle Harold. Even my cousin Barbara (Harold's daughter) and I would help them occasionally in the store.

We lived in Omaha so my father had to commute to Council Bluffs. He did this every day for 28 years. When I was in grade school, almost every Saturday I would go with my father to my grandparents' house or hang out at the store. When I was at my grandparents' who lived at 108 N. 8th Street, we'd often walk down to the store which was no more than six blocks down Broadway. They did machine shop work in the back, so there was grease everywhere. I remember the smells...the wooden floors absorbed all the odors. When I was older, my Uncle Harold's daughter Barbara and I would take the sales slips and check them against the inventory. Everything was done by hand then. There was no air conditioning.

Joey: Hot and greasy. Fun!

Janie: Luckily, we had fans. The store seemed very big to me because I was a kid. As a matter of fact, Bobby (Harold's son) and I were in the store recently and the back is still the same; wooden floors. It's a flower shop now. There are now apartments above that strip on West Broadway where they've restored a lot of the older buildings.

My father and Uncle Harold also opened some stores in some smaller towns, in the southwest corner of Iowa: Glenwood, Clarinda and Bedford. I remember the same city plan in each of the towns: the court house in the middle and businesses around it. It was fun being with my father, I felt important. He was very gentle, the whole Fox side of the family was very gentle, and we have what we call the Fox Family Humor -- very dry. My cousin Bob does, too. One-liners.

On Saturday mornings, when I went with my father over to Council Bluffs, we'd walk from the store to the Home Café, a little restaurant down the street, to have breakfast. Best pancakes in town! Or he would drop me off at my grandparents' and I'd spend the morning there. It was a treat to go over there. Grandma Sarah was very neat and sweet. I never, ever heard her raise her voice. Never. Sometimes my father would show up for lunch. He liked her spinach borscht.

Friday night was pretty big in the family. I just loved being with the aunts, uncles and cousins. I looked forward going to my grandparents for *Shabbos* and holiday dinners. Oh my God, whatever Grandma cooked was wonderful! I remember stuffed veal pocket, sweet and sour cabbage rolled up, her pancakes were…I've never had any since that can match them, and believe me I have tried cooking them myself. Very often we would walk to the little synagogue on Mynster for services after dinner. The sanctuary was arranged like the European synagogues; the *bimah* was in the middle and the women sat upstairs.

I explored my grandparents' house often. I remember Grandma had a huge walk-in closet and I'd look at her clothes and shoes. She was a very small woman, like me, always dressed very neatly, hair was always in place. The upstairs was one or two huge rooms where the children slept. I liked looking at the old furniture and imagining what it was like living there. I found the basement scary, and the kitchen seemed very big to me.

Joey: It was the center of the home?

Janie: Yes. They had an alcove with a refrigerator, she called it The "Frigidaire." I remember they had bottles of milk with the cream on top. Right across from the fridge was a hallway of cabinets where my grandfather kept his schnapps. He'd come home on Saturdays from work and had a little shot.

My grandmother and I would walk to Joe Smith's drugstore on Broadway, not far from the house. It always had a certain pleasant odor to me. I think they had a soda fountain, I remember Sealtest ice cream. We'd have chocolate sodas or sundaes. To this day, you can't find a decent soda fountain in town. Of course' we'd stop in the Peoples Store -- definitely went to the Peoples Store, probably dress shopping.

I love telling this story because it's happened so much in my family. My father's brother Lester married my mother's first cousin, Helen, so I'm doubly related to my aunt and uncle. Then one of my dad's first cousin's daughter, Joan, married my mother's brother Richard, so I'm doubly related to them also. My uncle is my cousin and my aunt is my cousin. Another cousin of my mom's married another cousin of my dad's; there was no problem with families getting to know each other because they already knew each other. My grandfather Dave's sister Ida married -- not related -- Morris Fox.

Joey: She didn't have to change her initials!

Janie: No, and my Uncle Morris started F & F Cough Drops in the Beebe + Runyan building on South 9th Street in the Old Market. The business way very successful. His brother-in-law was Jacob Fregger, thus F & F stands for Fregger and Fox.

Joey: Sounds like a law firm.

Janie: It does! Since I started this genealogy with my cousin Bob and Sue Millward, we've come across a lot of interesting family trivia. When my brother Dan was living in Kingman, Arizona, he went antiquing one day and, lo and behold, in one of the antique shops there was this huge poster advertisement of F & F. Oh my God, he was ecstatic! He literally had to beg the woman to sell it to him. So he brought it back to Omaha and we had it framed.

Incidentally, the Fox family name in Kreminitz, Russia, in the town district of Shumskoya, was either *Fuchs* or *Fiks*. In German it means fox. Rumor has it this Fox family were furriers in Europe.

Joey: Interesting, Fox/furrier.

Janie: Maybe that's how they got the name because they didn't have last names.

Joey: Clearly, family is incredibly important to you and has had a big impact on your life.

Janie: Yes. My mother especially made sure that no matter which side of the family, whether her side or my father's, if we went to Chicago or to L.A., or wherever, we would visit the aunts, the uncles, the cousins. Nobody does that anymore, and they lose track of each other and they don't see each other. My mother made sure that we saw everybody. It's carried over to me and probably somewhat to my son, Jay. On my mother's side of the family, there is a big sense of family and Bobby has picked it up also. Every couple of weeks he'll call me with something new he's found.

Joey: He does the research; you reap the benefits.

Janie: I do, just little tidbits…He and I went to the *Nonpareil* website and found articles about my father; that's how I knew he was active in the Chamber of Commerce, was on the high school Honor Roll, and editor of the A.L. yearbook.

Joey: Modern technology has helped you discover family stories you might otherwise not have found.

Janie: It has. I never thought about my ancestors or asked because I was young. Keeping memories alive! So important.

Joey: How does that contribute to your sense of belonging, your sense of family?

Janie: Well, I claim a lot of cousins. We have mutual cousins; everybody in Omaha does. They had big families back then, and they all married Jewish. On my husband's side, oh my gosh, the cousins all married each other and they all have the same name. I'm very family conscious. I'm friendly with cousins on down the line.

Joey: So family bonds have influenced your values.

Janie: Yes. My older son could care less and, again, my younger son is into the genealogy stuff. Not that he wants to go see everybody.

Joey: They are fascinating, lovely people on paper!

Janie: Exactly. My mother just loved her family, and it rubbed off on me.

Joey: What was your family's relationship to B'nai Israel?

Janie: I actually have a picture of my father and my grandfather standing at the new synagogue in Council Bluffs. The first synagogue burned down, and my Aunt Rose, my father's sister, and another Jewish lady who may have been an Endelman, ran into the synagogue and saved the *Torah*. The last four years I have gone to Rosh Hashana and Kol Nidrei in Council Bluffs because my cousin Jeff Taxman conducts the services there.

Joey: Another cousin! How are you related?

Janie: My great grandmother Ida Trustin Sherman on my mother's side and Jeff's great grandfather Motel (Martin) were brother and sister. My mother used to refer to him as Uncle Trustin. The name in the old country was *Trustinetsky*. They were from Bratslav, Russia. Apparently, Harry Trustin was over in Europe and found there was a bridge named after a Trustin in that area. I keep wondering if we still have relatives over there.

Joey: So, what relatives are buried at Oakhill?

Janie: On my father's side, my grandparents Sarah and Dave, my Aunt Rose Fox Schneider, Uncle Al Fox and his wife Esther. Also, my Uncle Sam Saltzman and his wife Irene and various other Saltzmans we didn't know we were related to. But Bobby found the connection. All these Saltzmans; who the heck are they? They were from my father's family, especially on his mother's side. It turns out that my great-grandfather, Hertz Saltzman, had a brother, Moses, that no one ever talked about. Cousin Bob managed to find Moses' descendants in California, who I met when I was in L.A.

We didn't know this, but my grandmother Sarah's brother, Hazreal, is buried there. Again, "Who the heck is this one?" Bobby tracked him down. He became ill just after he arrived in Council Bluffs from Russia and died at 20. Bob and I visited his grave which was in need of repair. John O'Connor, Oakhill's groundskeeper, reset the headstone and cleaned it up so it was legible. Just a few years ago we found out my grandmother Sarah's father, Hertz Saltzman, had a brother. We'd go over to the cemetery and see this other Saltzman names and didn't know who in the devil they were. After doing some research, Bob found that my great-grandfather Hertz had a brother, Moses Saltzman. A whole new branch of the family was discovered. When I was in L.A. I met two of the great-grandchildren. Talk about a small world! They are even related to Omahan Jerry Hoberman.

Two interesting side stories: my grandmother Sarah Fox had two sisters and a brother, Sam Saltzman. He married a woman by the name of Dorette. They divorced and she moved to California in the 1930s with their son Marvin. Marvin married Barbara Freed, whose father was Arthur Freed who produced and wrote music for *The Wizard of Oz* and *Meet Me in St. Louis*. He also sang with the Marx Brothers on the vaudeville circuit and wrote material for them. He helped the careers of Gene Kelly, Frank Sinatra, Lena Horne and others.

Also, Sarah's sister Molly Saltzman married Abe Marcus and they had two daughters, Beverly and Darlene. Darlene married Kurt Hershinger who was born in Germany. I found out from their daughter, Debbie, that Kurt, as a youngster, met Hitler because his father was a tailor. I believe he did work for Hitler. Kurt's father Herman, whose boss was Hitler, was a social worker in the German prison system. Hitler told Kurt's father and Kurt that the Jews would be okay. Kurt's father saw the writing on the wall and they immigrated to the U.S., I think to New Jersey, and we all know what happened to the Jews in Europe.

Also, Sarah's sister, Molly Saltzman, married Abe Marcus and they had two daughters, Beverly (whom I mentioned earlier) and Darlene. Darlene married Kurt Hirschinger, who was born in Germany. I found out from their daughter Debbie that, as a youngster, Kurt met Hitler. Kurt's father Herman, whose boss was Hitler, was a social worker in the German prison system. Herman liked Hitler's personality. In 1934, when Kurt was ten-years-old, he and his father went to a ceremony where Hitler gave Herman the Iron Gross, which the family still has.

Debbie relayed this story to me: Hitler looked Kurt and Herman in the eye and said, "I never will do anything to hurt the Jews." Herman believed him. Meanwhile, by that time, Hitler was rounding up the Jews and wouldn't let the professional Jews work anymore. Grandma Henrietta Hirschinger and her sister Sorma Kaufman didn't trust Hitler. Henrietta told Herman, "Either you come or you stay, I'm leaving with Kurt, Walter (Kurt's brother) and Sorma." Before they left –– Herman included –– the women sewed valuables into their umbrellas. When the family reached the German/Holland border, they were strip-searched, yet the authorities didn't find anything because they didn't look in the umbrellas. In 1934 or 1935, when Kurt was 12, they left Europe, landed at Ellis Island and decided that since they were coming here, they'd only speak English, not German. I think they settled in New Jersey, and we all know what happened to the Jews in Europe.

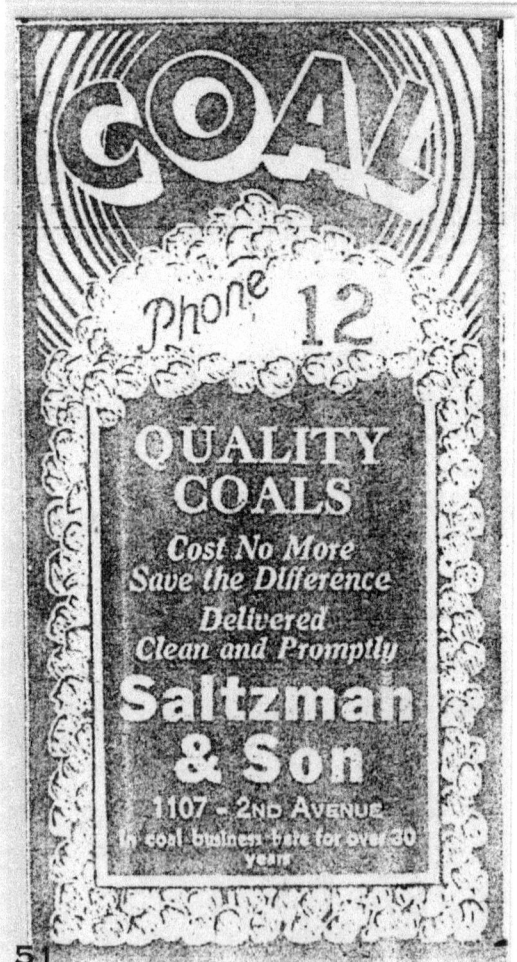

49. Fox Clothing advertisement
50. Hertz Saltzman on his 90th birthday, 1947
51. Coal advertisement

52. Alma and Bernie Fox, Joan, Richard, Dora and Phil Rosenblatt
53. Dave and Sarah Fox with family on 50th Anniversary

Dave and Sarah Fox, Rosa Fox Shneider, Harold, Lester, Al and Jack

HAROLD ABRAHAMSON
1927 - 2017

MY MOTHER WAS Fannie. She was born, I think, in Lithuania. She came over here when she was about 10 through Ellis Island. My dad Ben Abrahamson, was born in 1895 in Omaha. His father Isaac was from the old country. There's a story that my grandfather Isaac told: I think he originated someplace in western Russia. To get to this country, he emigrated through about six or seven countries –– he spoke seven or eight languages! English, Yiddish, Hebrew, probably Norwegian. He went through Germany, Poland, Norway…I think that's how we got the name Abrahamson. In Norway, Abrahamson is a very common name. In fact, there are a lot of Abrahamsons in South Central Nebraska who aren't Jewish. I think that was the name of one of the foster people who sponsored him, so he took that name in honor of his sponsor.

I was born April 23, 1927 in North Omaha. We lived around 23rd Street and Laurel. My dad and his brother had a little grocery store there called the Beehive, it didn't work out well for them so when I was about three-and-a-half or four, we moved to Council Bluffs because my dad got a little one-story grocery store around 21st and E or F. It was a one-man grocery store and my mother would go in and work part of the time. It was operated…well, at a loss, I'm sure! It was during the Depression and it was tough for a number of years. Our store, as I recall, was not a great success, we were barely scraping by.

The store eventually went under and we moved around. Dad tried various things, like selling insurance, which was really tough. How do you sell insurance during the Depression? He'd go around trying to collect premiums which were about 25 to 35 cents a week. You have no concept of the Depression until you've gone through it. It was a big deal when it came to spending money. If you had three or four cents, you'd be among the relatively rich. We're talking pennies. When we lived on 25th and Avenue A where the streetcar line ran, it was a gravel street. There were guys out from the government, the WPA (Works Progress Administration) digging ditches in the streets. I'd listen to their talk, it was rough. These guys were working for somewhere between four and 10 dollars a day. It was 1936 or '37. At that age, I didn't realize how rough things were. I just knew what we could and couldn't do.

Dad was having trouble getting and holding a job. Finally, in the late 1930s/early '40s, he got a job in Omaha tending bar for Art Rosinsky at 24th and Cuming. That's when we moved to Omaha and he was a bartender there for quite a few years. He worked there 'til midnight every day, I think he went to work around 12 or 1, so he put in 12 days. My dad had a tough go. My mom worked all over, including Omaha and downtown Council Bluffs at some of the grocery stores. Mom worked eventually for the Peoples Store in Council Bluffs as a general clerk. I remember she would send home groceries. They had a delivery truck, I think, and in those days, the oranges came in a big crate which had three wooden partitions and she'd fill that up with groceries and send it home for us. Her comments were something like, "It was really expensive, a whole crate cost two-and-a-half or three dollars." She was working like a dog. I think she made something like 12 or 14 dollars a week.

At the Peoples Store, there was a ready-to-wear store on one side and a grocery store on the other. They had everything in there. You'd go there and buy shoes and I remember they had an X-ray machine, which is really dangerous now, but in those days, I got the biggest kick out of putting my feet under there and seeing how the toes fit in my shoes. You stood on a little platform and this thing came up in front of you, and you could see whether your toes were crowded or how the shoes fit!

When I was four, I started off at Avenue B School. They gave me an exam so I could go early. I liked the funnies, but I didn't want to read, so I'd sit on my folks' lap but they found I wasn't reading, so they sent me back half a grade! In Council Bluffs, they had kindergarten, then first grade and first grade section two; so it was divided into two semesters or levels. It was an incentive for me to begin to read. I discovered I liked reading and did nothing but reading for a number of years.

In Council Bluffs, we lived in four different places: 22nd and E, I think, 25th and A, then 22nd and C and 25th and B. All on the west end. We were "West Enders." I had a lot of non-Jewish friends there. The majority of the Jewish community at that time lived in the east end of Council Bluffs. There were three or four Jewish families on the west end, a couple blocks west and a block or two north were the Passers who had a grocery store. There were two or three Jewish kids in school -- that was a big deal. Eleanor Passer was at Avenue B School with me. She was my girlfriend, but I was too bashful to do anything. I was 11 or 12. At Fairmount Park in eastern Council Bluffs, I got to meet with her, and I think I finally got a kiss!

When I finally got to be 12, I got into Boy Scouts. That was a big deal for me. We met behind Thomas Jefferson High School. Camp was expensive; a week cost seven dollars, I think; and nobody in my Scout troop had seven dollars! So what we did every week was buy stamps for a quarter and you had a book. Once you had the book filled, you had enough to go to camp! That's the way we did it. We were talking real Depression days -- real Depression -- when a nickel or a dime was big money. Movies cost a whole dime to get in, I think, if you were under 12 or 13. If you were older, I don't think it was more than about 20 or 25 cents.

Boy Scouts shaped me a lot as far as moral tendencies, I worked my way up to be Assistant Scoutmaster. At Scout camp, I was one of the guys who ran the camp. We'd camp out, go on long hikes and so forth. I hit the rank of Life Scout. I was a few badges short of being an Eagle, but one of the merit badges was a 12-mile hike. You'd hike out to a campsite north of Council Bluffs which is six miles. For an 11 or a 12-year-old, that's a long walk with a pack on your back. You'd stay there overnight at the campsite; and then, the next day, you'd cook breakfast and hike back in. I remember all of us were just dragging our tails, barely making it, but we made it. A lot of times, our camping would be in pup tents. In our Scout troop we had a bunch of pup tents and we could check them out. A lot of times we'd check them out and put them in our backyard and sleep outside overnight.

I got a bike for my 12th or 13th birthday. It had balloon tires and it was red and white. That was a big deal for me, to get a bike. I rode to *Talmud Torah* -- that was the

Jewish school in the synagogue on 6th and Mynster in the basement -- but when I didn't for some reason or other, I'd take the streetcar which ran on Avenue A, which was an unpaved street at that time. It was all gravel with streetcar tracks running down the middle of the thing. It was a nickel, or six tokens for a quarter, which was big money in relation. We're talking about the 1930s now, see. So, anyway, I would ride my bike down to *Talmud Torah*; then we'd meet with the gang outside and talk and I'd either ride back home or take the streetcar. I had a lot of Jewish friends: Maynard Telpner, Stan Katelman and a whole bunch of others. My friends were all "East Enders." They were good friends and we had good times together.

The rabbi taught us four days a week. I can remember the room we sat in right off the basement community area, and then the older men would come in for services in the evening, so I guess Hebrew school sometimes lasted 'til sundown. That's probably when I was taking the streetcar instead of the bike. *Talmud Torah* was sort of boring, but I learned how to read Hebrew (my Hebrew name is *Hershel Maier*) and learned to say a few words in Hebrew. Not like they teach it now, not at all. It didn't have that appeal, you know? It was something I had to do because I wanted to be Bar Mitzvahed. I wanted to be Bar Mitzvahed because my folks wanted me to be! I didn't say, "I don't want to be Bar Mitzvahed." It was just a given fact. It was, "When is your Bar Mitzvah?" not "Are you going to have a Bar Mitzvah?"

For the holidays, we'd get into our old car. I think Dad had a 1931 Chevy. I remember it was a sort of maroon color. We'd get in that and drive over to Omaha and park two blocks from the *shul* because you weren't supposed to ride during the holidays. We rarely went to B'nai Israel for the holidays. It was always Omaha because the rest of our family was over there, about five blocks south of 18th and Cuming. After *shul*, we'd go to my grandparents' house on 30th and Lincoln Boulevard, one block north of Cuming. Isaac, my grandfather in Omaha, said prayers every morning and I remember he'd go for *seder* or some dinner and he'd be sitting at the head of the table saying prayers for another hour. He was very religious.

To his left was the kitchen where the women cleaned everything up. The men were in the living room with the kids. There was no TV, of course. Sometimes we listened to the radio; most of the time we talked. It was a family feeling.

Our whole family was close on both sides. We'd go there almost every Sunday to visit and they'd have a card game going. They would play bridge and we'd horse around, play outside…If you went outside through the back door, half a block south was Reed's Ice Cream stand. They had them all over town, little stands. There'd be one window in there and they'd give you ice cream which was in these big round tubes. They'd slice it off, stick a little stick in one side of it, peel off the wrapping and stick it in a cone. It was either a nickel cone or a dime cone, and the dime was twice as big. Vanilla was my flavor.

At that age, eight or nine, my folks half the time would go over and play poker with my aunt and uncle, mostly at the Bordy's house (my dad's sister was Bertha Bordy, they lived about a block or so away from my grandparents) and I'd go with them. My dad was considered one of the worst players in Omaha, my mom was pretty good. They'd play until late and I'd be sleeping by the time they'd be done. Then we'd go home to Council Bluffs.

My brother Norman was nine years older than I was. My sister Lucille is five years older. I was the baby, and she'd walk me to school when I was five or six. I remember my brother was in high school and I was in grade school and he was on the wrestling team. I'd go over there and he'd wrestle and I'd be in his corner giving him massages! He was a good wrestler and a mediocre football player. I was never a good sportsman, but I could swim. In the summer, I did a lot of swimming at Crystal Pool in the Bluffs. I think it was around 20th or 19th and 5th Avenue. I was a lifeguard.

In fact, in my career I pulled a couple kids out! Once when I was in Scout Camp outside Atlantic, Iowa, one of the kids started going under. I swam across the pool and got him. The lifeguard was doing something else with a group on the other side, but he didn't hear me; so I dived in and went across and saved him. Anyway, I was the camp hero for a day or two.

For fun, we went to the movies. The Strand was the quality theater. The Broadway Theater was fairly decent. Right across from the Strand was the Liberty. The Liberty was the Saturday thing. They had Saturday serials like Roy Rogers. You'd go and they'd leave you hanging on the edge so you'd come back next week. Before you'd go in the theater, there was a little candy store next door. They had penny candies, and you'd go in and go, "Oh, two or three for a penny? I'll take some of those." And you'd end up either taking four -- or maybe if you were really rich, a whole nickel's worth of candy -- into the theater with you! For a nickel you could get a great big Hershey Bar. It was enough to feed the whole family.

At the Strand, I think probably on Saturday night, they had drawing nights. I think it was called Bank Night. It was a big deal. They had big barrels of tickets on the stage, then they'd pick somebody from the audience who picked a number, if that was your number you won the drawing. That way they'd fill up the theater. I remember one time I met my mother at the Broadway Theater when she worked across the street in the Peoples Store. I think it was Saturday afternoon and she said, "Well, we gotta eat lunch" and I said, "I made lunch for both of us," probably some sandwiches or something, and we went and ate lunch in the theater watching from our seats.

We didn't own our homes; we rented, and it was a time when if you paid 15 or 20 dollars a month for rent, that was a lot of money! 25th and B, the last house we lived in, that's when I went to Avenue B Grade School and T.J. (Thomas Jefferson High School). There wasn't any middle school; you went from grade school to high school. I went through eighth grade at Avenue B School until 1940, then did one year at T.J. in 1941. When the war broke out, I remember hearing it on Sunday listening to the radio. I was 13. It wasn't hard for me to comprehend, but it was hard to get the meaning of the war, you know? Shortly after that, we moved to Omaha. I went to Central and was in AZA #1 there, I was Alef Godol president. At UNO, we formed the Jewish fraternity AK-something-or-other. They elected me president. Every outfit I was in, I was president.

During high school, I got into ROTC; and after I graduated I went into the Navy. Here's a famous saying of mine: when I was ready to graduate high school in June of 1945, the Germans heard I was graduating and enlisting so they quit! So I went up into the Naval station out at Great Lakes Naval Academy north of Chicago where I got my basic training. I signed up for the Jewish choir there. One time, they had us gather onto the field and that's when we heard an announcement: the Japanese surrendered. Just then, we looked up at the clouds and saw a big V. Was it a sky writing signal from the Navy or a natural phenomenon? I don't know. Anyhow, the Japanese saw I was graduating from boot camp so they gave up.

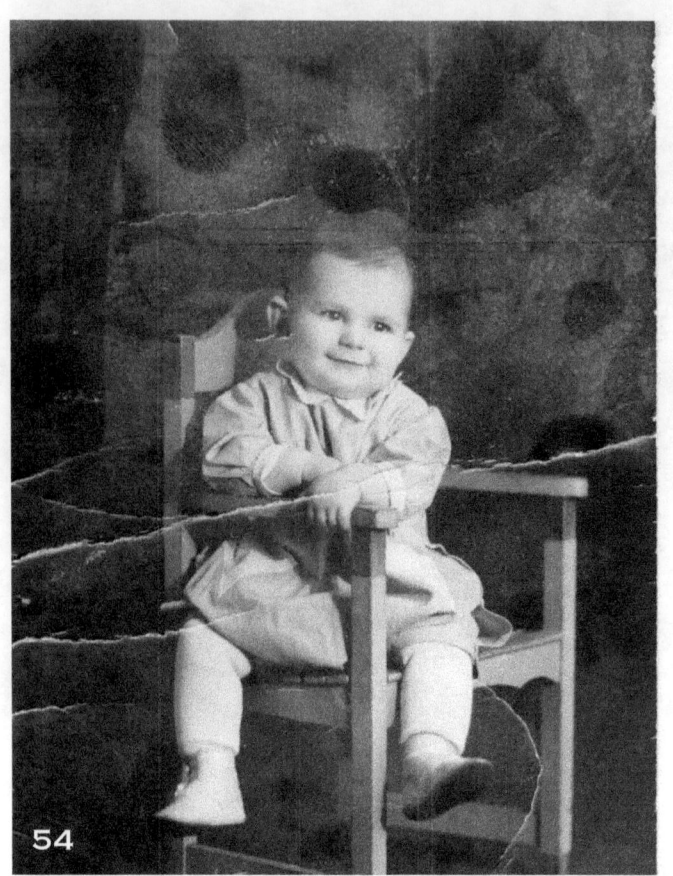

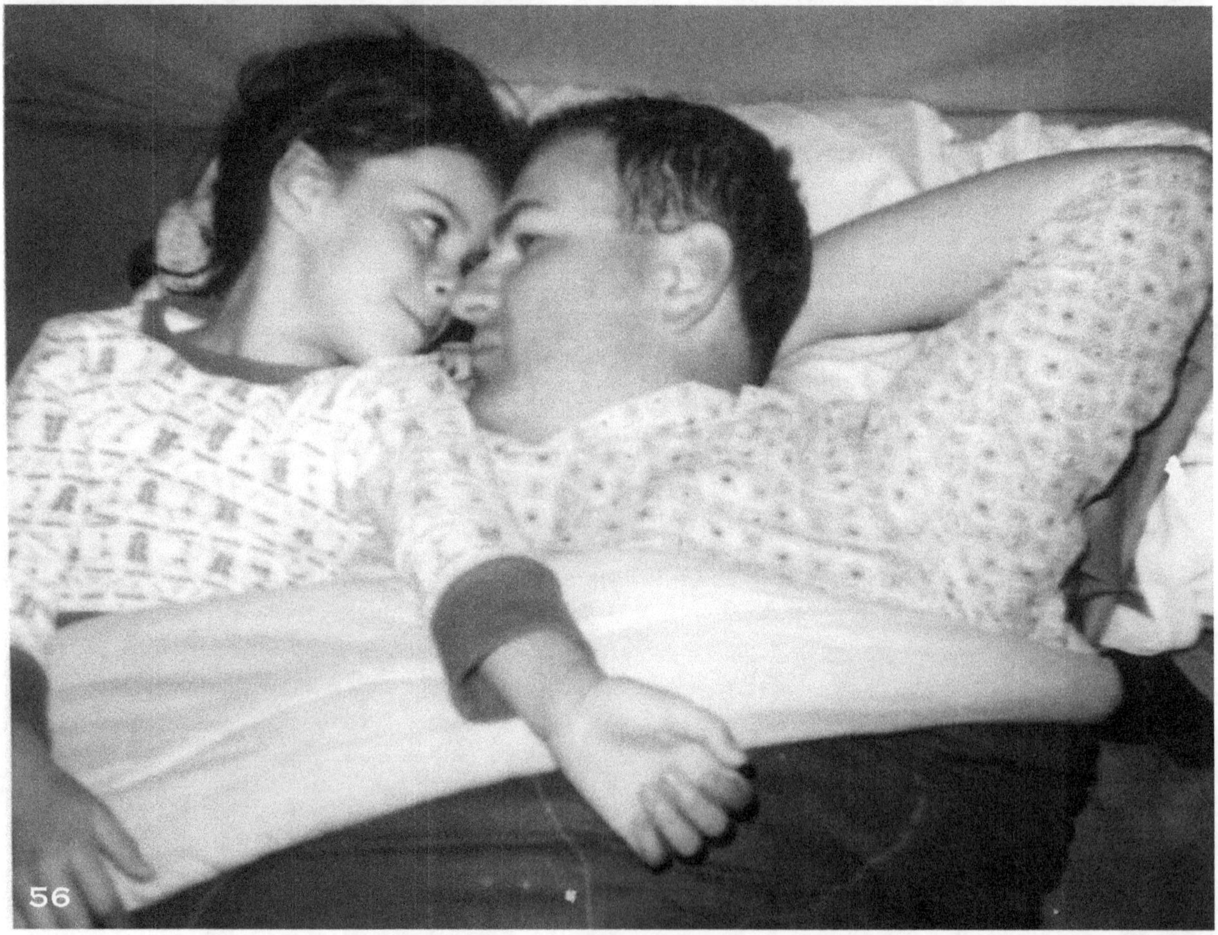

54. Harold Abrahamson, infant
55. Harold Abrahamson in U.S. Navy uniform
56. Harold Abrahamson with daughter, Ellene
57. Harold and Helen Abrahamson

CHICKIE PASSER LINSMAN

BORN JANUARY 30, 1930 in St. Louis to Shirley, who grew up there, and dad Louis Passer, who grew up in Council Bluffs, Chickie recalls how her parents met: Louis and Lou Katelman were army buddies in WWI and belonged to the American Legion. After the war, during an American Legion convention in St. Louis, Lou wanted to stop and visit cousins. One of them was Shirley.

"My mother's maiden name was Passer, and she married a Passer, my dad. Their two fathers were first cousins," she says.

The two settled in Council Bluffs where Chickie's grandfather Morris owned a grocery store -- Passer's Grocery, one of the first in the city -- and promptly passed it down to Lou. All the Passer brothers had independently owned grocery stores in Council Bluffs, all called Passer's, but in different parts of the city.

"We were in the north end of town, my uncle Ben was in the south part, my uncle Joe in the east. They were never in competition. Our grocery store was in an Italian neighborhood. All the stores were neighborhood stores, not chain stores, and they all made a nice living. Our folks all had nice homes, and the kids were educated and dressed beautifully from their little store. They saved and bought little rental homes. They went into real estate a little bit, not big-time. My uncle Joe was bigger than the others; he did a lot in real estate."

On Military Avenue, roughly five blocks from the store, lived the Passers, in an enclave of fellow Jewish families -- the Sacks's, the Gordons, the Meyersons, the Shykens, Chickie's grandparents -- who bonded like one extended family, reminiscent of the old country.

"I remember walking on Rosh Hashanah and Yom Kippur. We'd always walk to the synagogue. As we would walk (the *shul* was quite a ways, a good 10 to 12 blocks from our area), we'd meet the other families on the way. It got larger. Everyone walked, no one drove. Harry and Anne Cohn also lived in Council Bluffs. Harry had Iowa Clothes Shop and lived right across the street from the synagogue. During the break on Yom Kippur, everyone would go to Harry's house for the rest instead of walking all the way home. On the corner where Harry and Anne lived, was a Maid Rite. They made the best sloppy joe hamburgers in the world, they were unbelievable. So during the fast, Harry would take all the hungry little kids to the Maid Rite to eat. What a sweet man!"

At B'nai Israel, of course, being Orthodox, women sat upstairs and men sat downstairs. Chickie recalls a seating chart of sorts in her section of female family and friends. "In my mind, I know where all the women would sit, where all the Passers sat," she says.

"We had this whole area of pews: Harry Cohn's wife Bertha Cohn, Dolly Passer, Eva Passer, my mom, Shirley and grandmother Bertha Passer. I mean, it was just a whole section of Passers and Cohns. It was just a wonderful time. They're all gone now.

"All the Jewish kids knew everyone. I ran around with Omaha kids because I belonged to BBG. They had AZA and all different kinds of clubs. They had meetings, bowling league. The JCC on 20th and Dodge was where all the kids hung out; that was the meeting place."

Chickie remembers she was the only girl in her Sunday school class. The class had Marvin Suvalsky; Leslie Krasne; Larry Roffman; Buddy Bear; Kenny Sacks and Milton Gordon. They have all since passed. After Sunday school, an assembly was held in the B'nai Israel social hall. Mrs. Frieda Suvalsky led the kids in Hebrew song. Chickie remembers Esther Sacks Gallner playing the piano.

Oakhill (Bikhur Cholim) is like an extension of *shul*. "We're still together, my family of Passers, Katelmans, Cohns and others. Years ago, my Dad Lou Passer started a tradition of honoring all the Jewish veterans buried there. They'd raise the flag and say *Kaddish*. It was very moving. To this day, Patty Lee Nogg continues the tradition," says Chickie, adding, "Council Bluffs gave me roots. My husband Melvin and I have a plot there. My grandson said to me, 'Why did you have plots in Council Bluffs?' I answered, "Because it's home. I know everyone buried there; they were like family." It was such a nice community.

58. Chickie's father, Lou Passer
59. Shirley and Louis Passer with daughters, Alice and Chickie
60. Louis and Shirley Passer

Shirley and Louis Passer

Scherry Gloria Passer Linsman - Chickie

MARTI NERENSTONE

Marti: I've been in Council Bluffs since 1984. I'm a transplant, born in Ft. Belvoir, Virginia. I went to high school in D.C., graduated in 1972, and then to college at Oberlin in Ohio, with my middle year at the Hebrew University in Jerusalem, so I was there during the Yom Kippur War as a student. I got out of college in 1975, enlisted in the Army and spent almost four years on active duty.

Joey: Nice Jewish girl in the Army? I love it.

Marti: I was a Chaplain Assistant. I was in the Army for almost four years active duty; part-time in the states; two years I spent in Germany. When I was in the Army, my mother's address was my address. At the time she was living in Massachusetts. She got married and they moved to Iowa City. My stepfather was a librarian.

Because I was in the service, I became an Iowa resident in the 1970s. When I got out of the service, I went to Iowa City because my mother and stepfather were there. I ended up going to law school on the GI Bill at Iowa Law, graduated, passed the bar, went to Alaska for two years for Alaska Legal Aid, then moved to Council Bluffs in 1984.

Joey: Why Council Bluffs?

Marti: I got a job offer. I worked as a Chaplain Assistant, including in Germany for an Orthodox rabbi, which is where I learned lots of stuff, like how to run services. In 1988, July I believe, a tornado hit Council Bluffs. At the time, my spouse, Ann, was running a stained glass business in Council Bluffs. When the tornado hit, it broke the windows of the synagogue and Sandra Kurland called Ann. "Can you come fix these windows?" So I went with her to the synagogue, we talked about the synagogue, and that's when I started becoming involved. In high school and college I was a Jewish song leader, and I play guitar. So I became a song leader and somewhat of a lay leader at the synagogue.

Joey: How many members were there and how active was the synagogue?

Marti: It was very small. There was no rabbi, I don't think we met every Friday night, maybe every other Friday, and some holidays. At the time, they were attracting younger people.

Joey: What do you think attracted younger people to travel to Council Bluffs where there wasn't even a rabbi?

Marti: I think they were looking for something that wasn't one of the "established" synagogues. We started getting some younger families: Marty Rosenberg and Ellen Fennick, the Blooms…With the Blooms the connection was Doc Bleicher. Some of the families also belonged to another synagogue, but they were still coming here for some things. We started doing religious education with the kids on Sundays. Not one kid lived in Council Bluffs; they came over from Omaha. Also, there was a family from Harrison County that came down, which is between the Missouri Valley and Logan, so about 20 miles. We had a family coming from Harlan, which is 50 miles away.

Eventually, religious school moved from Council Bluffs to West Omaha. For a while, we were renting space at a community center that had been an Omaha Public School near 108th and Center, then we moved it to the JCC later on. We were from all sorts of different backgrounds, and it was a process of looking at the Reconstructionist movement. We brought in a series of student rabbis from the Reconstructionist seminary in Philadelphia once a month and for the High Holy Days.

We all came from different backgrounds, everything from secular to ultra-Orthodox. Some had tried other synagogues in Omaha for a variety of reasons and weren't happy. It was eclectic. The Reconstructionist movement is much more egalitarian, much more participatory. So I'm sure some people in Omaha thought we were kind of this ragtag group of Jews. By the fall of 1989, we had our first student rabbi. Before her, we had somebody come in from Arizona and run high holiday services. And we had somebody who lived in Logan, a dentist, Mitch Siegel, who served as the Cantor for high holidays.

Joey: A grassroots idea.

Marti: Yes. I was basically serving as Cantor at that point. There were some issues after several years; part of it was funding for student rabbis; part of it was the building. At one point, law enforcement talked about a gang that was there; there was no parking; people were afraid to come at night; and the building was in constant need of repair. The roof is flat, it seemed like it was always leaking. There were concerns about asbestos and a variety of things. And so there was discussion and, frankly, I think, disagreement. "How are we going to expend resources?" Which were not a lot. Everybody chipped in.

I worked at the time at Legal Aid, in the early '90s. I'd get calls from law enforcement; somebody's broken in, it's been vandalized, whatever, and I'd be going over there and checking out stuff. It was like, "What are we going to do?" So there was a split of the congregation, and part of it was…let's move the congregation out of this building. We were running a school and none of the kids were from Council Bluffs. Most of them were from Omaha. At one point we were having services in two places. Once a month we were in Council Bluffs, and we rented space at the second Unitarian Church in West Omaha.

We were going back and forth, and part of it was, "Can we attract new members?" You know, it's not just "our congregation" or the Jewish community, but it's like, the road only seems to go one way, from east to west. You can see it with the established synagogues in Omaha, everybody's moving further west. That's where the Jews are.

By then, we moved to the JCC and we were there for a number of years. So the congregation split, it was very traumatic. I think it was about the allocation of resources. Is a synagogue the people or the building? I understand the desire to maintain that building, but it was like a money pit, and I thought, was it dangerous? I don't know. We only have so much money. Are we going to invest it in programs and people, or are we going to pour it into this brick building? And I suggested moving everything; we could take all the stuff down and move it to Omaha. Part of it was, "Do we grow or not grow?" And they were less willing to come to the Bluffs.

Joey: How sad. So what did you end up doing?

Marti: The breakaway congregation ended up adopting Rabbi Kripke, Meyer Kripke, the retired rabbi from Beth El, but he was really a Reconstructionist at heart. He was a wealth of information, a wonderful resource. We had kids growing up, so we were starting B'nai Mitzvah. He didn't want to run services and that was fine; so he came to Kol Nidre and B'nai Mitzvah services. I ran the service; I'm the lay leader at this point, running all holidays and Friday nights. *Note*: Reconstructionist Judaism is a modern American-based Jewish movement based on the conceptions developed by Mordecai Kaplan (1881–1983). The movement views Judaism as a progressively evolving civilization. It originated as a semi-organized stream within Conservative Judaism before it seceded. The movement developed from the late 1920s to 1940s, and it established a rabbinical college in 1968.

Marti: Rabbi Mordecai Kaplan was a Conservative rabbi at the Jewish Theological Center. He thought this concept of community and Reconstructionism would be part of the Conservative movement, and it turned out he created a new movement. Kripke was a student of Kaplan's –– we had it practically from the founder's mouth. We adopted him, and he adopted us. It was a wonderful relationship that lasted for more than 10 years, until he died.

Joey: Then what?

Marti: After the second to last kid, we didn't grow. We were done with B'nai Mitzvah, and we became more like *Havurah*. *Beyt Shalom* was the name of the new congregation. We did a wedding several years ago of a kid whose Bat Mitzvah I officiated. That was fun.

Joey: Chills!

Marti: We don't have a building or rent space anymore, but we get together for holidays, *seder*, plus I do some service leading at the Blumkin Home for *S'lichot*, *Rosh Hoshana*, and *Yom Kippur*.

Joey: What do you call your merry band of thieves?

Marti: *Beyt Shalom*.

Joey: Meaning?

Marti: House of peace.

Marti Nerenstone celebrating Hanukah at B'nai Israel, early 1990s.

SISSY KATELMAN SILBER

If Sissy had run for president of Council Bluffs, chances are she would have won in a landslide. Affable, affectionate, quick with a quip, her signature greeting ("Hi, Doll!") helps people feel like they've known her for years -- which most onetime Council Bluffians have. The Katelman name is synonymous with success, goodwill and a work ethic which rivals most. Sissy and her mom Rose, with an avant-garde style, earned accolades in both business and in life. Sissy had several firsts: she was the first Jewish girl in Council Bluffs to have a Bat Mitzvah at B'nai Israel. She was 12. She was also the first Jewish person asked to participate in the Mardi Gras ceremony, Council Bluffs' version of the Aksarben Ball. Rose, a girl born and raised in Burlington, Iowa who lived and worked in St. Louis, one day went on a first date to watch the St. Louis Cardinals play in the World Series. Her companion? Council Bluffs' own Lou Katelman.

"Rosie" (as Sissy called her), with her husband Lou, ran L.H. Katelman Company, the family hardware store founded in 1934, while raising two small children, Sissy and her older brother Buddy. They struggled to make a living, "but the store gave my brother and me a lot of fun years," Sissy says. "It was a fabulous time, so many interesting customers. When I was a little kid, Meyer Lansky came in because he was running the dog track. I think he came in just to *kibbitz* with my dad. They were contemporaries in age.

My dad knew Yiddish but he seldom spoke it. He grew up with parents who were immigrants and spoke Yiddish often. Meyer liked to talk Yiddish with him. Once in a while, he would invite our family to partake in an activity which probably was against the rules." 'Bring your kids to the races,' Lansky would say, and much to Sissy's delight, Lou agreed. "My dad wasn't a gambler, but we would go down there just to see the dogs run. I thought Meyer Lansky was a very nice man. He loved kids. At that time, I don't think my dad knew he was a gangster."

What Lou Katelman did know was his business. Sissy grew up with nuts and bolts. "I remember working the adding machines as a little kid. Dad gave me a pile of numbers to add up, and I remember sitting on a tall stool at a high desk." While their parents busied themselves with their business, Sissy and Buddy could be found rummaging through the upper two floors of the four-story building jam-packed with junk (now antiques) left behind by the prior owner.

"I can't tell you how many Edison Victrolas were up there. We'd crank them up and sing 'Japanese Sandman.' We used to play with all this junk that would be worth a fortune today. It was always like a playground, but you could kill yourself up there! And if you worked the elevator which was as big as a room, you'd start it by yanking a rope."

But in 1950, good times came to a halt when a potbelly stove inside a beer joint set the whole 100 block of Main Street afire, burning down buildings housing a wholesale drug store, a harness shop and L.H. Katelman Company. "It was a huge loss both emotionally and financially, so my dad had men digging to see what they could salvage out of this fire. I think the fire was on Thanksgiving eve and my parents had been to a wedding in Omaha and had returned home late. During the night, they got a phone call from the fire department and we all went over and watched the building burn to the ground. Because of the fire, A.L. High School which was close by, canceled classes for the rest of the week because the power was cut off. It was a tough, tough time."

Still, Rose and Lou persevered. They wouldn't give up. Soon, they bought land and the following year built a new store at 714 West Broadway. Through the years, Lou had ongoing back problems, starting when he was working at his dad Julius' scrap metal business in his younger years. Periodically, he would be laid up in traction so he finally went to Iowa City and underwent back surgery performed by a renowned orthopedic surgeon. While her husband recouped, Rose ran the store with little help. "It was the Depression, times were tough. If they took in 20 dollars a day that was a lot of money."

After graduating from A.L. and then Iowa with a bachelor's degree in sociology, Sissy joined Rose and her folks in the family business which specialized in farm and industrial hardware. Then, in 1962, the family was dealt another blow. "My dad died and my mother and I continued the business," she says.

Two women at the helm of a hardware store was a rarity, and mother and daughter became quasi-darlings of the local press. In a December 11, 1972 article in the *Nonpareil* entitled, "Women In Business Love Work," a photograph shows Sissy's signature smile as she stands high on a ladder before jam-packed shelves. The caption: "Climbing a ladder is part of the daily routine for Sissy Katelman. Customers say she's up and down the ladder hundreds of times each day getting hardware items for them."

Also in the story, written a decade after Lou's death, Rose confessed: "It's the most interesting business in the world. It is something I've lived with for 45 years and I love it. In the beginning, I was just hoping to make expenses. If I found I was falling behind, I would have sold out. But now it's about six times bigger than before." According to Sissy, Rose was "the brains of the operation. I push nuts and bolts…There's a lot of psychology in being in business –– and it doesn't hurt to be sociable either."

Whenever possible, Katelmans honored special requests. Nothing was too small, or too big. "Our inventory was primarily heavy hardware, but if someone asked for something really odd, like a hand-cranked cherry stoner, we'd go digging for it," she says. The only females in an over-testosteroned industry during the early years of women's lib, Betty Friedan would have *kvelled*, but what about men?

"The ones who had done business with us knew we could do it. When contractors came from out of town, we were the only one in town that had most of their needs. They would be surprised at first, but once they knew we knew the territory and business, we were accepted."

When Urban Renewal hit in the early '70s, L.H. Katelman Company, then one of the oldest businesses in Council Bluffs, was forced to face the reality their building would be involved. In a February 4, 1981 *Nonpareil* article, Rose said relocating would have been her first choice, "If I were younger," and selling out would have been her second. But moving the massive amount of stock was too big a task, so they shuttered the doors in March of that year to make way for the Kanesville bypass.

"I waited until the last possible minute to offer the community the service as long as possible," Rose said. "It's my baby, and it's been my baby for 50 years." Sissy's response? "It was time. My mom was getting older and I was married, Howard and I were moving into a house and we wanted to travel and we got Rosie interested in travel as well. So when we attended conventions that involved travel, we'd take Rosie with us. She had the best time because she worked all her life and never really had a chance to do some of those things. She had time for social activities that she didn't have while she was working. For instance, she took a Yiddish class and traveled with Molly Delman's senior group, including a memorable trip to Israel."

The family's Council Bluffs history dates back to the early 1890s when patriarch Julius Katelman and his wife Rosa (née Katelman, a distant cousin) both Russian immigrants, moved to the small western Iowa town where he started a scrap business. The couple had 10 children born roughly two years apart: Firstborn Lou in 1895, followed by Sam (whose daughter Lee was Mark Eveloff's mother), Jenny, Joe, Morris (father of Rick Katelman), Abe, Marian and Toby. In between, they lost two children: Oscar, who was run over by a fire wagon at the age of four, and Fanny, who died in her 20s shortly after she was married.

Sissy suspects part of the reason Julius and Rosa had a big family was so they could put the kids to work, hardly uncommon then. "My dad had to quit school in 8th grade," she says. "They had a load of scrap that needed to be delivered to Chicago and young Lou and a hired man delivered it. All the kids started off working in the scrap yard where Morris and Joe continued until the business was sold in later years and, meanwhile, Abe and my dad started their own businesses."

Sissy's uncle Abe, very involved in the Jewish Council Bluffs community, ran Bikur Cholim/Oakhill cemetery virtually solo for years. "Abe was a doll and he served in World War II in the SeaBees," she says. "When I was little, I loved sitting in his lap, but then when he was home on leave one time, he contracted the mumps from me which, for a grown man, could have serious results!" Abe's first wife Edna died a year or so after they were married, then he married Lucille Krasne Gross. "He raised and loved her two daughters as if they were his own."

Abe founded Katelman Foundry, a highly successful operation, the fruits of which could be seen around town as most manhole covers bore the Katelman name. When Abe died in 1977, he bequeathed the business to his nephew David ("Buddy") Bear who also had his own structural steel business in Des Moines. Buddy operated both locations for years and when it came time to sell, the new owners kept the Katelman name.

Sissy's uncle Joe too was a highly-regarded member of the Jewish community. He bought and donated a stately house on South 8th Street which became the Jewish Community Center, a hub of Jewish life. "Joe's thing was real estate," Sissy says. "He'd go to all these auctions where they were selling parcels of land. They'd go into foreclosure and he'd buy them reasonably. He did well buying and selling, and he donated nice pieces of property to the community." In 1976, the city built Katelman Pool in his honor.

"Joe was always interested in politics; he loved it," Sissy says. "He became an alderman early on and he would go to every council meeting even when he wasn't on the council. He loved politics so much, they called him 'The Watchdog of Council Bluffs.'"

Joe served as a councilman and later became mayor, earning praise from a writer who published an editorial after his death which read, in part:

"I expect to leave a name in Council Bluffs that will be known for years to come," City Councilman Joe Katelman told a reporter in March. They will know that there was a Joe Katelman here and that he was one of the progressive movers that built this town, that he put his money where his mouth was…Joe was a prominent and outspoken part of the political scene for 50 years…Yes, the people knew Joe Katelman was here. They saw him, they heard him and he did put his money where his mouth was. The great amount of property he owned is testimony to that. There were probably few people in the Bluffs who haven't heard of Katelman. He was well known to those who attended political and civic banquets. He owned four dogs, and it wasn't unusual for him to take a cardboard box around the table to collect bones scraps for his animals."

Over the years, curious folks have caught wind of a quirk in the spelling of the family's surname. "Often people would ask why there were 'le' and 'el' Katelmans since we're all related. In Council Bluffs, we spelled it 'el' and the Omaha branch spelled it 'le.' There was a joke my Uncle Abe would tell that I think now was for real. Their father ordered a big sign for the front of the junkyard and the sign painter switched the spelling and it became 'el.' It became easier to change the spelling of our name rather than buy a new sign. Having looked at my dad's World War I discharge papers I saw his name had been spelled 'le' so I think at the beginning we were all 'le's.'

Harriet Maxine Katelman was born October 16, 1934 at the Old Methodist Hospital in Omaha, "even though we lived in the Bluffs because Rosie's doctor was there," Sissy says. "They had hand-written birth certificates and mine just read, 'Baby Katleman.'" Sissy's Depression-era girlhood was marked by low finances and high spirits. "Times were tough. See? Everybody worked hard and nobody had a lot of money, but you just didn't expect it. I don't know if there was anything I felt I was deprived of. I could still go to the movies for 10 cents, spend all day, go outside and play, it was wonderful. Bayliss Park wasn't far from us. On weekends and evenings they'd put up a big screen and we'd have sing-alongs, 'Follow the bouncing ball.' It was very neighborly. On Sundays, we'd get in the car and just go for a ride in the country. Nobody had air conditioning so that's how you cooled off. When I was five-years-old, I remember people knocking on the back door of our house, guys who were hungry, and I remember my mom making sandwiches for them. All they had to say was 'I'm hungry.'"

The Katelman house at 215 South 9th Street cost a colossal $7,500. "My folks thought that was a million dollars," Sissy says. "It was a very interesting neighborhood, the 'Gold Coast' they called it, I think because it was in the center of town. The rest of the town hadn't been developed yet much. The center was all businesses in the oldest part of town."

As a kindergartener, Sissy had an unlikely companion escort her home from Bloomer Elementary School.

"My Irish Setter Red would meet me at school and take me home," she laughs. "That dog was like a babysitter for me. He was so smart, so darling. If he came too early to pick me up, the teacher, Mrs. Davenport, would let him come in and sit in the room."

Sissy's bonds, both canine and human, helped create a sense of camaraderie -- particularly in the Jewish community. "All the Jews in Council Bluffs knew each other. They were mostly involved in the synagogue. Everybody was family." Mom Rose and her gal pals got together frequently at each other's homes, dubbing themselves the "Gin Club" (a reference to Gin Rummy, not Tanqueray). "They'd talk and they'd laugh. They were friends for years and years. I think the youngest one was Judy Bobrick. Then there was Mary Kubby, Etta Yudelson, Freda Suvalsky, Eva Passer, Celia Saltzman, Dorothy Krause, Jeanette Katelman after she married Joe, Shirley Wohlner who later married Sam Meyerson and, once in a while, Annie Cohen, Patty Nogg's grandma. In good and bad times, they were always there for each other, which was wonderful."

Sissy and Buddy attended *cheder* (Hebrew school) at the synagogue, like many other Jewish kids in town. "There was a variety of rabbis during those years and I recall two memorable days when I was in class: one day somebody came in and said FDR died; and on another occasion, somebody told us the armistice had been signed and World War II was over. Also, we learned to read Hebrew but we had no clue what we were reading and couldn't interpret it. They didn't stress that and now I can't read it at all," she laughs.

Some of the Jewish kids from Sissy's generation who came to *shul* were Buddy and Larry Roffman, "Boonjug" Telpner, Marcia Gordon and her two brothers, Joanne Krause, Howard and Phyllis Wohlner, Barbara and Steve Frankel, Elaine and Vernon Sternhill, Sharon and Biff Bobrick, Linda and Jerry Passer, Alice, Chickie, and Chubby Passer, Milt Brown, Jeanette Siegel, Stan Richards and his sister and brother, Natalie Marcus, Ted, Millard, Ruth and Norma Seldin, Gilbert, Arnold and Stanley Davidson, her cousins Buddy and Max Bear, Kenny Sacks (his wife Velma was a sorority sister of Sissy's in SDT) and Les Krasne.

"Les was such a wonderful guy and was very observant. His dad Lawrence had a very fancy Pierce Arrow, the Rolls-Royce of its day. It looked like a limousine. We were all fascinated with that car. He'd drive it to synagogue while the rest of his family walked because he wasn't as religious."

At B'nai Israel, multi-generations gathered to worship and mingle. Grownups got closer while youngsters got *shpilkes*. "Everybody went to synagogue," Sissy says. "You'd get dressed up for the High Holidays; it was like Easter for the Jews. Services were an all-day event, nothing was abbreviated. They dotted every I and crossed every T. For a kid it was pretty hard to sit through; so we often would go outside and sit along those side banisters or on the steps. It was a social event. I sat upstairs with my mom until one day she decided to go sit downstairs with my dad. She must have discussed it with her Gin Club because several of the others did the same. From then on, everyone sat together except for Leah Krasne and Fanny Gordon. It was out of respect to their parents, I think."

Like most men of his time, Lou Katelman was very involved in *shul*. He was a *minyan* regular, "but two men were more involved: Sam Sacks and Simon Shyken who led the community." The family lived close to B'nai Israel as her dad did not ride on *Shabbos* and he could easily walk to synagogue. Did Lou work on Saturday? Yes. But curiously, he did not ride or write. During the synagogue fire in the original building, Lou was one of the congregants who ran in to save the *Torahs*.

Sissy (Hebrew name *Hannah Motel*) was Bat Mitzvahed at B'nai Israel, "an interesting experience for a 12-year-old," she says. "Milt Brown, the sweetest guy about my brother's age, reminded me that at my Bat Mitzvah he read the *Torah* because I don't think women read the *Torah* in those days." The *Nonpareil*'s formal announcement reads:

"Mr. and Mrs. Louis Katelman have announced the Bat Mitzvah of their daughter Harriet which will be held this evening, December 27th, 1946, at the B'nai Israel Synagogue, 618 Mynster Street. The service will begin at 8 PM and will be conducted by Abraham Katelman and a group of post-Bar Mitzvah boys under the direction of Rabbi Kramer of Council Bluffs. Rabbi Henry Joel will be the guest speaker that evening. He occupies the pulpit of Tiffereth Israel Synagogue in Lincoln. All relatives and friends are invited to attend, no invitations have been issued."

The synagogue remained vibrant for years to come, but as the older community diminished and young people were educated and moved to bigger cities, the Jewish population dwindled. "For a long time, the synagogue sat idle and along came

Doc Bleicher. He re-kindled interest in the synagogue. He persevered. In fact, he didn't go out and look for people to come and attend; but little by little, people who had a warm feeling for Council Bluffs and the synagogue came. Regardless of whether they were Orthodox, Conservative, Reform or Reconstructionist, their own opinions were respected."

Joined in his efforts were Alan and Sandra Kurland who also dedicated themselves to the cause. "When Doc Bleicher died, the Kurlands continued to maintain both the physical aspects and the history of the synagogue. Sandra has created volumes of memorabilia in scrapbooks which is a testament to our history. The Kurlands deserve a lot of credit. They kept it going. At one point, it was more and more time-consuming for them and it necessitated creating a board of interested people. On my part, it was memories from the heart; for others, I think it was kind of a new vision for celebrating Judaism. People were impressed with the history of the building and they wanted to preserve that."

B'nai Israel is on the National Historic Register, an architectural coup. "Our place is like a museum," Sissy says. "It's very significant that the building is on the national registry. That's our history -- the history of the Jews of southwest Iowa.
It would be a shame to see it disappear. The synagogue was never far from my mind, just as Council Bluffs isn't. It's all part of my heritage and I felt that it was too significant to just let it collapse. What's interesting is that most people involved now weren't raised there, but I'm grateful for their interest. I'm there because of memories. It's important to me that we keep it alive and going."

Over the past few years, attendance for *Shabbat* services -- held the second Friday of every month -- has grown. "When we first started this up, just our own little bunch, sometimes only five people would show up. Now we get 25, 30 or more. The secret is having speakers with interesting subjects. We have them talk about their lives or current events." To help increase membership, the board, which includes Sissy, Nancy and Phil Wolf, Rick Katelman, Carol Lainof and Marty Ricks, set membership dues at a nominal $250 a year. "Some who can afford more, give more. And for those who can't afford it, we're not keeping them out. It doesn't matter how religious they are. If they're interested in coming, we're glad to have them. We even have some non-Jews with warm feelings or a Jewish connection. Whoever wants to worship is Ok."

Bikur Cholim/Oakhill Cemetery, the final resting spot for many Katelmans, including Sissy's parents and paternal grandparents, all the brothers and sisters except for Marian who is buried in California and her husband Howard, provides an opportunity for the third-generation Katelmans to ensure her family and the larger Council Bluffs Jewish family have a dignified and peaceful place to call their own.

For Sissy, like her Uncle Abe before her, it is essential to prolong and preserve the cemetery. For the past few years, she has served on the board and logs hours as a volunteer, ensuring the place meets the standards her ancestors would have set.

"They needed people from different generations," she says. "Now they need young people to perpetuate the care and look after the cemetery. We have to keep it up. It's part of our history. It's going to be there forever, I hope."

That Sissy has not resided in Council Bluffs for decades is besides the point. "Believe me, I live there. I do. My heart lives there. I love Council Bluffs; I love the people. I even meet my high school classmates once a month for lunch there at Tish's."

Katelman Hardware at 714 W. Broadway

Everyone says Sissy is a carbon copy of Rosie, and everyone would agree that if her mom were still alive, she'd be *veklempt* over the girl she groomed; her legacy; a still-impassioned member of the Council Bluffs community. And if Rosie were still around, "She would want to go see all her old customers from the hardware store. I can tell you that."

61. Louis Katelman with daughter Sissy Silber
62. Lou Katelman Family, Sissy, Lou, Rose and Buddy at 215 So. 9th Street
63. Sylvia Telpner, Jeanette Katelman and Ann Marcus

64. Lou and Rose Katelman

65. Herman Krause, Sam Meyerson, Sam Saltzman and Lou Katelman

Passover at Grandma Katelman's on Oakland Ave, 1940s

MILLARD R. SELDIN

I LIVED IN Council Bluffs for 34 years, from 1926 when I was born on August 8th, to 1960 –– except for two years (June 1944 to June 1946) while serving in the Navy Air Force. In 1960, I moved to Omaha when I married my wife Beverly.

K-8, I attended 8th Street School, then Bloomer Junior High and Abraham Lincoln High School. My fondest memories, not necessarily great, were of always having to walk to school especially when it snowed or rained. In junior high, I tried out for the basketball team but was the shortest person at that time with no talent. I did not last very long.

My best childhood memories of growing up in Council Bluffs? I learned how to play chess from Marvin Richards and subsequently was able to beat him and also beat Eddie Cherniss. They both became doctors and moved to California. During high school days, Stanley Katelman used to have parties in their basement recreation room.

I also learned to play poker in Stanley's basement at an early age using pennies. During WWII, Stanley worked for his uncle Abe Katelman's foundry and had extra gas stamps that we used to go to Omaha for dates. We also went to Beth El for the dance socials they regularly had in their recreation room. There were not many Jewish girls in Council Bluffs, but Omaha had a good selection. During WWII, our high school let everyone out of classes to seek scrap metal. Stanley and I toured the farms in his pickup, for many miles, picking up scrap metal for the war effort.

I was a member of B'nai Israel and AZA #7, which was very enjoyable, especially playing basketball against the Omaha teams at the old "J" on Dodge Street. I walked to Hebrew school every night and also to Sunday school. While waiting for classes to start at Hebrew school, three or four of us would play tackle football between the curb and sidewalk in a space of maybe four or five feet. Also, downstairs prior to going through the door to the main room and classes, there was a small square opening west of the door and away from the pipes, near the ceiling. We would utilize the opening for a basketball hoop using a tied up rag as the ball.

It always seemed the World Series took place during the High Holidays. After services, we would adjourn and go to the home of someone and listen to the baseball game. That was big then.

My Jewish friends remained close to me, although I also had many gentile friends. After WWII, I became friends with several older Jewish guys and shared many social activities including poker games, going to the races, and traveling.

A few of my Council Bluffs Jewish friends included:

Owen Meyerson – Lived one block away in elementary school and was a college roommate at University of Iowa

Donald Vann – High School

Norman Cherniss– High School

Marvin Richards – High School

Eddie Cherniss– High School

Art Sommer – High School

Milt Gordon – College Roommate

Kenny Sacks – (My brother Ted's age)

Stanley Krasne – High School

Les Krasne

Jack Brown – Elementary School, AZA, Phoenix

Orville and Billy Fried – AZA

Jerry Passer – College

Mickey Roffman – Elementary School

Marvin and Selwin Sulvasky – AZA and Sunday School

Herb Tepperman – AZA and College

Maynard Telpner - AZA

After WWII:

George Brown

Sam Bittner

Les London

Eugene London

Al Passer

Bob Yudelson

Sam Eveloff, when he came to Council Bluffs to marry Leona Katelman

I went to an Orthodox Synagogue and read Hebrew without understanding the words. I was brought up in an Orthodox home, but later realized the old ancient customs were necessary thousands of years ago; but present health conditions do not require them. Except for tradition, I feel the world has changed. We have autos, electricity, refrigeration and can handle food and health issues differently. In 1960, I joined a reform Temple.

My Bar Mitzvah was not a big deal because the country was barely coming out of the Depression. For my party, I took a few friends to a Saturday movie (either the Strand or Liberty Theater).

Other memories about growing up in Council Bluffs during the Depression: Quaker bread had a large round 1¢ coupon on each loaf's cover. Save 10 and you could go to a movie. If you had an extra five coupons, you could buy popcorn.
In the winter, milk was left by the kitchen door and on cold mornings the cream would rise and pop off the paper lid.

It was also a task keeping the house warm with a coal furnace that needed to be attended to throughout the night.

In the summer when the ice man delivered ice for our ice box, he always would give me a small chip from the truck to cool off (it was a hot day and night without an air conditioner).

When I was about 10 or 11, I went door-to-door selling Liberty magazines -- it wasn't easy. Later on, I had a paper route with the *Nonpareil* that paid me \$2.03/week of which I used 50¢/week to purchase my bike.

My father Ben came to Omaha from Russia in 1913 when he was 16-years-old. His brother Eli previously came there in 1913. My mother Bertha was born in Sweden and my dad met her in Omaha and they married. I believe they originally moved to Council Bluffs to open a grocery store. Ben also joined the army in WWI and was stationed at the Omaha Balloon Corps.

As a child, I would travel with my father selling life and general insurance to various grocery stores in Council Bluffs. He always picked up a few groceries and that helped in his selling the grocers insurance.

In 1949, my father and I started building houses in Council Bluffs. I would build them, and Ben would sell them. Ben posted $500 as collateral to secure a construction and FHA loan to build our first house on a vacant lot we were purchasing. We built Milt Katelman's house on Kenmore as well as bought steel fabrications from him, purchased steel I-Beams from Abe Katelman's foundry and hardware from Lou Katelman's Store.

In the '50s, our office at 24 North 6th street was just a block from the synagogue and when my dad and I would get a call, we would rush over so they would have 10 men for their *minyan*.

My parents spoke Yiddish, but I never bothered to learn. My sisters Ruth and Norma did, as they were interested in what was being said. My wife Beverly can still speak Yiddish. My father went to Boyles College to learn English. He could also speak Russian, German and Yiddish.

In Sunday school in the middle 1930s, Mrs. Sulvasky always spoke of the "Blue Box" for Palestine (the Jews' homeland). Since Israel again became a country after WWII, Palestine became the name for the Arab settlements.

Growing up Jewish in Council Bluffs has probably kept me humble, understanding that wealth can come and go. I grew up in a blue-collar neighborhood and assimilated with Italians, African Americans and the wealthy. Many times I was subjected to anti-Semitism at an early age, but it also made me more tolerant and understanding of others and why and where these unfortunate comments arise from.

My dad Ben Seldin was very active in the Jewish community. He helped finance the rabbi's house adjacent to the *shul*, and the *shul* when it needed repairs or had financial problems. My mother Bertha was active in Hadassah and always baked great desserts for their events. She was an excellent cook and, after traveling worldwide, I realized how special she was.

Millard R. Seldin And Florida Girl Plan Vows

From Miami Beach, Fla., comes announcement of the approaching marriage of Miss Beverly K. Seidel of that city and Millard R. Seldin of Council Bluffs. Her parents, Mr. and Mrs. Harry Levin of Miami Beach announce the plans.

Miss Seidel and Mr. Seldin are to be married Nov. 27 at the Seville Hotel in Miami Beach. Mr. Seldin is the son of Mr. and Mrs. Ben I. Seldin.

His fiancee attended schools in Philadelphia, Pa., and Miami Beach. The two met while Mr. Seldin was in Florida on business.

He is a graduate of Abraham Lincoln High School and the State University of Iowa. He received his bachelor of science degree in commerce there.

He is associated with Seldin Homes, land developers and home builders in Omaha and Council Bluffs. He is a member of the City Planning Commission of Council Bluffs and is second vice president of the Omaha Home Builders Assn.

66. American Legion Drum & Bugle Corps., 1938
67. Millard Seldin engagement announcement

68. Millard Seldin promotional photo for Seldin Homes, 1957
69. Family: Denise Silverman, Stan Silverman, Norma Silverman (Millard's sister) Beverly Seldin, Millard, Bertha & Ben Seldin, 1964
70. Ted Seldin, Ben Seldin and Millard Seldin, 1964

JERRY SLUSKY

WHEN YOUR FAMILY owns an amusement park, chances are you have no shortage of friends. "Toward the end of every school year, the kids knew my birthday parties were always at Playland, so I became the most popular kid in class for the last month or two of the school year," says Jerry, whose August 17th birthday fell during high season at the Holy Land of Fun.

Jerry's father Abe had a decidedly different childhood. Abe, who immigrated from around Kiev in 1910 to 1912, settled in St. Joseph, MO and had three older siblings: Rose, Sam and Louis. Tragedy struck the Sluskys when their parents died at early ages leaving Rose, then 14, to raise her three younger brothers. This life blow, however, helped transform the orphans' loss into an opportunity for growth, self-reliance, and, for the family, a career in creating joy.

"The family across the street owned a popular local amusement park," says Jerry. "They put the boys to work which is how they learned the business. They'd bring home every dollar they made, put it in the cookie jar and Rose, from 14 to 17 years of age, used it to run the house."

Years later, once again, fate -- and faith -- intervened. AZA (Aleph Zadik Aleph) and BBG (B'nai B'rith Girls), the local chapters which sponsored regional events in Omaha, Des Moines, Sioux City, St. Joseph and Kansas City, unwittingly made a *shidduch*, as Abe met Ann, his future bride. Several years later, Abe and his siblings moved to Omaha to run Krug Park, an amusement park in Benson. Abe and Ann met again and ended up getting married in the late 1930s.

When the Sluskys moved to Benson, the Louis Paperny family who lived across the street from their home at 52nd Street and NW Radial Highway and owned Louis's Market in Benson, took the Sluskys under their wing and developed a friendship that lasted for 50 years. The Sluskys later moved to Houston in the early 1940s where Sam enlisted in the Navy. By that time, Abe and Ann had a son, Howard, and another, Jerry, who was born in Houston in 1945. By then, the Slusky brothers had honed their chops, built their own funplex in Houston and dubbed it Playland Park.

The Sluskys built 20 rides, a stock car racing track and the first roller coaster in the Houston market -- one of the only true, genuine wooden coasters built by Philadelphia Toboggan Company, the oldest and finest roller coaster manufacturer in the world, says Jerry. Playland Park Houston was on a roll; yet, in 1947, Ann (née Fellman) missed her family in Omaha, so the Abe Slusky Family packed up and headed north, purchasing 40 acres of land in Council Bluffs just across the Missouri River from Omaha. In the spring of 1948, the gates to Playland Park of Council Bluffs/Omaha opened, with 20 rides ready, games-a-plenty and a stock car racetrack, the likes of which locals had never seen before, or since.

"The roller coaster was almost a mile long," says Jerry. "Before the interstate, it crossed all the way down Broadway, from the current Missouri River levee on the west and to where the exit to 35th Street is now on the east, then turned around and came back. It had a 70 foot drop." Rides came at a hefty price: 15 cents per, 10 cents for each additional go-around.

Remember the smaller park rides? "The Octopus, with eight arms and a tub at the end that spins, goes up and down, around. I wouldn't ride it then or now, made me sick," Jerry laughs. "I love roller coasters, bumper cars -- can't have a park without bumper cars -- Ferris wheel, Tilt-A-Whirl, and a Scrambler, which was closer to the ground than the Octopus, four arms, the whole ride turns, it gets going pretty fast so you have centrifugal force going all the time. The most thrilling ride was the Roll-O-Plane; it looks like a bullet, it's nicknamed "Bullet," it starts going around, bullets spin around and twists. A lot of debris, let's call it, under that ride," he laughs.

Roll-O-Plane sentiments aside, nothing got Jerry pumped quite like the stock car track. Still does. "I have a little secret: I loved to drive. I was able on three or four occasions in my early to mid-20s to get stock car driver friends of mine to allow me to use their car in a real race. It was as much of an adrenaline rush and as much fun as I've probably ever had in my life."

The only asphalt track in the midwest, so rain wasn't a worry, the speedway was built and operated as a dog track in the '40s by...guess who? "The state allowed Meyer Lansky to come in and they legalized dog track betting for four years." Drivers owned their cars, but not all could afford one -- especially the Super Modified $10,000 to $25,000 model -- and Jerry, eager to offer the masses a chance to get in the game, created a more affordable class of car: the Bronco.

"Anybody could put together a $500 race car and be eligible to race on Saturday nights at Playland Speedway," he says. These standard stock cars were outfitted with roll bars, seat belts and shoulder harnesses, sans big-time engines or tires.

The Bronco class was very successful. By August of 1967, after starting with 20 cars, "we had over 100 cars coming in the pit, starting at 6 p.m., crowds lining up for the gates to open at 7. Popcorn's popping, hot dogs cooking, beer getting cold...Watching the warm-ups, it just felt like you were in a wonderful entertainment experience with the smells: smell of exhaust fumes and the sounds of loud pipes (these cars didn't have mufflers). So you had, collectively, sounds of any 20 cars in a race, going around the short track, constantly at a high rpm, very loud, very smoky. The cars hit 60 to 70 miles per hour on the straightaway, brake and downshift into 30 to 40 miles per hour and back out again. It took quite a bit of driving skill."

What also took quite a bit of skill, albeit it came easily to him, were Abe's social graces. "Most of the Jewish community visited the park and would head to Abe's office. It was a well-known thing that if you stopped by the office, Abe would take care of you with free tickets. We used to kid him about being too generous. That was his family. But you didn't have to be Jewish, it was family and friends."

Slusky senior worked hard in the summer season. Jerry too? "Only from age five to 25, except when I was away at the University of Oklahoma. At five, we had a boat ride which had Briggs & Stratton three horsepower motors in back of the boat so that you could go on the pond and steer the boat. Some nights I hung out with the boat operator who taught me how to tear down the engine and put it back together."
But it wasn't all work. "I rode bumper cars for three hours some nights, always pretended I was in a race, had to win every race. I became pretty adept at bumper cars."

On weekend nights, Mom worked in the office, Dad walked around making sure things were working properly and Jerry "knocked around with operators and cashiers. My older brother Howard and I learned about how the park operates: the games, rides, later stock cars, winter repairs. It was like, 'Wow, this is a glorious business.' Two men walked the coaster every day during the season; they had cleats and were looking for loose boards on a track. They had to climb up 60 or 70 feet. It was fascinating to me, to watch them."

Playland had two key men who were responsible for operations and maintenance of all the rides: Mac and Jack. "Jack ran the roller coaster and supervised the operation, extremely important for success of the park. Jack had a bit more personality and Mac was the straight man, very serious about his job. He walked the park at night to ensure everything was working properly and did safety checks on all the rides including their brakes and hydraulic engines. Dad built houses for them behind the park. They worked a long time there, very loyal. Family. He took good care of them."

And Council Bluffs Jews took care of each other. "Dad bought insurance from Ben Seldin for the park. I remember being in Ben's office as a kid, one little narrow office in Council Bluffs. Dad took me there and they talked about insurance, my introduction to the business. Ben and Abe had a lot in common, they shared ideas for business and furthering the growth and the success of Council Bluffs. Ben was an overall very, very good guy."

Imagine; Little Jerry Slusky, tagging along with Abe, unwittingly learning the ropes, now a partner at Smith Slusky Law who does some work for Seldin Company. "I got to know Ted and Millard through real estate, their specialty," he says. Small-town friendships come full-circle.

As all eras end, so did Playland's. Abe died suddenly at 59 on Jerry's birthday in 1970, just as he was finishing Creighton Law School. He had a job lined up at the County Attorney's office, had been operating stock cars during this time yet couldn't operate both, so he sent the rides to his brother. "It was painful, very emotional, because Dad died in mid-August, and we closed the park Labor Day. I was certainly still grieving about our loss but knew I had to get the rides shipped out in the fall before winter came."

Specialty carriers who knew how to tear down rides helped Jerry and Howard coordinate the multi-truck shipment to his brother who owned Frontier City in Oklahoma City, part of Six Flags, still in operation. When the state acquired the property for the interstate highway, it included the roller coaster. It was the first time in the nation's history a governmental authority had condemned a roller coaster, taken for public use.

Though the park was dismantled, part of it survived: the stock car track -- Jerry's baby -- which he pushed into a smaller area and continued to run while practicing law until 1972. "The city owned the balance of the land and we had a lease. When the lease ran out in 1973, they asked me if I wanted to name the land for my dad. No, I thought, he would appreciate it more if they named it "Playland Park." The sign still stands.

In the same vein as Playland Park, River's Edge (official name: Tom Hanafan River's Edge Park) is now being developed in partnership with the Iowa West Foundation. "I'm very proud of what's going on over there. I asked a number of people involved with the redevelopment to make it "River's Edge at Playland Park" to keep the history alive. I'm hopeful."

How did Playland, his parents and the community, make Jerry Jerry? "The biggest lesson I learned was how to treat people and, frankly, how to entertain people. I saw, as a young person and into my stock car years, what it took to draw people out and provide an appealing entertainment package. Whether it was the amusement park or stock car races, I learned what people responded to, and I have used that in my legal career in a variety of ways, particularly when I am making zoning presentations to a City Council or a Planning Board. I have an understanding of how to shape presentations as attractive and to provide content that people want to listen to."

Playland Park, Council Bluff's own Disney World. Memories seared like a well-grilled frankfurter for the thousands who flocked to their childhood fantasyland, Jerry included. "I have tremendous nostalgia about it. I have five grandkids, since the first ones were three we have been going on annual trips, the first eight to amusement parks," he laughs.

Remember Jerry's little secret? Loved to drive, the stock car experience in his DNA. "Saturday nights at Playland Speedway, we've never had more fun. Those Saturday nights were special; it was like a family between the drivers and the patrons. There were five or six people who worked on cars, the pit crew, who brought family. And the spectators...it was like a love fest. We drank a lot of beer and ate a lot of hot dogs, I can tell you that."

71. Playland Park Roller Coaster
72. Playland Park, 1951

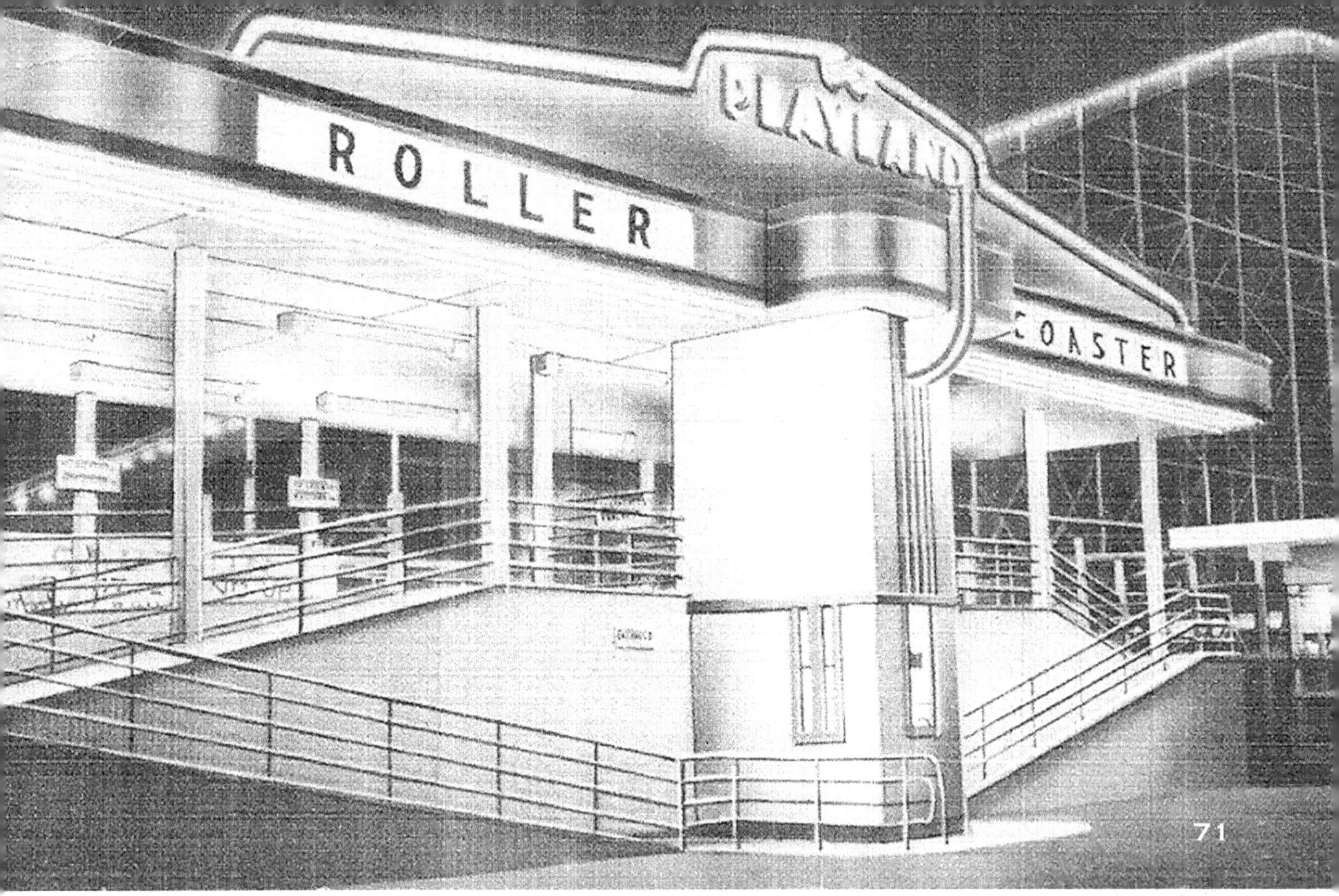
PLAYLAND
ROLLER
COASTER
71

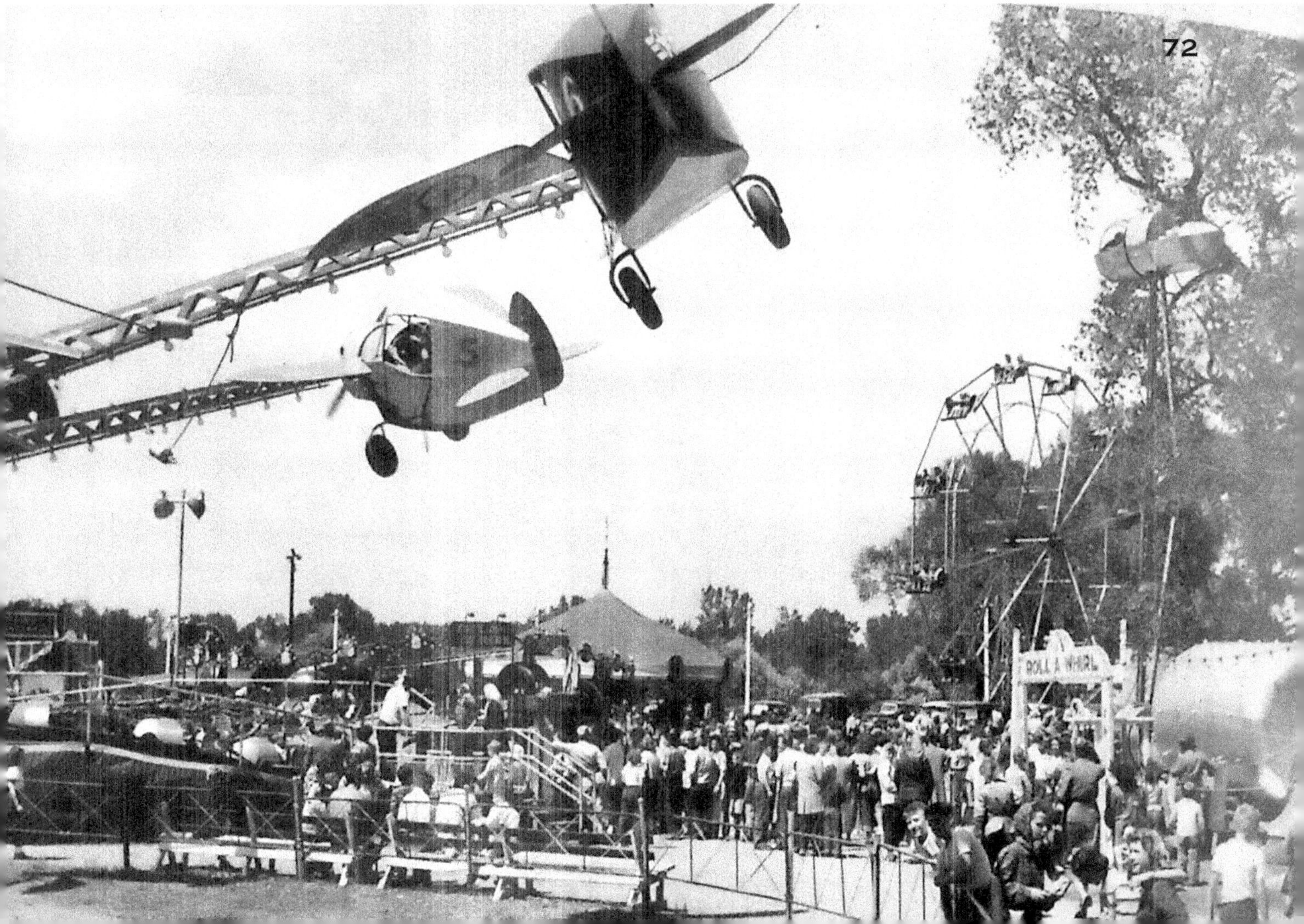
72
ROLL A WHIRL

73. Playland Park Entrance
74. Jerry Slusky

JAN SCHNEIDER LUND

IT WAS HARDLY your typical news story -- even for Small Town USA. "A deer jumped in the window right where I was playing!" says Jan about one October day in 1950 when she was two. "The deer went back into the dining room of the house where my newly-born sister Lynn was in a bassinet, and my mother screamed and ran with us out the back door and so did the deer! The deer jumped through the back window and turned into another apartment!" Their tale garnered the Schneiders notoriety when the *Nonpareil* featured the story, photo re-enactment included (sans deer).

Born at Jennie Edmondson Hospital on June 23, 1948, Jan lived at 143 Vine Street until she was six. In 1955, her parents built a house at 246 Kenmore Avenue at the top of the hill where Kenmore and Keeline meet, in a neighborhood replete with Jewish families.

"We all grew up and came of age on Kenmore," she says. "The Jewish kids on the two streets all knew each other from Sunday school, of course, and most of us continued through the Council Bluffs public schools, although a few went to Omaha to high school and some to private schools. It was an idyllic kind of place where, in the summers, one of the (non-Jewish) families opened up their gorgeous swimming pool for all the neighborhood kids to have lessons (it was all very official and we earned the Red Cross water safety level badges). Classes were taught by one of Council Bluffs' prominent pediatrician's daughter who lived on Keeline). At Halloween, the neighborhood was amazing because everybody was out on the street in costume, and there were lots of parties after that. At Christmastime, the non-Jewish houses on the street were all decorated and lit up, and the *menorahs* burned in the windows of the Jewish homes. On Kenmore, we had so many kids to play with. We'd go to this house and that house with our Barbies and paper dolls, and we could ride bikes all over; it was safe. The boys commandeered one of the islands between the two streets and made it a sports playground. It was really neat; the life of a ten-year-old couldn't have been better. Everybody in Council Bluffs in the '50s and '60s had a Leave It To Beaver/Father Knows Best upbringing. We had the run of the town."

Jan attended Washington School and when the family moved to the Kenmore house, she transferred to Hoover Elementary School for 3rd through 7th grades. "We didn't have junior high yet in those days, so I finished 7th grade in the elementary school; and by the time I was in 8th grade, I went to East Side Junior High School for 8th and 9th. That's the location of the present-day Abraham Lincoln." Jan graduated in 1966 and in 2006, she was inducted into the A.L.H.S. Hall of Fame.

Her parents were Ben and Beatrice (Krause) Schneider and her Council Bluffs grandparents were Herman and Dorothy "Dora" Krause. Her other grandparents, Abe and Sadie (Fishkind) Schneider lived in Omaha. Her parents met before World War II and they married just before Ben was to be shipped off, first to Oran, Algeria and then to the Euorpean theater. When Ben returned from the war, he and Bea settled in Council Bluffs and started a family. At first, Ben was in his father's business, Schneider Portland Cement Company, which did stucco work on many homes in Omaha. But later, he joined his father-in-law in the family business, The Bargain Spot at 618-20 West Broadway.

The Bargain Spot was founded in 1938 by Jan's grandfather Herman Krause, born *Chiam Kravitzky* in a village near Minsk, Russia (now Ukraine) who came to the United States via Bremen, Germany and went first to Philadelphia. He moved to Lincoln, Nebraska and there met the Davidson brothers; and through them, at a Jewish community dance, he met their sister Dorothy. It was a *bashert* relationship which led to love and marriage. Dorothy Davidson, née *Dwojka Datzkowsky* also from a little village, *Gordishe*, which is in the present day Ukraine, had come to the United States in 1906 as a three-year-old via Liverpool, England and on to Lincoln, Nebraska. Two of her older sisters had already married and settled in Lincoln, and the rest of the family -- parents and seven younger children -- joined them there. Herman Krause joined the American army and fought in World War I, and stayed in the Argonne Forest area after the war to help resettle refugees. When he returned from the War, he and Dorothy were married in 1919. The couple had three daughters, two of whom were born in Lincoln and one in Council Bluffs. They lived in various small towns in Nebraska including a little place near Red Cloud where Herman had a small store. He would also travel to neighboring towns and buy up stock from stores that were closing. This is what may have led them to Iowa and, by 1928 they were in Council Bluffs where Herman established several retail businesses, culminating in the opening of their permanent store, The Bargain Spot, 10 years later.

Herman and Dorothy Krause ran the store together, and their eldest daughter Beatrice helped them. Bea Krause was very smart and artistic. She had a scholarship to attend Drake University in Des Moines, Iowa, but it was the height of the Great Depression, and they couldn't afford to send her. So upon graduating from Abraham Lincoln High School in 1939, she attended beauty school and became a beautician during World War II. Bea had met and fallen in love with Ben Schneider from Omaha by then; and when he enlisted in the United States Army, they were married and moved to Camp Crowder while he was in basic training. Soon, he would be shipped off to Oran, Algeria and later to the European theater. Bea moved back to Council Bluffs and lived with her parents at 311 Fuller Avenue.

When Ben Schneider returned from World War II, he initially went with his father in their family business, Schneider Portland Cement Company in Omaha. He and Bea were living in Council Bluffs and soon to start a family of their own, so Ben decided to join his in-laws' business and he and Bea partnered in the management of The Bargain Spot, eventually taking it over completely from Dorothy Krause, and stayed there until it closed in 1978.

Herman Krause died of a heart attack in 1952. Though Jan only knew Herman when she was a little girl (he passed away when she was four), "I remember him always laughing and smiling, always happy. He was intelligent and very beloved in Council Bluffs, one of those gregarious people everybody liked," she says. Herman and Dorothy Krause epitomized community commitment, and Herman's legacy continues to this day as the blue arm chairs he procured first for the Jewish Community Center were later moved to the synagogue and are now in the Irving Cohen Lodge chapel in the synagogue's lower level.

Ben and Bea Schneider had two other daughters besides Jan. Lynn was born two-and-a-half years after Jan, and Hermene ("Mimi") was born in 1962. Jan and Lynn both took active roles in the life of The Bargain Spot from a very young age. Before they were really old enough to actually work in the store, they would still go in and be put to doing chores like straightening tables and racks. Later they were taught how to do gift wrapping, and the first real job they had was wrapping presents for customers during the holiday rush. Both girls worked at the store during every vacation from school, eventually taking on all jobs associated with selling, doing stock work and being the cashiers. The cash register was inside a little booth in the middle of the store, surrounded on three sides by counters. Three counters, one register, one busy girl.

The Bargain Spot left an indelible mark on Jan. "Now," she says, "I feel nostalgic for it." It started out in one building, grew to take over the space next door and was divided into small departments: on one side was women's and children's clothing, intimate wear, baby items and accessories (hats, scarves, gloves, purses), outerwear, toys at Christmastime, and on the other side was the men's department with some dressy clothes, but mostly Big Smith jeans and overalls, flannel shirts and other items catering to the working man and his family. Once the new space was created, a burgeoning shoe department was set up on floor-to-ceiling shelving, stocking everything from baby shoes to school shoes for boys and girls, women's shoes and, of course, work boots.

"What I wouldn't give now to have some of the costume jewelry we sold, which at the time I thought was dowdy and now realize it is vintage treasure!" Jan says. But even though she worked alongside her parents and even though she and her sisters had the "run of the place" and could have pretty much anything they wanted from it in the way of clothing and shoes, she really didn't want to get her wardrobe for high school especially, from her own store, which was by intent, a business catering to the working man and his family.

"My sights were set on Brandeis! We wanted name-brands like Bobbie Brooks and Garland to wear at A.L. The most "in" outfits in the mid-1960s were matching wool skirts and sweaters in pastel colors with socks to match and penny-loafers. I got the shoes at our store, but not the rest of it.

"Retail was very hard, our store was open from 9 'til 6. Two days a week we stayed open from 9 to 9 and we were open on Sundays sometimes, too." Later on, they worked 9 to 9 all the time and during Christmas. Shopping was changing and the downtown along with it. They had to compete with the nascence of the big box stores like K-Mart and Woolco (later Shopko) which morphed out of the dime stores, Kresge's and Woolworth's. "My parents could rarely, if ever, take real vacations because they couldn't just close up the store for two weeks like the shopkeepers do in France, for instance."

The Bargain Spot was one of several Jewish-owned businesses in the town. A few doors east was Marcus Department Store owned by Jan's classmate Mark Eveloff's family. And many other stores including Iowa Clothes Shop, Kayper's and the Peoples Store were businesses whose owners' kids all went to Sunday school and Hebrew school together.

Ben Schneider served many terms on the Council Bluffs Chamber of Commerce and one of his jobs was procuring the city's Christmas lights that were placed on all the street light poles throughout the downtown. He was also on the Board of Children's Square which had previously been known as The Christian Home. More often than not, Council Bluffs folks supported each other, no matter their faith.

During the Missouri River flood in 1952, Ben moved his family over to Omaha to stay with his sister; but then he rushed back to the flood plain to stock sandbags at the banks of the river. In the mid-'60s, when Marcus Department Store was robbed and stock was depleted ("one of those crash and grab thefts"), Ben Schneider donated stock to tide the Eveloffs over until the next day. After Ben died in 2008, Jan ran into two high school classmates who told her, "Your dad and mom gave my parents credit and if they hadn't, I wouldn't have had any back-to-school clothes."

Herman and Dorothy Krause were not part of the founding families of B'nai Israel Synagogue, but they were both very active in the life of the Council Bluffs Jewish Community. A memorial award was established in honor of Herman and Dorothy who took on leadership roles including president of Sisterhood and service to Hadassah. Bea served with her mother in both of those organizations, along with women like Ida Perlis, Sally Telpner, Edythe Krasne, Esther Gallner, Rose Katelman and many others who raised money for B'nai Israel's ritual supplies, supplied food for *onegs* and sent funds and support materials to the Hadassah hospital in Tel Aviv.

Ben Schneider became very involved in Council Bluffs Jewish life. He was on the synagogue board, was elected president of B'nai Brith's Irving Cohen Lodge in 1958, rising to the position of Cornhusker Region president in the 1960s.

"As president of the local B'nai Brith Lodge, my dad was actually presented with the Herman Krause Memorial Award for contributing the most to the lodge during the year," Jan said. The event, too, was covered by the *Nonpareil*, which wrote that the prominent Council Bluffs physician Dr. Ike Sternhill presented the award given in the name of Herman Krause, calling him, "a model father who loved his family, his home and his fellow men. He had equal fervor in his love for the country of his adoption."

Jan attested to her father's double delight, receiving a distinguished award from the Jewish community in which Herman Krause -- his father-in-law and her grandfather -- was his role model. Ben continued to be active in the Council Bluffs synagogue long after Jan left the Bluffs, even during an era around 1975 when B'Nai Israel's attendance was waning. "My dad also participated in *minyans* and helped with services at the Blumkin Home for a long time."

Jan and her grandmother Dorothy were extremely close all through Jan's childhood and teen years. Almost every Friday night — before football games would interfere with it -- Jan would accompany Dorothy to *shul* which became a tradition Jan grew to cherish. "Services were sometimes in the basement, in the social hall if I recall, if there weren't enough people present to have services upstairs," Jan says. "I guess Friday night wasn't as popular as Saturday morning, but I remember I always liked Friday night services. Because of the ritual chanting and the music, I pretty much learned all the prayers. But I can't recite them too well now because we chanted them rather than saying them. If I hear the chants, I can do them perfectly, but if not... I'm pretty nil, "Jan laughs.

A girl and her grandmother, the relationship was seared in Jan's heart long after her dearest was gone. Though Dorothy died in 1972, Jan's relationship with her is still alive. "She was one of my best friends growing up, she was my mentor, very literate if not very educated. She didn't go to college, but was very well-read. And she was very liberal! My aunts tell the story of how when they were growing up on Fuller Avenue, that house was the one where all the kids hung out because my grandparents let them smoke! They said something to the effect of, 'Better to be doing it out in the open than to go off and sneak cigarettes.'"

Jan continues, "I got much of my love of family, traditions, taste in furniture, clothing, art and even photo preservation from her. She and I would put photos in albums, and my love of scrapbooking started with her. The house on Fuller Avenue was even more my taste than my own modern one on Kenmore. They had bought it during the Depression when it was going for a song, and they also purchased the contents that came with it: victorian furniture, beautiful crystal sconces on the dining room walls, heavy brocade draperies. I just loved that. I spent as much time with my grandmother in that house as possible. She also taught me how to cook rice pudding, amazing cinnamon rolls and mandel bread. She was a great Jewish cook, and while I didn't hang around her apron strings all the time learning that skill, I did help her and my mom make homemade kosher pickles. My mother's chicken soup and *latke* recipes were from her mother, too, and I make those to this day. My sister and I would also stay overnight many times on Fuller Avenue in a spare room with a hide-a-bed, which was a newfangled thing for us. And my grandmother had the first color TV in the family, so we would go over there to see the beautiful screen and especially to watch the NBC peacock spread its tail."

Jan's paternal grandmother Sadie Schneider, "was quiet," she says. "Her English was not so great. I had a close relationship with her and my *Zaydie* Abe because every Friday night when we were really little, we went to their house at 52nd and Military in Omaha. Abe was fabulous, very sweet and loved his grandchildren to death. We were the younger ones -- our older cousins lived in Omaha -- and he doted on us all. He had also come to America from a *shtetl* near Minsk, Russia, spoke fluent Yiddish and spoke English with the same accent as my grandmother. He'd take us to Louie's Market up the street from his house across the Radial Highway and buy many wonderful fruits and candies for us. My grandfather even wrote poetry for all the special occasions in our family, including my wedding."

Jan's Jewish education was like that of her contemporaries. She attended Hebrew school and Sunday school where students performed mock seders, reciting the four questions and learned all the other blessings, too. Hebrew school was every Thursday.

"The boys were naughty," laughs Jan, who outs Pete Lee, Mike Gallner, Richard Selo (the one well-behaved boy), Mark Eveloff and Greg Mann as the culprits. "They were sometimes so disobedient they were put in the corner and would sit there to peel the wallpaper. Steven Perlis would sometimes bring sock monkeys he made and we all played with them. We giggled a lot; Rabbi Korb didn't like that. He didn't have much control over the class, let's put it that way."

Besides Jan, the other girls in the class were Deborah Mezey and Judy Cole. Jan and Judy shared a B'nai Mitzvah on May 20, 1960. "I was one of first girls in the Bluffs to have a Bas Mitzvah party," says Jan, who notes the difference between Bas and Bat. In the '70s, there was a pronunciation change to go more Israeli and so S's became T's. Shabbat instead of Shabbos.

"My party was on our patio at 246 Kenmore, and it was a pretty dressy affair. My Bas Mitzvah outfit was a white nylon organza dress with a full skirt and embroidered rose buds up the front. I wore my very first pair of 'heels' that were squash heels, so not high at all, but I felt like I was very tall. My cousin Harold Schneider from Omaha, who was older and went to Central High and worked part time at radio stations, was the DJ. That was a big deal. He played records for us all night with the hits from Ricky Nelson, my favorite, and the Everly Brothers and Brenda Lee. We did have trouble getting the boys to come outside from watching the NBA playoffs and dance, however. My non-Jewish friends from the sixth grade at Hoover School were all invited; and for many of them, it had to be their first ever Bas Mitzvah party or for that matter, the first time they ever had been inside a synagogue."

The Council Bluffs synagogue drew the Jewish community together on many occasions, including, most importantly, the High Holidays. In keeping with tradition, congregants attended services for two days for Rosh Hashana, and, of course, Yom Kippur, which was the most important holiday on the Jewish calendar even as Chanukah held the principal allure for kids. "On Chanukah, my parents often worked long hours, so we didn't celebrate until they got home — sometimes after nine at night. That was late for us."

Though Jan's family was observant, they didn't always live by the book. "The tradition in our family was this: my grandmother Dorothy didn't know when her birthday was, so she chose December 25th –– probably because that date was 25 *Kislev* (the third month of the civil year and the ninth month of the ecclesiastical year on the Hebrew calendar). On Christmas Eve day in our teenage years, Lynn and I worked in the store so the (non-Jewish) help could be at home that night. After closing, we all went to my grandmother's house on Fuller Avenue where each place at the table had a small pile of presents. We also had presents on Christmas morning from Santa Claus in my early childhood, but never a tree. The dominant American culture permeated our lives," Jan said, and explained that another tradition they had was going to Brandeis in Omaha to see the Christmas windows and marvel at the wonderland on the tenth floor.

When the Brandeis downtown store closed in 1981, she wrote an op-ed story for the *Omaha World-Herald* about what that store meant to her as a child, especially at Christmastime when the prevalent American culture was a stronger draw than the religious one she lived otherwise. "My parents just caved," she laughs.

When asked about the presence of any anti-Semitism in her life growing up in Council Bluffs, Jan admits she did not experience it like her dad did in school in Omaha during the 1930s. But she did recall an instance of what she considered blatant discrimination. Jan experienced anti-Semitism when she tried out for American Field Service.

"It was my whole life, my Alpha and Omega. I wanted to be an exchange student more than anything else. We had AFS students living with us three summers in a row. I was in the AFS group at school; we were all very active in it. I think I was an officer. So when some of us tried out to be exchange students, I thought I had a pretty good chance. We all went through the interview process, and I thought it had gone well.

"The next thing that would happen was the announcement of the winner, and the way it worked was that the committee showed up at one's house to do it. But on the night they were due to come –– and we were waiting with heightened anticipation –– they didn't come to my house. I was completely devastated but didn't think it was because they didn't like me. There were a lot of my friends also trying out; I had to be happy for the girl who got picked, she was a friend of mine. As it turned out, shortly thereafter my grandmother happened to be across the street from the store at the gas station where she was filling up her car and talking to a guy who she knew to have had something to do with the AFS Committee (though he wasn't the person who actually made the decision). And she said, 'I'm wondering how my granddaughter didn't get chosen' and he said, 'Well' (and he named a very prominent person in Council Bluffs), the person made it clear to the committee that Council Bluffs couldn't send a Jew.' That was a real eye-opener to me. My father wasn't surprised, but I was shocked."

The good things about growing up in small-town America surely outweighed the bad, in Jan's opinion. She noted that the Jewish kids and the Gentile kids mixed fairly well in school. "I visited many churches with my friends in grade school and high school. I was always treated kindly." And the country club in Council Bluffs, then known as the Elks Club, allowed people of all faiths to be members, unlike some of the clubs in Omaha. "We were a family who did not take long vacations, as I mentioned," Jan said, "So Lake Manawa was our vacation spot. My sister and I were dropped off every day in the summers; and after the store closed, my parents would come out, play golf and let us swim at night when the pool was lit up. Later, in high school when I could drive, if I wasn't working in the store, I was at the Club."

Jan did move away and has lived in San Francisco and Europe then back in Omaha since 1974. But whenever she's in Council Bluffs, it always makes her feel happy to reminisce about her life there and revisit old friends and old haunts.
"Things change," she says. "A lot of the downtown is fairly unrecognizable from the 1950s and '60s. But the Fuller Street house is still intact, and the Kenmore/Keeline neighborhood has been preserved almost (not quite!) just as it was; so it is always nice to drive around up there. I like the fact that the Council Bluffs synagogue got put on the National Register of Historic Places. I hope that assures its unchanged existence long into the future."

Wedding of Dorothy Davidson and Herman Krause, 1919

Left to right; Ben Schneider, Jan Schneider (age 2), Beatrice Schneider, Shirley and Edward Cherniss, bride and groom, Joan Krause, Dorothy Krause and Herman Krause, 1952

Wedding of Shirley Lou Krause and Edward Cherniss Looking at bride are Dorothy and Herman Krause and Beatrice Schneider, 1952

75. Sunday School of B'nai Israel taken on steps of Council Bluffs Jewish Community Center-Jan Lund second row, 4th from the left, 1954

76. Harry Cohen (seated) and Herman Krause, 1950

77. Ben Schneider, Rabbi Korb, Harold Bernstein

78

Nonpareil Sunday Sept 17, 196

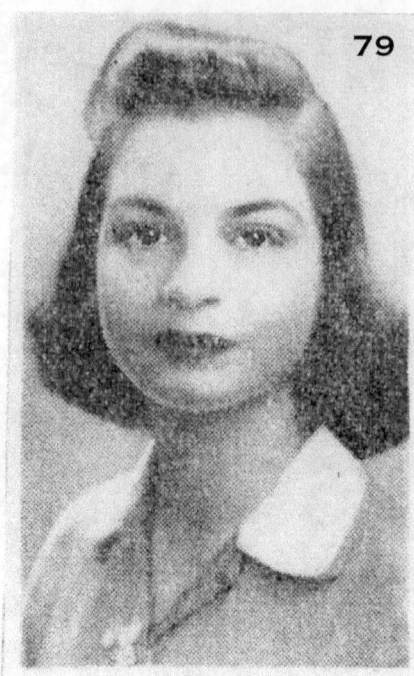

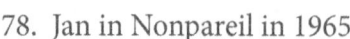

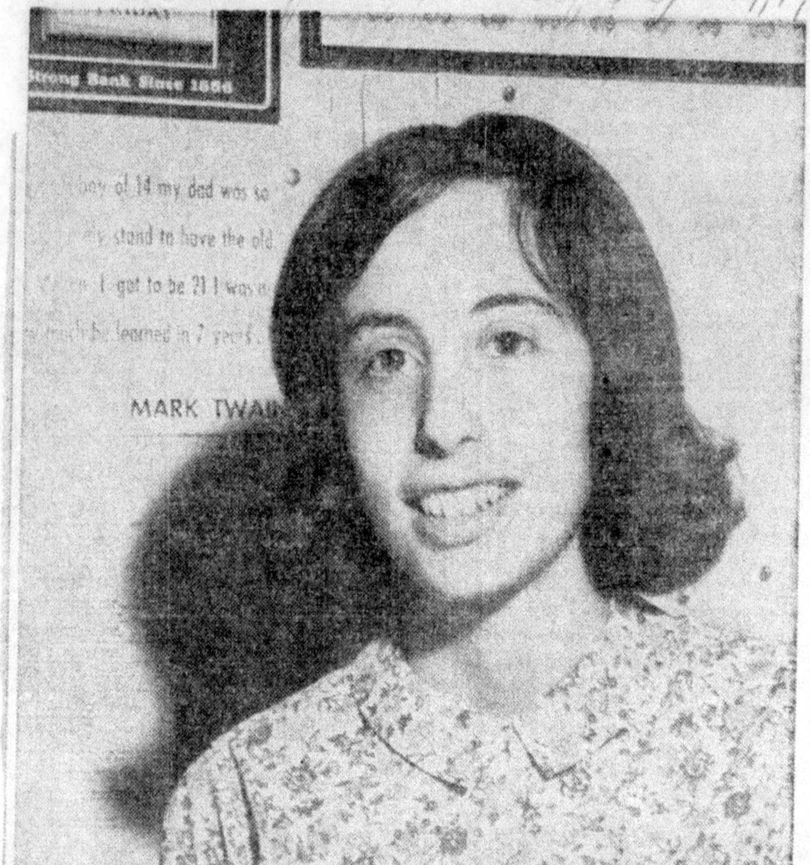

Jan Schneider . . . of Abraham Lincoln High School is the 17-year-old daughter of Mr. and Mrs. Ben Schneider. A National Honor Society member she is interested in reading, spectator sports, writing music and drama. She is a member of Future Teachers, Spanish and Drama clubs and American Field Service Club. She has two sisters, **Lynn, 15,** and **Miml, 3.**

79

Miss Beatrice Krause

COUNCIL BLUFFS.

Mr. and Mrs. Herman Krause announce the engagement of their daughter, Miss Beatrice Krause, to Ben Schneider, son of Mr. and Mrs. Abe Schneider of Omaha.

Miss Krause is a graduate of Abraham Lincoln High school. Mr. Schneider is in the enlisted reserve of the signal corps in Omaha.

80

78. Jan in Nonpareil in 1965

79. Jan's parents' engagement announcement

80. Bea and Ben Schneider in front of The Bargain Spot, 618 West Broadway

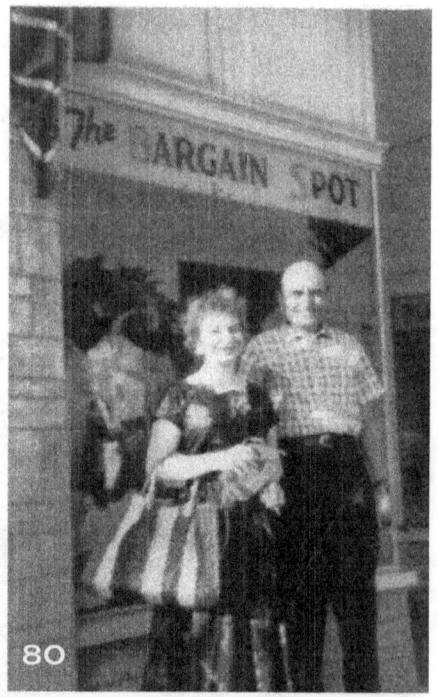

81. Sunday School of B'nai Israel on steps in front of Jewish Community Center in Council Bluffs, 1961
Jan Schneider Lund, top row, last person on the right

82. The Bargain Spot, 618-20 West Broadway, Council Bluffs

83. Dorothy Krause and Bea Schneider at Bargain Spot, 1970

Lloyd Krasne and Bea Schneider at last Council Bluffs Hadassah meeting in 2002

Jan Schneider Lund and Bea Schneider at last Council Bluffs Hadassah meeting in 2002

GARY KATELMAN

Gary: I was born in Omaha, my mother Anna Jane was from Omaha and my dad Stanley grew up in Council Bluffs. When they got married, they both moved to Omaha. She didn't want to move to Council Bluffs.

Joey: Why?

Gary: Women's prerogative [both laugh]. So, on my mother and father's first anniversary in 1948, my grandfather, Sam Katelman, bought a clothing store for my dad named Herman's Clothes Shop on Broadway and Main in Council Bluffs. In those days, it was a lot of work clothes and jeans, overalls, boots, a few suits, casual slacks like Haggar, a few nicer things. We had Levi's brand which was very exclusive back then and Van Huesen was another hot brand. The downstairs also had some western wear in it and the second floor of the building was the tailor shop. Above that there was another story that was vacant. As I remember, being five-years-old, we would go over every weekend with my dad. It was wonderful! I spent all day with my father so…

Joey: So it was about family.

Gary: Yes. And my grandfather was in the store quite a bit, too. He was in the real estate business; he put together a deal, a lease with the original Mr. J.C. Penney. He had a 40-year lease on a large building between 5th and 6th Streets on Broadway, the J. C. Penney Building. Every month Grandpa's rent was a percentage of their sales. It was a very lucrative deal back then for Sam. Above that building, there were two other floors he converted into sleeping rooms, so-called apartments, mostly for a lot of railroad people. Back then, the Union Pacific Railroad stopped in Council Bluffs. When he was out of town, I usually managed the apartments, and I was getting anywhere from, depending on who the occupant was, around 30 dollars a month. I worked at the store my whole life, even during college. I went to the University of Nebraska at Lincoln and was home every weekend and worked.

Joey: Was that by your design or your parents?

Gary: That was my parents' idea; that's how I earned my money to pay for my gas and a few items I needed at school. This was in 1968 to 1972 and my weekend pay was $30 dollars, which was a lot back then, so I was never really short of cash for gas or beer during that time [both laugh].

Joey: Hopefully not both at the same time. How did he get introduced to J.C. Penney?

Gary: Well, Grandpa knew a lot of people from around the country and Council Bluffs was a pretty active town back then. A lot of railroad business, a lot of merchant business. The Jewish population were all close-knit families and they owned most of everything in Council Bluffs at that time: the haberdashery stores, the textile stores, the hardware store, the junkyard, the foundry. These were all my ancestors and there were a few other families over there as well. Council Bluffs was a booming city, especially during the war, as I understand. The old-timers stopped when they couldn't get any farther. Most of our family came in through New Orleans from Russian Romania on both my parents' sides. My grandfather was born in Council Bluffs in 1899; all his siblings were born here. My grandfather's parents were actually first cousins.

Joey: What were their names?

Gary: Katleman and Katelman. One spelled it K-a-t-l-e-m-a-n and the other spelled it K-a-t-e-l-m-a-n. So there are two sides of this family that were all related. The "le's" and the "el's" were all related, one family across the country. So the two first cousins married and it had to have been my great-grandfather who changed it to "el" and that's how we are the "el" side of the family.

I went to work every day in Council Bluffs starting when I was about five. It was great; we'd have breakfast at the Seventeen Club which was right in back of the store. I remember as a kid, the president of the Council Bluffs Savings Bank was there every morning, and my dad and a group of friends. At the store, I swept floors in the basement; then as I aged, I worked in the office, some bookkeeping. I was on the floor selling since I was 10 or 12-years-old.

Joey: What did you learn about working at such a young age?

Gary: I have the same work ethic today. I don't stop. I have no other hobbies other than work, which I thoroughly enjoy. On the weekends, I'm up early and working. Working retail back then, it was always two nights a week, Monday and Thursday, and Saturdays. A lot of hours. You had to know everybody; we took good care of our customers. If they came to Council Bluffs and bought a suit and they lived in Omaha, I would bring the suits home with me at night and they picked them up at my house. I would take things to certain people's homes, fit for them.

Joey: So you were a tailor, too. Did you always have a piece of chalk in your pocket?

Gary: Always. At the end of the day, what was in your jacket was emptied on the counter. Personal service was all we did, took care of a lot of friends down in Lincoln as well. They would call me up, tell me what they needed and I'd bring it down. We carried the hottest dress lines back then, like Christian Dior.

Joey: How much would a Christian Dior gown go for back then?

Gary: You could buy one for probably $800.

Joey: Did your mom work in the store?

Gary: No, she used to come and take home what she wanted [both laugh].

Joey: Tell me about your fondest memories of the store.

Gary: The camaraderie between my dad and my grandfather and myself -- we were like three thieves. That was the most important part; you always had somebody to talk to. I learned a ton from my grandfather about life and street smarts. He said, 'If you know nothing else in this business, you've got to add and subtract in your head and you've got to do it fast.'"

Joey: Did you?

Gary: Oh, yeah. I can still do it. He also taught me, 'Smile when somebody says, "I want to Jew you down."' That was very common back then. It didn't bother me, I was expecting it. I remember when the *Hasidim* would come through town begging for money. They'd come into the store and all three of us would run up to the office and lock the door [laughs].

Joey: Tell me more about anti-Semitism.

Gary: All kinds of comments. Way back when, the Jews had to go into business for themselves because nobody would hire them. If you look at my grandfather's family back in the 1930s, every one of them owned something because how else are you going to make a living? I mean, Mrs. B took her cart, that's how she started. Borsheim's, same thing.

A lot of the gamblers back then were all Jews. You had the Ziegmans and the Abrams and Grandpa's cousin Katelman who built the El Rancho in Las Vegas, which was one of the first strip hotels out there. Most of all that was controlled by Jews. I knew one of Meyer Lansky's guys from Kansas City, I used to have lunch with him at Lane Drug Store with my grandfather, next to the Iowa Clothes Shop, Patty Nogg's family, on the corner of 5th and Broadway.

Joey: Wow! Who stood out? Mentors or big personalities...

Gary: My grandfather was my mentor. Uncle Joe was the mayor of Council Bluffs. I remember I had an aunt over there by the name of Toby Richards; she was five-feet-eight or more. She married this guy, he wasn't five feet and he smoked this great big long cigar...Uncle Nate.

She used to pat him on the head [both laugh]. We have a lot of longevity in the Katelman family; they either lived a long time or died young. My grandfather lived to 96, my grandmother on my mother's side lived to 107.

Joey: Did she eat a lot of bacon?

Gary: I don't know, but she was a prima donna. She was wonderful to us! Growing up, my grandfather had a three-story house on Bayliss Park. In there, he had Grandma's parents, his wife and then all the kids. He had built a dance floor in the basement and all the kids used to come over and dance on the weekends. Everybody still talks about that. Everybody knew Sam. He was a pretty well-connected guy around the country. He didn't talk about it, but I had that feeling and, as more and more comes out, I have more of that feeling.

There were a lot of businesses run with my family in Council Bluffs, like owning a junk yard. Joe and Maurice Katelman, my grandfather's brothers, owned the junk yard: Katelman Brothers Junk Yard. That's Rick Katelman's dad. Maurice ran the junk yard, and Rick and I used to go over there and fiddle around with cars. We were driving cars by the time we were 12-years-old. Old junkers.

Abe Katelman ran the foundry, and he got called to World War II. They made steel components, melted and manufactured steel. Then when they went to war, my grandfather and my dad who was 4F, which indicates an applicant has been deemed unfit for military service (he could only hear out of one ear and was disqualified to go into the service, so he never went to college), they went down and ran the foundry and they were making bullets and made a lot of money. They had all the gas stamps in town and they'd end up with new cars every once in a while and they supplied the whole city with tires to their friends, because of the government contracts.

Joey: What did your dad and grandpa do after they sold the property?

Gary: Dad moved to Florida with my mom and Grandpa was already in Phoenix.

Joey: Why didn't you stay in the business?

Gary: Retail was evolving. I was a finance major in college. My dad got sick in 1973 with herniated disc problems, so I ended up in the store, which was fine. I mean that's all I knew. I just assumed the role of what the family has to do. In 1982, they built a new highway through a lot of this old property and we were able to help guide that highway, Kanesville Boulevard. It was a bypass road and it took a lot of the property out from the families. They bought out family property from us, the Eveloffs and Dad's sister.

Joey: How did you feel about that after having a family business there?

Gary: It didn't bother me; retail was hard back then, during the advent of department stores, marketing dollars and loyalties. It was much more difficult to operate one or two units than it was to operate a lot more.

Joey: It was a hub for your family, though.

Gary: It still is. I still have very fond memories of Council Bluffs. I'm over there probably once a week. To this day, we still have a lot of friends over there. The cemetery is over there and almost the whole clan are buried there. As a kid, my dad made us go to

B'nai Israel on the second day of Rosh Hashanah and the second day of Yom Kippur and they were always short of *minyans* on Saturdays. Either Ben Seldin, Abe Katelman or Sam Sacks usually ran the services by the time. I reached age 13. Every Saturday they were running around town trying to drag somebody into the synagogue. So once I reached 13 and had my Bar Mitzvah, I was the one that got shoved out the door of the store.

My grandfather Sam was married to Goldie Marcus; and when I was five-years-old, she passed away from breast cancer. They were living in the Chieftain Hotel so they could have proper care for her. My grandfather, in memory of my grandmother, built the kitchen that's still there today.

Herman's Clothing, Council Bluffs

July 14, 1978 MIDLANDS BUSINESS JOURNAL 7

Gary Katelman, left, and Stanley in the suit department of Herman's Clothes... Volume at the store has grown every year for 30 years.

84. Gary and Stanley newspaper photo

85. Four generations of Katelmans: Gary, Bret, Sam & Stanley, 1980

86. Bottom right: Katelmans in Herman's

SARA WOLFSON EPSTEIN
1923 - 2015

My name is Sara Wolfson Epstein. I was born in 1923 in Riga, Latvia, to Boruch Meyer Wolfson and Anna Fineman Wolfson. My parents followed my uncle, Judah Wolfson, to Omaha. My father came first to escape being drafted into the Russian army, and my mother, sisters, paternal grandmother and I followed when I was less than one-year-old. I attended schools in Omaha.

My husband Harold Epstein was born in the back of the tailor shop in Omaha. Our families knew of each other and my husband was in elementary school classes with my older sisters. Harold and I dated when he returned from World War II and we married in 1947. My husband took a job with the IRS in Sioux City in 1948. Our daughter Karen was born there and we enjoyed living in the community. In 1953, Harold was promoted to run the IRS office in Council Bluffs. We were very excited to move back to the Omaha area where we both had family. Shortly after moving, our son Jerry was born.

I was raised in a very Orthodox home in Omaha in a neighborhood surrounded by Jewish families. My parents spoke many languages, but in our home we spoke Yiddish, so my first language was Yiddish. Now, I seldom have the opportunity to speak with others in Yiddish. My father was a rabbi but was never attached to a congregation. To earn money, he repaired *Torahs*, was a *shochet*, led services in neighboring communities and tutored boys for their Bar Mitzvah.

My husband grew up in an immigrant neighborhood. His parents had a tailor shop. His mother kept kosher, his parents associated with Jewish families, were part of the Workman's Circle, they celebrated the Jewish holidays and his mother was very active in Jewish organizations and activities. By the time he was born, his parents understood English. They spoke to him in Yiddish and he would respond in English.

In our home, together we celebrated all of the holidays and kept the traditions over the 65 years we were married. For example, on Fridays I changed the beds, cleaned the house and made chicken for dinner, just as my mother had done. We would have wine and challah and say the blessings on Friday nights. For Chanukah, we always had *latkes* and played *dreidel*. I changed the dishes for Passover, removed bread from the house and we would have two *seders* every year. The children loved listening to the *Megillah* being read by Harold every Purim and they always were eager to drown out the name of *Haman*. And twice a year, before Passover and Rosh Hashanah, I would thoroughly clean the house.

In 1953, we bought a house at 111 Midland Dr. in Council Bluffs. While I was unpacking, I received a knock on the door from an older woman neighbor. I came to the door in work clothes. She did not want to come in but did come by to see what Jewish people looked like. She had heard the new neighbors were Jewish and had never met a Jew before. I always wondered if she thought I would have horns. At that time, most of the women in the neighborhood did not work. They were cordial and did have a surprise baby shower for me shortly after we moved in. There was neighborhood friendliness but none were close friends.

Very few Jewish people lived in our area of town. And we found that most of the 80 Jewish families were related to each other. However, through the synagogue we met many nice people. Our closest friends were Lotti and Sam Colick, Betty and Ike Sternhill, Harold and Lillian Finkel (who lived on the next street) and Irene and Rudy Selo. There was also a couple who were Holocaust survivors: Abe and Guta Goldfelt. They had two daughters our children's ages and, as I remember, the Council Bluffs Jewish community sponsored them after the war. They lived in Council Bluffs for a short while, then moved to Los Angeles.

Also, we were close to Phil and Margot Falken and their children, Elaine and Steven. The Falkens retired to Sun City and their daughter married Jack Oruch and settled in Lawrence, Kansas. While we lived in Council Bluffs, we saw all of our friends through Jewish events in town and enjoyed sharing meals together in our homes. For many years after we left Council Bluffs, we exchanged Rosh Hashanah cards and maintained contact.

The center of our life was the Jewish community. Rabbi Korb led the Jewish community, and he was a very fine, kind man who tried to meet the needs of all. The community owned the synagogue, a community center and the rabbi's house next to the synagogue. The community center was an older house that had a big central room with classrooms around the perimeter. The central room had probably been the living room and dining room in the home. All of the children in the Sunday school could fit into that central room, and every Sunday morning when the Sunday school was in session, the children would sing songs together in that room. The singing was led by the rabbi who had a very nice voice and the singing usually ended with *Hatikvah*.

We regularly attended services on Friday night and services were held in the basement of the synagogue. Sunday school and community dinners were held at the community center. I worked closely with the rabbi to coordinate the Sunday school and I taught the confirmation class for many years.

Twice a year, the confirmation class students would come to my house for a cooking class, boys and girls included. The teenagers learned how to make *challah*, *latkes* and other traditional Jewish dishes. They always had a good time and the class would end with eating the food they prepared together.

Holidays were celebrated throughout the year by the Jewish community. A *sukkah* was built next to the synagogue and it was decorated with fruit. There was a Purim party every year and the children would come dressed as Purim characters. There was a mock *seder* with the opportunity for children to taste all of the special foods.

Before the internet, it took a bit of searching to find *bauxer*, St. John's bread. I would order it and it would arrive by mail. You could always tell when it came because of the strong, unusual odor. In Sunday school, all students had the opportunity to taste it every year and I'm not aware of anyone who had a taste for it. It was an experience!

There was no gift shop associated with the synagogue or community center, so I approached the Krasne family who owned the Peoples Store and asked if they had a glass cabinet. They were generous and donated one. It was placed in the Jewish community center. I purchased items such as jewelry, *mezuzahs* and *menorahs* to stock it. It was open after Sunday school and was a popular place to buy wedding gifts, graduation gifts, confirmation and Bar/Bat Mitzvah gifts.

Harold and I were active in the men's and women's Jewish groups in Council Bluffs. I cannot remember now all the offices we held, but I am sure that we were either a secretary or treasurer of each group. The children remember a yearly dinner for adults at the community center. It always smelled good with roasting brisket that was cooked by one of the members. In the afternoon, prior to the meal for the adults, we would bring our children to help set the tables.

There was always a big crowd of people at the synagogue for the high holidays. The main level of benches in the synagogue was always full and it was common for the balcony to also be full. For children it was a long day, so they would often play in the basement. Of course, they would make noise while having a good time and their noise would carry upstairs. Their play in the basement would eventually be terminated by an adult who would go to the basement to have them stop. Sometimes, their play would then move to the front sidewalk.

Many of the downtown stores were owned by Jewish families. The children fondly remember going to the Peoples Store. There was a candy counter that was never missed, and the owners were very generous in sending the children home with Golden Books which they treasured and read until the books fell apart.

At the time Karen started kindergarten at Gunn Elementary School, there were no other Jewish children at the school. Early in the school year we went to the school's open house. There, we saw a picture of Christ on the wall of the kindergarten room. At about the same time, Karen started saying a prayer she learned at school thanking Christ for food. Harold and I spoke with the teacher, the principal and the school district superintendent. We were told that praying to Christ was up to the teacher. At that point, Harold contacted the ADL and they intervened. When our son started school, these issues had been worked out.

Karen started going to Hebrew school when she was eight-years-old. She would take the public bus twice a week into the city center, get off at the town square where the library was located, then walk to the community center. The Hebrew school class was very small and all of the other children were transported by their parents. If it was snowing, Karen was frequently the only one to attend. The class was taught by the rabbi, who was especially kind because if it was snowing, he would take Karen back in his car to the Medical Arts Building where she could wait inside to get the bus, or he would take her to Harold's office near the synagogue.

Looking back, there was a rhythm to the year. Jewish life, family and the school were the focus of our lives while we were raising children.

Every summer, I had a difficult time with allergies. The last year we were in Council Bluffs, I was hospitalized for a significant amount of time. We needed to move from the area, so in 1960, Harold got a job in San Francisco which was a better place for me to live. It was difficult leaving friends and family and it took a while to develop close friends to share holidays and special events. It is special that many of these people are still alive and are still part of my life. My husband passed away unexpectedly in December, 2012.

It was nice having the opportunity to look back over the time my family lived in Council Bluffs. It was a happy seven years.

232 | S. WOLFSON EPSTEIN

87. Sara with Rabbi Korb, unknown woman, Lillian Finkel and Elaine Falken

88. Abe and Guta Goldfeld in 1960

89. Harold and Sara with Jerry and Karen

90. Harold Finkel with daughter Leslie and Karen Epstein

91. 92. Harold and Sara Epstein

93. Harold looking for afikoman

94. Lighting Chanukah candles with grandchildren, Jessica and Jacquelyn Epstein

BOB SUVALSKY

ONE CHANCE MEETING led to a lifetime of love, family and furniture. "It was love for a long time," says Bob of his grandparents Saul and Frieda (née Goldberg) who met because he ran out of money.

Born in Kolno, Poland in 1896, at 14, Saul, leaving behind his parents, three sisters and four brothers boarded a train to Belgium, embarked on a three-week voyage by ship to Ellis Island and a new life in New York City, thanks to his Uncle David who sponsored him. His formal education stopped in elementary school at the 6th grade, but no matter. The kid from *Kolno* learned street smarts as a delivery boy who ran sweets from a wholesaler to candy stands, and as an usher with Fox's Follie Theatre for a hefty $7 a week.

He'd need loads of caffeine, because after finishing 8th grade in night school, Saul ricocheted from city to city, working odd jobs, joining the Army -- he was stationed in Fort Dodge, Iowa, where he obtained his citizenship -- an industrious young fellow finding his way; yet he never lost faith, only his Polish accent. Fantasies of San Francisco were dashed after he boarded a train in 1915 and made it as far as Columbus, Nebraska where he ran out of cash. Plan B? A job painting the Union Pacific Bridge in Omaha.

Unbeknownst to him, love was afoot.

Thanks to Omaha-based relatives Isadore and Sophie Sokolof who knew someone in Council Bluffs, Iz got him a job in retail at the Peoples Store where he worked from 1919 to 1922. Like many families back then who opened their home to boarders to earn extra money, Saul rented a room in the Goldbergs' house, where eldest daughter Frieda caught his eye, then his heart; eventual partners in life and in business.

"Man and wife, side by side," says Bob of his grandparents, who opened and ran The White Front Market in the 500 block of Main Street from 1922 to 1944, sold out and started a small appliance business which eventually morphed into Master Furniture & Appliance Company located first at 224 West Broadway, then 149 West Broadway, the Hughes-Irons Building, a two-story beaut on the Historical Register owned by the Seldin family and whose second floor has been converted into sleek, modern loft apartments.

"It is so cool to be able to see some of the featured units and remember that part of the warehouse!" Bob says. "The Seldins did an amazing job with that building, and I know that my dad and uncle would have been very proud of it!"

Saul handled operations while Frieda managed the office and public relations. Suvalsky brothers Marvin, Bob's father and uncle Selwin ("Sel") joined the family business where they worked until both retired in August, 1997. The *Nonpareil* featured the store's closing –– big news in small Council Bluffs –– and cites the most important lesson they learned from their father: "Always treat your customers as you would like to be treated because when you pass away, there is only one thing you leave and that's your good name."

The Suvalskys earned their good name by doing business the old-fashioned way: catering to second and third-generation families, calling them by name, even making house calls. Yes, they would tote sofa cushions to a customer's home to ensure a proper color scheme and style. "This has been more like a family than a business," Sel said.

Zeph ("Boonejug") Telpner, a family friend, also weighed in on Master Furniture's closing in an article he wrote for the *Midlands Business Journal*. "Marvin will ask me about my children and my wife," he says. "Dotty and Reva (Marvin and Selwins' wives) never fail to check on my family. Their concern isn't a rehearsed routine. They even remember where our conversation left off when I was last in the store."

In Frieda's words: "One of the joys of selling to the public is knowing you have a part in making better homes –– and in making people happy." Indeed, they made Bob happy too. "My grandparents were a very unique couple, devoted to each other, active in the Jewish community –– Frieda in Hadassah, Saul in *shul* –– love for life and love for family."

Saul, whose parents were from Poland, lost a lot of family in the *Shoah* and spent much of his life trying to reconnect with family. He found a brother in Chile and another one in Israel, the only survivors. "Grandma was big about the family getting together and hosted "The Goldberg Family Reunions" which were every few years at her house. They rented out motels for family members and grilled in the backyard....It was a big festival for four or five days and it kept getting bigger as the family grew. It meant so much to her."

Bob's Jewish Council Bluffs was decidedly different from his parents' and grandparents' who carried traditions from the old country, kept Kosher and attended *shul* every Friday night. Saul even ran services with Sam Sacks after Rabbi Klein, the last full-time rabbi, left B'nai Israel. "It was a very unique experience and everyone knew everyone," says Bob, who loved attending *shul* with his grandfather. "It brought him so much pleasure to have me there, especially in the end."

As Jews moved away and generations gave way to the next, the population dwindled, along with Bob's sense of belonging, socially, at least. "You knew you were different as I was the only Jewish kid in my neighborhood," says Bob, who lived across from Hoover Elementary which he attended with area, non-Jewish children. While most Jewish kids lived off of Keeline and Kenmore, they lived on Corrine Avenue. Why?

"My dad was not your typical Jewish kid." On Sundays, when they weren't with his grandparents, Marvin flew planes -- an Aero Coupe, a Piper Cub -- and often took his son for a spin. "We'd fly to farming communities, small, regional airports, woke at the crack of dawn. Me and my dad, it was fun stuff." Since Marvin's flying buddies lived in that neighborhood, he wanted to stay close to that community.

Most Sundays, Bob spent time with his cousins at his grandparents' house, his only real exposure to other Jewish kids. "We'd all pile in the Rambler station wagon, all five grandkids, stopped at Christy Creme on North Broadway and went for a drive along Lake Manawa, I believe. Hearing my grandfather telling stories of growing up and coming to the U.S., it was a bonding experience with my cousins and it's all I really had."

He did have, however, a claim to fame he still holds today: he shares Ringo Starr's birthday, plus he turned 18 on 7/7/77.

In his age group, the only other Jewish kids were Susan Sacks (Gelb) and her sister Karen, Patty Lee (Nogg), Edie Colick and the Telpner daughters, Marcy, Heidi and Sari. "I didn't think twice about it," he says. "I think it bothered my parents more than me. I didn't realize what I was missing until my Bar Mitzvah." His sister Linda and cousin Marti were the last girls to get Bat Mitzvahed in the synagogue in 1969. The last education Bob had in the Bluffs was at *cheder* with his teacher Mrs. Gurtenstein from Omaha (via Brooklyn) who wore a *sheitel*, and also taught Susan, Edie and Karen.

"It was neat having her come over from Omaha to Council Bluffs three times a week to teach prayers. We started with the *Shema* and ended with *Hatikvah*, the Israeli national anthem. Once I left Hebrew school and *shul*, it was back to Bluffs World." He took guitar lessons after school at Walter's music store downtown for $3 a lesson. Afterwards, he'd walk with his guitar to his dad's store, wait until closing, then ride home with him in the company van. "It was a nice bonding time, sitting in front of the TVs at the store watching Hogan's Heroes and Gilligan's Island. I was one of the first kids to watch color TV; that was wild!"

Since there was no rabbi at B'nai Israel and no more *cheder* in Council Bluffs, his mother Dotty *shlepped* him after school across the river to Beth Israel, where he befriended Omaha Jews. "It was a great mitzvah," says Bob, whose parents decided if he and his sister Linda were going to have Jewish association, they'd have to move, which they did, between Bob's 7th and 8th grade years. "Perfect timing, I was just at that age, becoming aware of my Jewish identity. Wow!" He quickly became a Jewish joiner: initially *Tovim* and *Kadimah* (Beth Israel's youth groups), and he became president of Chaim Weitzman AZA 1510 and Beau of Hevrah BBG.

Still, Council Bluffs was in his blood. After Bob's Bar Mitzvah in June, 1972, he was called many times by his grandfather Saul for a *minyan*. "There were so few Jews in Council Bluffs, we used to get that phone call at 7:30 am on Sunday. 'Bobby? We need you to come to *shul* to be our 10th man and we can't start services without you.'"

Decades later, his parents' sacrifice remains seared in his heart, as his father was born and raised in Council Bluffs, where his parents had a business. "Imagine the resistance to leave? That was a tough one," he says. "It was the best thing my parents could have ever done, because they gave me that Jewish identity I was lacking in Council Bluffs. In the end, when you're a Jewish kid in the Bluffs, you know you're different, unless you have other Jewish friends. You assimilate like everybody else, you're always known as being Jewish. You can imagine, especially in the late '60s and early '70s, I was singled out as the Jew in school, and sometimes harassed. It was difficult being a Jewish kid in Council Bluffs. I was the last Jewish kid at Hoover Elementary, the last of the Mohicans."

Frieda and Saul Suvalsky wedding picture

Saul, Frieda, Selwin and Marvin, 1930s

95. Marvin, Frieda, Saul and Selwin Suvalsky 1949-1951
96. Dotty, Reva, Ronda, Steve, Linda and Marti Suvalsky, 1959
97. Bob, Dotty and Linda Suvalsky at home in back yard of 146 Corrine Ave., 1961

Saul Suvalsky and Sam Sacks at B'nai Israel, ca. 1963

98. Velma Sacks, Marv and Dotty Suvalsky, 1967

99. Sulvasky Family, 1965

100. Closing of Master Furniture, Marvin and Selwin Suvalsky

Paige, Lisa, Bob & Erin Suvalsky in Jerusalem, 2010

Bob and Lisa Suvalsky, 2013

MAYNARD TELPNER

Maynard was so affable, civic-minded and legally savvy, he could have been Mayor.

Oh, wait. He was.

"When I was mayor, one of the highlights was when I held Marci, our youngest daughter, then three, when we turned on the Christmas lights at Broadway and Main. A Jewish mayor turning on Christmas lights," he laughs.

Council Bluffs' first Jewish mayor was heavily involved in a project that today -- particularly for those who were not around during that time -- some might take for granted: the construction of the interstate system. And if that teeny project wasn't enough, here's a snippet from his resumé that would make law students perk up.

- President of the Pottawattamie Bar Association
- A founder of the Human Relations Council, dealing with minority-related issues
- A founder of the Legal Services Commission, a volunteer service for people who couldn't afford a lawyer
- On the Board of Governors for the Iowa Bar Association
- Mercy Hospital Heritage Award recipient for business

Perhaps most impressive? That same year (1999), Maynard was inducted into the Abraham Lincoln High School Hall of Fame.

"I was the MC for every high school class reunion," he says. "As we got older, I could tell the same jokes and nobody could remember them."

Born at St. Joe Hospital in Omaha on March 23, 1928 to mother Sylvia and father Ben, Maynard recalls details of a Depression-era childhood that define destitute.

"I was privy to a conversation between my mother and father where they talked about the fact we didn't have seven dollars for a ton of coal," says Maynard, whose family lived at 704 Madison Avenue. "We didn't have seven bucks. I remember a conversation between them and Mr. Voss, the coal company owner, who wouldn't let them charge it. In our furnace, we started burning boxes, cardboard, wooden orange crates, furniture…dining room chairs! You burn what you think you can most do without."

When they were fortunate enough to scrape up enough, the delivery man drove his truck up to a chute in the foundation that led to a coal bin in the basement. "It took a long time for the coal dust to settle, it filled up our basement," he says.

"We were so desperate, I used to sit in the corner of the living room and hear Mom and Dad quarreling over some of the desperate things we were dealing with. Today, I almost cry. We had an ice box; the ice man came and put ice in the box. You put a sign in the window whether you wanted 100 or 75 pounds of ice. We finally bought an electric refrigerator in the 1930s. In order to pay, you had to put a quarter in a box that was on the side of the fridge. It had a slot; you'd push a little button to make the quarter drop into the box. I remember, again, being privy to a conversation, that we didn't have a quarter which would operate the fridge for 24 hours. My mother would say, 'What'll happen if the food spoils?' We paid for it by the week. Mr. Dempsey, who worked for Continental Keller where we bought it, would come to our house every weekend to collect the quarters. That's assuming we had seven quarters to put in there," he laughs.

The Telpners, of course, also included siblings Gene, Audrey and Zeph (a.k.a. "Boonjug"). Ever wonder where he got that moniker? "When Zeph was little, he'd sleep on his face with his tush up in the air. My sister thought he looked like a June bug. When he started to talk, he pronounced it Boonjug."

Not surprisingly, the family of six didn't have a hot water heater. When his mother wanted to bathe him, she'd heat a bucket of hot water on the stove, pour it into the tub then add cold water to make it more comfortable.

"That's what our lives were like at that time, and I just thought everybody lived that way. Boy, those were the days," he laughs.

Still, some aspects of Council Bluffs life reflected a time in which the folks at 704 Madison felt safe. "We didn't lock our doors. I had a friend who had a key and I asked, 'What is that?' I didn't know people locked their doors."

Pre-Depression, Ben owned Madison Avenue Grocery at the top of South First Street. He, like most merchants, allowed people to charge items and pay their bill at month's end. But once hard times hit and customers were unable to pay, he was forced out of business. Instead of collapsing into his own depression, Ben stepped up and survived. Maynard even pitch hit.

"He started peddling vegetables off a truck. As a matter of fact, when I was not even 12, when he'd have leftover vegetables he couldn't sell, I'd load them in a little wagon and knock on people's doors."

"Jews helping Jews" could have been a Council Bluffs tagline. In a twist of fate, coupled with consequences of war, the Telpners and the Meyersons epitomized this concept. When WWII started, Ben, a vet, got a job digging ditches during construction of an air base in Alliance, NE. Meanwhile, a war plant in Council Bluffs was established which manufactured radio crystals for the Armed Forces –– Scientific Radio, Leo Meyerson's company.

"Dad had lots of skills and a nice personality and was hired as Superintendent. That lifted us out of the Depression." And just as young Maynard peddled vegetables to help his family, so, too, did Gene, who enlisted in the Army one month after the war started.

"In those days, in the Army you made $21 dollars a month. Gene sent home a much-needed one dollar. I remember we were so glad to get that dollar. Shortly after that, we recovered from our hardships."

At war's end, Ben returned to the grocery business: Madison Avenue Grocery. Same location, same name. During his stint away, others operated a grocery there. Call it *bashert* or coincidence, but one of the owners? Leo Meyerson.

Jewish kids had their own mini-community, particularly during Hebrew school. While serious study may have been on the teacher's agenda, horsing around was on the pupil's. Some boys were less than perfectly behaved, but not Maynard.

Yet.

"I wasn't as naughty at that time as I was later on," he laughs. "That was not the zenith of my career as a naughty boy.

"At first, I walked. Then I got a bicycle on September 1st, 1939, the same day England and France declared war on Germany," he says. "We used to play touch football in front of the synagogue before class started. Some of the gentile kids in the neighborhood joined us, like Mick Heck, who died recently. There used to be fighting within the synagogue before class. Marvin Suvalsky and Kenny Sacks used to have fights all the time, chasing each other in the hallways. The rabbi, we couldn't stand him. We had one thing in common, all the boys did; we hated him. There was a nasty manner about him, not good-natured, he was like a concentration camp commander. He made Hebrew school unpleasant."

For Maynard's Bar Mitzvah in March of 1941, he wore Gene's hand-me down suit which had to be altered. Also, "I can remember my mom and dad talking about whether they should have a bottle of whiskey there. There was a luncheon and everyone bought something: *kugel*, pickled herring…I don't remember if they agreed on the whiskey. My wife Sally and I still have the receipt for payment of the use of the synagogue. My parents had to pay five dollars.

"After I recited from the Torah, I gave my speech. Unlike what I see today, I wasn't allowed to read my speech, I had to memorize it. I remember the rabbi telling me, 'When you give your speech, look at your parents.' I did what I was told. I looked at my father on the main floor, and my mother upstairs. To this day, I remember I was absolutely petrified before synagogue because I knew I would have to do these recitations in front of all these people. Later, Maynard would become President of AZA and B'nai Brith.

Unlike today, when kids might throw a theme party or an extravagant soirée, Maynard kept it down-home. "I took eight boys to a movie, 10 cents each, a total of 90 cents. We saw a cowboy movie at the Broadway Theater starring Tom Mix. Of course, we always bought candy before the movie, but I didn't have enough money for everyone so they brought their own. I only had a dollar bill to get them into the movie."

And now...the zenith of Maynard's career as a naughty boy: "In 8th grade at Washington School, the science teacher wrote a letter to my parents saying I was the most incorrigible student he'd ever had. Miss Powers, our art teacher, left the room temporarily and when she returned, she saw me throwing chalk and called my parents. Miss Ivory, the Principal, called my parents about my behavior because she'd had so many complaints from teachers about me."

Sylvia and Ben may have logged more hours on the phone with staff than Maynard did paying attention in class, but he *mensch* up in high school. "I just grew up a little bit and got a little more common sense," laughs the terror-turned-A.L. Hall of Famer.

Maynard and Al Klein co-wrote a weekly column for the school paper called, "As You Were," which included a student's life history and baby photographs. Readers had to guess who it was, and the following week was the reveal. Perhaps he took a cue from his newsman brother Gene, who once served as the paper's editor and went on to become an esteemed journalist in Canada. "He won an award equal to the Pulitzer," says Maynard. "He was soft-spoken and brilliant."

Post-graduation in 1946, at age 17, Maynard attended Creighton for one semester, then enlisted in the Army, though he may not have known what he was getting himself into.

"They put me in the Counterintelligence Corps. They had a quota; they wanted a certain percentage of dumb people. I'd never heard of it. They had a lot of investigations of people who were Nazis and Communists."

After two years in the Army, Maynard graduated from Creighton, then Creighton Law in 1952 and swiftly opened a practice at 24-years-old. His career spanned exactly 50 years. Telpner Peterson, the firm he helped build, remains in Council Bluffs.

Why did he choose law? "I had no idea what I wanted to do. I went to the library one day and saw a notice on the bulletin board they were taking applications for law school and I thought, 'Why not?' I had nothing else to do."

For the boy who peddled produce, became mayor and amassed an impressive award collection to boot, one accomplishment was tops.

"The most important thing I did was to marry Sally Priesman," he says. "A lot of Jewish kids hung out at the JCC, across the street from Central High. She was going to UNO when we met in 1949 and I was going to Creighton. Bill Fried and I used to go to the JCC on Sundays to play basketball, meet other kids -- and hoped to meet some girls. Sally was a girl, she still is. I liked the way she looked, and she had a warmth and sincerity about her that I thought was quite unusual and not pretentious. I liked her right away."

On Maynard and Sally's first date, they went to a movie starring Danny Kaye. When he took her home, they did the unthinkable. "We kissed. That's a shocker. Boy! You could write a novel about that. Remember the song: 'If they asked me, I could write a book, about the way you walk and whisper and look…?'"

Married since 1951, they have three daughters: Heidi, Sari and Marci, and six grandchildren: three boys and three girls.

Though Maynard applied to law school on a whim, his career was brewing behind the scenes. "I always paid attention to politics. I ran for City Council in 1959 and took office in January of 1960. I was the youngest by far on the council, 32, and served for four years. The council then chose me as mayor in 1963."

Maynard's Jewish identity, particularly since his teen years, prompted him to speak out about issues which affected the community, both local and international. In cases a reader wrote a letter to the *Nonpareil* or *The World-Herald* criticizing Israel, for instance, he wrote letters in rebuttal.

"I always felt obligated to respond, that's how my mother inspired me. I'm always conscious of the fact my mother was so involved in the question of anti-Semitism and in support of Israel and sticking up for the underdog."

In the 1950s, Maynard, a founder of the Human Rights Commission in Council Bluffs and a free legal clinic, teamed up with a colleague and undertook a project to change ordinances to protect minorities. They challenged laws which stated blacks could not live in certain neighborhoods, and traveled to Des Moines to address legislative committees. Their relentless campaigning paid off. Maynard helped write the Council Bluffs City Ordinance.

Naturally, Maynard identifies with being a minority. On his right middle finger is a stainless steel Star of David, prompted by the resurgence of global anti-Semitism. "I want everybody to know I'm Jewish," he says.

These days, Maynard and Sally live in Ashland, Oregon, where they moved to be near daughter Sari and closer to their other daughters who lived in California. "We might have stayed in Council Bluffs if our kids hadn't moved away," he says.

In his free time, Maynard -- what else? -- volunteers at the Chamber of Commerce and at Legal Services in Medford, OR, at a free legal clinic where he interviews new clients.

Their synagogue, Temple Emek Shalom, threw a bash in honor of four milestones: 70 years since he graduated high school, 75 years since his Bar Mitzvah, 65 years since he and Sally married, and "88 years since my circumcision."

And how's he feeling?

"I'm so well, it's embarrassing."

101. Maynard on Council Bluffs City Council, 1962
102. Maynard Telpner, Mayor of Council Bluffs, 1963
103. Maynard Telpner

Case closed for retiring Telpner

TIM JOHNSON
Staff Writer

After practicing law in Council Bluffs for half a century, Maynard Telpner is leaving.

Case closed.

Telpner, 74, will retire Friday from Telpner Peterson Smith Ruesch & Thomas. He and his wife, Sally, will move to Oregon to be close to their three children and six grandchildren.

A reception will be held Wednesday from 4:30 to 7 p.m. at Telpner Peterson Smith Ruesch & Thomas, 25 Main Place, Suite 200.

Telpner said he will miss his friends, co-workers and clients in Council Bluffs.

"My wife and I have had a wonderful life here," he said. "We love the people here."

Telpner was born in Omaha but has lived in Council Bluffs nearly all his life. He graduated from Abraham Lincoln High School in 1946 and served in the U.S. Army for two years.

He trained as an infantryman but was assigned to the counter-intelligence corps, where he helped analyze intelligence information.

He met Sally at the Jewish Community Center in Omaha while attending Creighton University. They were married June 5, 1951.

Telpner received his law degree in 1952 and began practicing June 30, 1952, at the former Wright & Kistle law firm, where he had worked as a law clerk during law school. He started his own practice in 1970 and was joined in 1976 by Chuck Smith.

"Early in my career, I did everything – personal law, criminal, divorce," he said.

"Most of what I did was of family law and appellate work."

That included divorces, adoptions and appeals, Telpner said.

"Most of the appeals that I was involved in had to do with child custody and divorce cases," he said.

The work took its toll on Telpner.

"It's rumored that family law is the most stressful type of practice – and I would agree

TELPNER/See Page 5A

Attorney Maynard Telpner puts a notebook into a box to prepare to move out of his office at Telpner Peterson Smith Ruesch & Thomas.

Maynard in Nonpareil in 2002

COUNCIL BLUFFS/NATION

Thursday, June 27, 2002

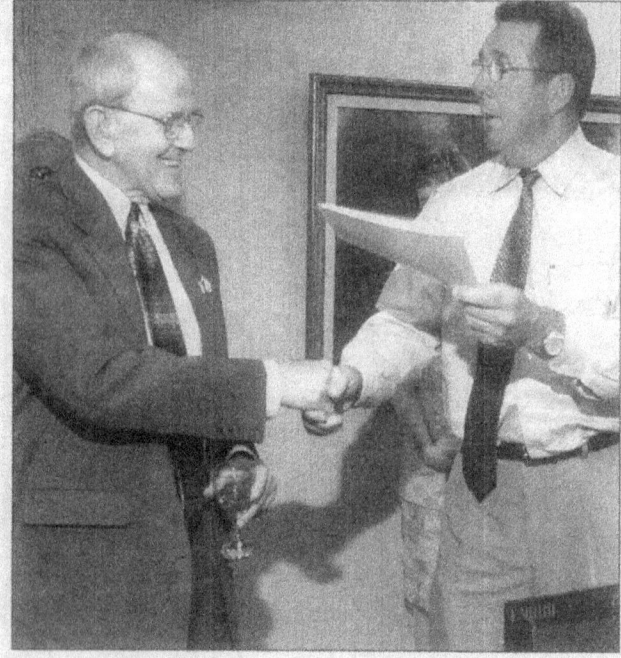

Staff photos/Jon Leu

Maynard Telpner (top) talks to guests about his 50 years as an attorney in Council Bluffs during a retirement party Thursday afternoon in the offices of Telpner Peterson Smith Ruesch & Thomas. Telpner will retire Friday. Mayor Tom Hanafan (bottom at right) was on hand with an official proclamation marking "Maynard Telpner Day" and noting his efforts for the city, including serving as mayor.

Maynard in Nonpareil in retiring, 2002

104

105

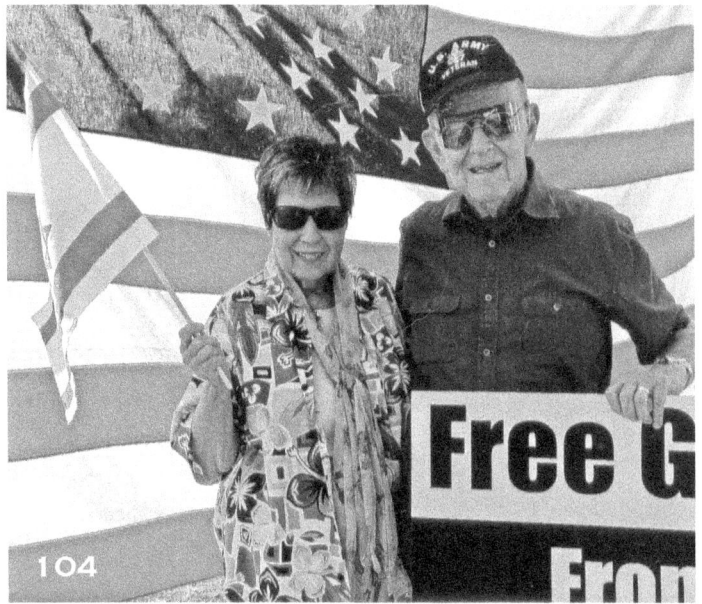

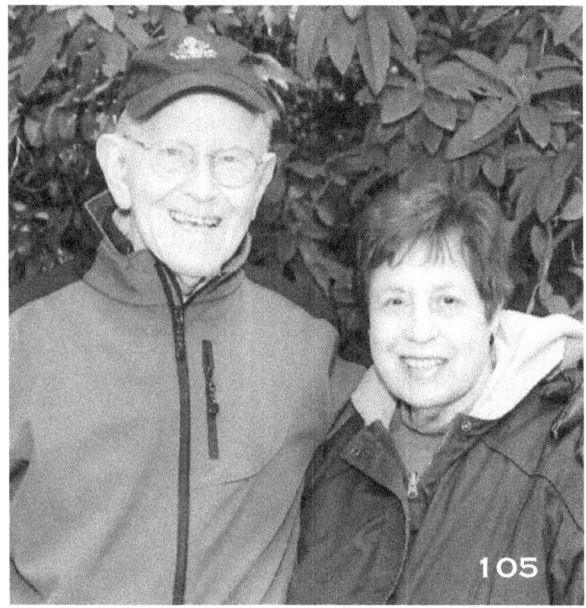

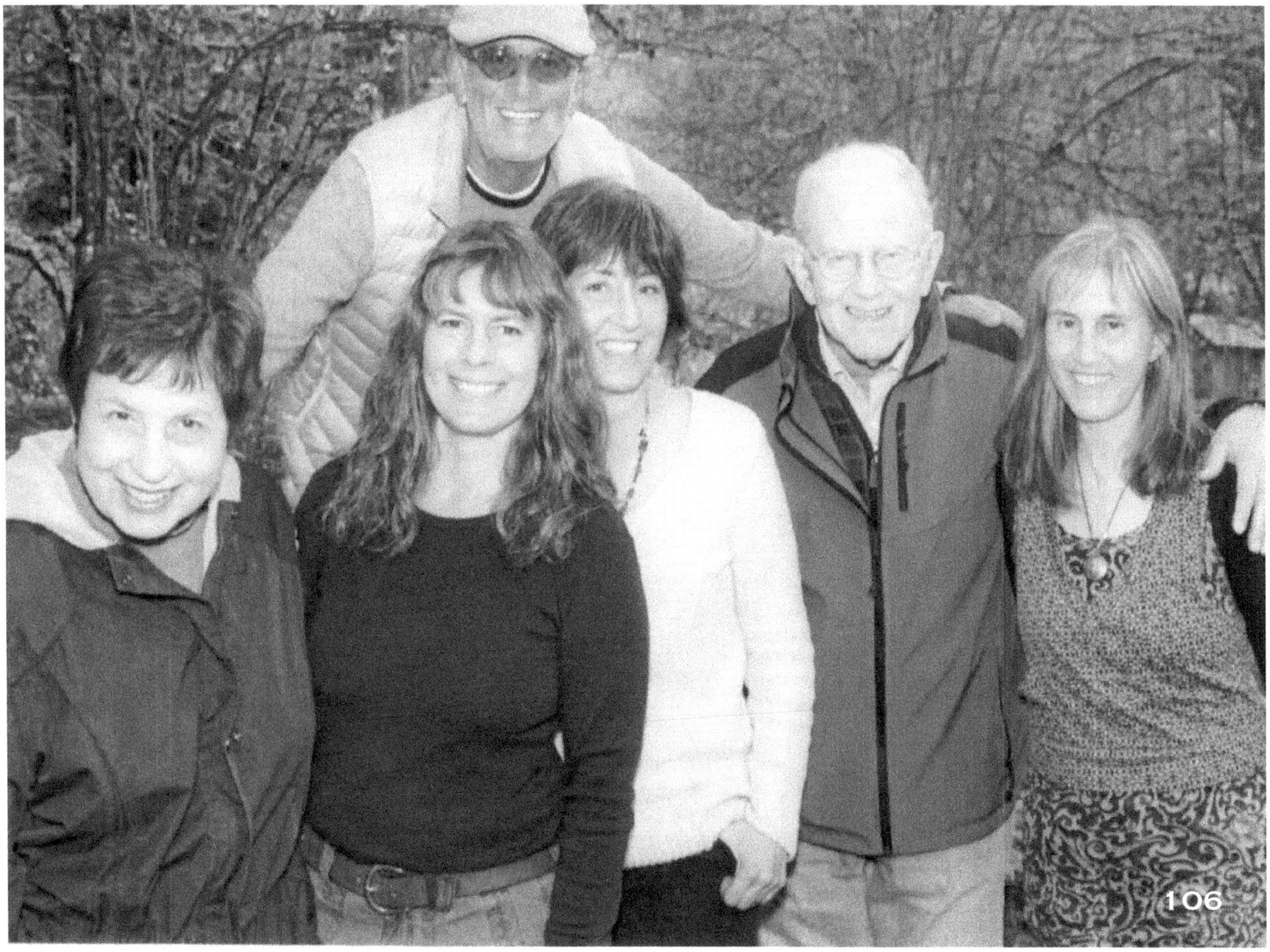

106

104. Sally and Maynard Telpner, Bedford, OR, August of 2014 (Rally for Israel)
105. Maynard and Sally Telpner on his 85th Birthday in Ashland, OR, 2013
106. Maynard's 85th birthday with Sally, nephew Ron Telpner of Toronto and daughters Marci, Heidi and Sari, 2013

SUE FRIEDMAN MILLWARD

I STARTED WORKING at the Peoples Store when I was 12-years-old. Grandpa Millard Krasne would take any of his grandchildren over if they wanted to go. I especially looked forward to going on Saturdays. Grandpa paid us…maybe 50 cents an hour, but I worked up to a whole dollar an hour by the time I was 16 years old!

We knew everyone in the store because a different branch of the Krasne family owned different departments. I remember Aunt Leah Krasne and her son Leslie owned the first floor. Leah was the daughter of Mordechai Krasne, she married Lawrence Krasne, her first cousin who was the son of Jake Krasne, one of the founders of the Peoples Store. Lawrence and Leah co-managed his portion of the store until he died in 1961, when I was only 10-years-old, so my memories of him are rather faint.

After his death, Leah managed most of the first floor that included the notions department with fabrics and sewing goods; fashion accessories such as gloves, hats and perfumes; men's casual wear and accessories; such as farm wear like overalls and blue jeans, shirts, belts and hats. We always went to her, or Les, for our blue jeans when I was young. They carried the Wrangler brand that was popular back then. The candy department was also on the first floor, so it was a great way of ensuring that we children would go to see her. She always gave us a couple of pieces to munch on.

Aunt Leah was a gentle woman who loved everyone, especially us grandchildren. In fact, all the Krasnes were like that, very lovable and caring. She was so happy to see us, she would give a big hug and make a fuss over us. She also introduced me to all the other Krasne ladies that I didn't know as well as I knew her, it wasn't until much later I understood the family relationships. I just remember these sweet, short, white-haired ladies: Aunt Sadie (Geffen), Aunt Grace (Bernstein) and Aunt Sarah (Pepper). These ladies were my Grandpa Millard's elderly aunts, all sisters to Millard's father, Herman Krasne.

Les Krasne was Leah's younger son and very active in the workings of the store. He was not a tall person, maybe 5'7," but he towered over his diminutive mother and aunts. They were cute together, Leah managed the day-to-day activities of the business and she managed Les as well. He didn't seem to mind because he enjoyed socializing with the customers. I felt it was a shame he never married.

The store itself had a long brick façade with large display windows. There were three floors inside, with hardwood floors throughout and a wide but rickety wooden staircase that went down to the basement level. When you walked into the store, the main floor was Aunt Leah's departments.

There was also a grocery store on that level. Downstairs was the shoe department that my grandfather Millard owned. He also owned most of the second floor. During different times in the history of the store, ownership of certain departments changed hands from one generation to the next. I don't really know about all of that, though. But, in the 1950s and 1960s, Grandpa owned the second floor departments including men's dress wear, women's wear, the infant department, toy department and the snack bar. The store's offices were also located in the back of this level.

Uncle Lou Bernstein and his son Harold managed the grocery and hardware departments. Both departments were on the first floor originally; but sometime in the 60's, the hardware department went into the basement of the store.

There was an elevator between the three floors; it was the old-fashioned style with a manual control. There were two elevator operators, Winnie was the primary one. She was a tall slender black woman who dressed immaculately in a two-piece wool suit, high heels and white gloves. She would open the gate, make sure everyone was in and push the lever that took you up or down. She had to make sure that the elevator was level to the floor before she could let you out.

Bill Rudd was the other operator. He probably wasn't very old at the time, but he seemed old to me. I don't know what his position was; he might have been the janitor for all I know; but he helped to sell things and spoke with everyone. He was a jovial black man who always made time for a hug and to share stories with me. We all loved him, and when I say all, I mean all of us kids and parents alike. Recently, I read comments on the Facebook page: "You Might Be from Council Bluffs

(Kanesville) Iowa If…" Bill was mentioned and he was remembered kindly by all the customers at the store (I met Bill again many years later when he was working for Phillips Department Store in South Omaha, and he had not changed a bit, still as lovable as ever).

The toy department was like my playground. That's where I started working when I was 12. I was very good at selling because I could share with customers about the toys I loved best. If a woman came in to buy a present for her daughter's birthday, I'd say, "I'll show you what my favorite thing is." I could sell. It was so much fun. At Christmas time, I learned to wrap presents. Gift-wrapping was free, so people would leave their gifts, such as toys or a box of clothing. Sometimes it was challenging if the boxes were not square, but I learned how to be creative. I also worked in the infant department, the junior department, and, finally, the women's department. I even helped in the men's department when they were short-staffed. But I didn't really know how to measure a man's waist and such. I could just show them were to find their sizes (if they knew them).

Grandpa and Uncle Bob Krasne (Millard's son) would go to the Peoples Store together every day and work from open to close. Back then, they opened at 10 o'clock and closed at 5 o'clock. The store was open six days a week, not on Sunday. Though they were not overly religious, the store did always close on the Jewish High Holidays. I know Aunt Leah and Les were very religious, but I also think they did work on Saturdays. Still, I don't think I ever saw them handle money. They would just pass the customer along to a cashier instead. The cashier would handle the transaction and when the sale was complete, the money was sent from the first floor in one of those tubes that went up and across the ceiling, to the back of the store and directly into the office of Catherine, the bookkeeper, on the second floor. I don't know if this system was used so that Leah and Les didn't have to handle money or not, but I know there were cash registers on both the second floor and the basement departments.

On Saturday mornings, my Grandpa, Uncle Bob and I would all ride in Grandpa's Cadillac from Omaha, across the Aksarben Bridge to the store in Council Bluffs. Before the store opened, we typically would sit down and have a donut from the snack bar. They'd have coffee and I would probably have milk or orange juice.

The snack bar was like a soda fountain with high spinning stools, and the ladies who managed it were always there cooking, getting food ready for the day -- it smelled great! I never missed a lunch because I loved the homemade tomato or chicken noodle soup of the day with egg or tuna salad sandwiches. I think they made malts or root beer floats there too.

I am one of four siblings. There is my older sister Anne, then me, then my brothers Howie and Tom (Tommy back then). We all thought that it was the neatest thing for Grandpa to have the Peoples Store, especially the shoe department where we could get cowboy boots. Recently, I found a picture at my Uncle Bob's house that shows us all in our cowboy and Indian outfits. I had the best pair of black and white cowboy boots of all! That reminds me of the funniest story: Tom is the baby of the family and was very proud of his red cowboy boots. One day the boots went missing. Tom claimed that a man got out of his car to admire the boots, and when the man asked if he could have them, Tom handed them over. We don't know what really happened to them, but the story stands as we never did find that pair of boots. Not to worry, though. Tom went to the Peoples Store and got a bright shiny new pair to replace them.

On our birthdays (my birthday is April 21, 1950), our grandparents Millard and Sara would always take great joy in letting us choose something special from the store, even if it was something our parents were not crazy about. When we were younger, we were allowed two or three toys, and as we got older it was clothes or jackets. Usually they took us to the store for the day. We'd have lunch and spend the day with "The Peoples Store" family. It was very special.

Every year when school started, we, the Friedman siblings, were allowed to go get new clothes. I remember it as a whole new wardrobe! When I say that, it was all wholesale for us, if something cost $12, we got it for $6. Grandpa would put it on a charge account, and I assume my parents paid for it (I really don't know). When I got older and there wasn't a Peoples Store anymore, I realized how much clothes really did cost! Garland was a popular brand when I was a teenager. I would often wear a pleated tartan plaid skirt with a cardigan, a blouse (you always wore a blouse whether it was with a cardigan or a pull-over sweater) and penny loafer shoes.

The most memorable thing about the Peoples Store were the people I met there. I mentioned before about the great-aunts, but there were other family members who shopped there as well: Rae Brodkey and Pauline Friedman, Harold Bernstein's sisters were often there, as was Shirley Goldstein. I remember seeing Penny Krasne (Endelman) with her mom there, too. John and Kay Bernstein were there quite often working with their father, Harold Bernstein. John and Kay lived in Council Bluffs and I lived in Omaha, so I didn't see them often except at the store. Eventually though, we all started Hebrew School together at Temple Israel and became friends.

The employees at the store were wonderful, too. It was like a home. I knew all the people who worked there; and during the years I worked there, I became quite close to several and remember them well. In addition to Winnie and Bill Rudd, there was Ann Moore, manager of the women's clothing. She was a tall, elegant woman who liked keeping things orderly. Also, there was Mary Grimes, the head of the junior sportswear. She enjoyed having me work there and she taught me how to sell without being overbearing, how to ring up the sale and how to write up a layaway. I learned a lot from her. Other family members and employees were Albert Krasne, Chris Krasne and Henry Ginsburg. I am certain there were others I cannot recall just now.

The Peoples Store was a unique place and it became a second home for me during my growing up years. I learned so many valuable skills and lessons from the people who were a part of it and it has a special place in my memories. I was so sad in 1972 when the store was torn down for "Urban Renewal." The city of Council Bluffs tore down more than just the building, it also ended a way of life for so many people who were a part of it.

I remember Albert Krasne, a wonderful cousin of mine who worked in the men's department. He always was really nice to us, loved us kids and never had children of his own. There is a story on the Facebook page: "You Might Be From Council Bluffs (Kanesville) Iowa If…" that illustrates the caring and generous nature of the Krasnes:

"My dad, John Derry, was one of seven living Derry children. My grandfather had a shoe store on Broadway at one time. They made it through the Depression, but my grandfather was an alcoholic, so most likely lost the shoe store. They were very poor, and the kids worked to support the family. My dad, who was 16, worked at Peoples. My grandfather left CB to find work in Joplin, Missouri. He was hired by a shoemaker and sent money home.

One night, after he had gone to dinner at a restaurant in Joplin, he had to cross a highway to get back to his home (ironically, he had not been drinking that night). An enlisted kid, home from leave, passed another car on the highway and struck and killed my grandfather. Someone had to go get the body. My grandmother still had two kids at home, and there was no money to spend on a train to go to Joplin. Mr. Krasne gave my dad the money for the train to get to Joplin. All I know is, my dad was forever grateful to Mr. Krasne."

Clockwise-Sadie Krasne Geffen, Sara Krasne Pepper, Toby Goldstein Krasne, Grace Krasne Bernstein

Herman and Rose Krasne

107. Phil Krasne
108. Leo Krasne
109. Herman, Millard, Philip, Leo and Rose Krasne

110. Millard and Sara Krasne, with Tham and Bob Krasne ca. 1942
111. Millard and Sara Krasne, Bob and Tham (Krasne) Friedman
112. Millard and Sara, Bob and Tham (Krasne) Friedman

113. Herman and Rose Krasne
114. Millard and Sara Krasne, 1985
115. Sara Krasne and Tham (Krasne) Friedman
116. Krasne Family photo

117. Sara Krasne and Tham (Krasne) Friedman
118. Tham and Willard Friedman family
119. Friedman family, 1955
120. Tham (Krasne) Friedman and Bob Krasne
121. Sadie Krasne Geffen, Rose Bernstein Krasne, Toby Grossman Krasne, Grace Krasne Bernstein, Sophie Bernstein

Albert J. Krasne and Isaac Krasne ... check merchandise order at Peoples department store.—Nonpareil photo.

Father-Son Combination ...
Merchandise Business Is Also a Hobby for Krasnes

Fifty years as a merchant hasn't changed Isaac Krasne's cheerful outlook on life.

Now 77, the veteran Council Bluffs businessman is just as interested as ever in people and what they wear. From his vantage point on the second floor of the Peoples department store, he has watched styles come and go.

Clothes are his stock in trade, he admits. But his real interest is in the people themselves.

Young people, especially, appeal to him. In turn, he is a favorite with them.

Hundreds of youngsters greet him as "Uncle Ike."

Lives With Son

Since his wife's death in 1947, he has made his home with his son, Albert J. Krasne, 316 Grace street. The latter is merchandise manager of the second floor.

About the turn of the century, Isaac Krasne was a familiar figure in rural areas around Fremont, Neb. He drove a horse and wagon through the conutryside as a peddler for six or seven years.

Born in Bialystok, Poland, he emigrated to America at the age of 18. Oldest of five brothers, he was the first to try his fortune in this country.

His first venture in the field of general merchandise was in Genoa, Neb. Later, he operated a similar type of store in Aurora, Neb.

With one of his brothers, the late Frank Krasne, he operated a business partnership in Fullerton, Neb., for 12 years. The pair came to Council Bluffs in 1922 to assume management of the second floor of the Peoples department store.

Three other brothers were already in business in the store. They were: George, Jacob and Herman Krasne.

Only Herman Krasne is still living. He now resides at Los Angeles, Calif.

Merchandising has always held a fascination for Isaac Krasne. "It's been as much of a hobby for me as a business," he explains.

"Sometimes, though, I enjoy a good game of cards," he admits.

He belongs to the Chamber of Commerce and Woodmen of the World. His religious activities center in Chevra B'nai Yisroel and Beth-El synaogues, B'nai B'rith and Jewish Community Center.

Joined Store In 1918

Although he retired from active supervision of the store's second floor a few years ago, he still goes to work daily.

Reared in a store atmosphere, Albert Krasne early decided to follow in his father's footsteps. Coming here in 1918, he has been associated with the present business ever since.

Like his father, business has been his whole life. Buying trips though, have been somewhat of a diversion.

In short, clothing and related items of merchandise have become a hobby with him, too. Their display and sale has been tinged with an aura of adventure.

A member of the Chamber of Comerce and a Mason, he belongs to B'nai B'rith Temple Israel, Beth-El synagogue and Jewish Community Center.

He sees eye-to-eye with his father as to the future of Council Bluffs. It's becoming more and more the hub of southwest Iowa's trade territory, they believe.

"I've never been sorry I came here," declares the elder Krasne. His son shares the same sentiment.

Nonp. Nov. 19, 1950

Isaac and Albert Krasne

Lawrence S. Krasne

Director
City National Bank

Born September 27, 1901, at Fremont, Nebraska, Lawrence S. Krasne graduated from Abraham Lincoln High School in Council Bluffs, in 1919. Early in 1920 he became a partner in the Peoples Department Store and has been actively engaged in the retail business in Council Bluffs since that time.

Mr. Krasne is a member of the Masonic Lodge, Bnai Brith Lodge, Council Bluffs Chamber of Commerce and Bnai Israel Synagogue. He is a past member of the Board of Directors of the Iowa Retail Association, and at present is on the Board of Directors of the Bennett Building Corporation.

Mr. Krasne and his wife, Leah, reside at 242 Park Avenue. They have two sons, Leslie who is a partner in the Peoples Department Store, and Rabbi Stanley M. Krasne who resides in Brooklyn, New York.

Lawrence Krasne

122. Back row: Millward, Phil and Leo Krasne; Front row: Sara Riseman Krasne, Benice Ferer Kranse and Sylvia Ross Krasne

123. Bob and Elaine Krasne, Willard and Tham Friedman

124. Phil and Millard Krasne

Family View Report for Thama Lee Krasne

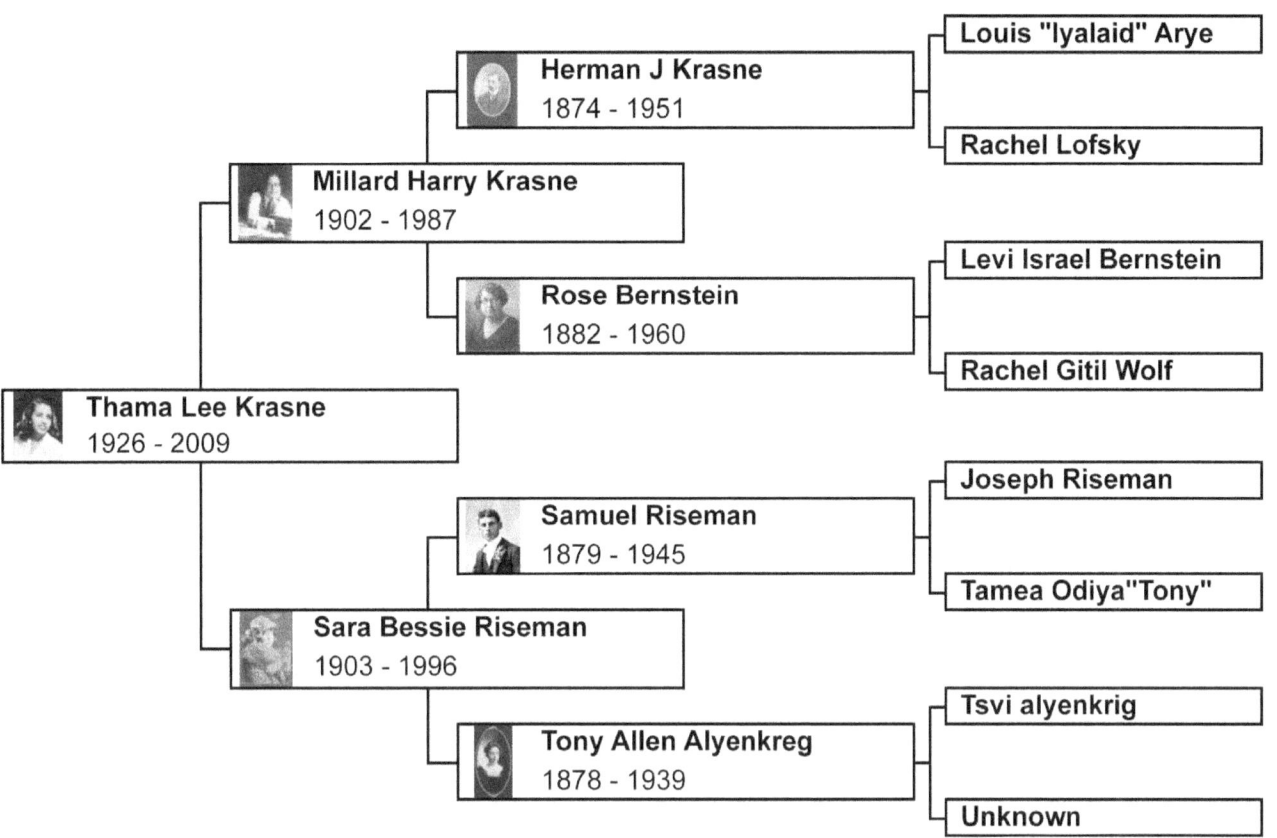

		Louis "Iyalaid" Arye
	Herman J Krasne 1874 - 1951	
		Rachel Lofsky
Millard Harry Krasne 1902 - 1987		
		Levi Israel Bernstein
	Rose Bernstein 1882 - 1960	
		Rachel Gitil Wolf
Thama Lee Krasne 1926 - 2009		
		Joseph Riseman
	Samuel Riseman 1879 - 1945	
		Tamea Odiya "Tony"
Sara Bessie Riseman 1903 - 1996		
		Tsvi alyenkrig
	Tony Allen Alyenkreg 1878 - 1939	
		Unknown

Willard Israel Friedman		Thama Lee Krasne	
Born:	17 Oct 1923 Omaha, NE, USA	Born:	20 Mar 1926 Council Bluffs, Pottawattamie, Iowa,
Died:	09 May 2008 Omaha, Nebraska, USA	Died:	27 Jul 2009 Omaha, Douglas, Nebraska, United

Marriage: 31 Aug 1947 in Omaha, Douglas, Nebraska, USA

Children:	Sex	Birth	Death
Anne B Friedman	F	13 Nov 1948 Omaha, NE, USA	
Sue F Friedman	F	21 Apr 1950 Omaha, NE, USA	
Howard J Friedman	M	26 Jan 1952 Omaha, NE, USA	
Thomas D Friedman	M	21 Dec 1952 Omaha, NE, USA	

HAROLD BERNSTEIN
1921 - 2017

GEORGE BURNS SAID: "Happiness is having a large, loving, caring, close-knit family in another city." The Krasne and Bernstein families are an exception. "Our family was very close; we got along great," says Harold, a one-time partner at Council Bluffs' retail Mecca: the Peoples Store. For 26 years, he worked and *kibbitzed* alongside relatives with whom he grew very close. The atmosphere was water cooler-like. "We saw each other every day! The whole day! We'd visit all the time. It was a different era."

The Peoples Store was a one-stop shop where folks could find bananas to baseball gloves. Though the building's exterior and interior morphed through the decades, the concept remained the same. "It was crazy the way it was set up," says Harold. "My dad Lou, his brother Mose, and my uncles, the Krasnes, all owned different departments in the store, but we all had the common name of Peoples Department Store and we advertised together a great deal."

One ad in the Council Bluffs *Nonpareil* newspaper dated October 21, 1943 features brands of yesteryear and prices which today seem comical: a three-pound jar of Crisco (68 cents), Rinso soap (23 cents) a one-pound package of Butter-Nut coffee (31 cents).

A NOT-SO-BRIEF HISTORY OF THE PEOPLES STORE

Louis Krasne, Harold's maternal grandfather, emigrated to America from Poland in the early 1890's with his oldest sons Isaac, Jake and Frank. According to the boat record, their original name was *Krasnuglowie*. After landing in New York they were met by the Hebrew Immigrant Aid Society (HIAS), given $10 and put on a train to their destination, Fremont, Nebraska, as they had cousins there. They began as peddlers with a horse and wagon; but as the story goes, when the horse died in Fullerton, they traded the contents of the wagon for a general store in Fullerton which they dubbed, "Krasnes."

In 1892, the rest of Lou's family came over after the death of his wife Rachael. "My grandmother was pregnant with my mother and she didn't come to America at the same time. It was her brothers and her father. Imagine, her father left his wife pregnant and was going to go back and get her! But she died when my mother was born, and it was her older sister Dora who brought my mother over as a baby. Imagine coming on one of those kinds of ships in those days to this country. She was brought up pretty much by her brothers and sisters in Fullerton."

In 1907, Krasne brothers George and Frank moved to Council Bluffs, joining their cousins Lou and Mose Bernstein, brothers who grew up in Omaha. "I don't even know how they got started. My dad was about 21-years-old by the time he opened the Peoples Store." The foursome purchased and operated a one-room establishment on the corner of West Broadway and Bryant. Over time, more Krasnes trickled into the business. On July 4th, 1917, Herman Krasne, who owned a women's apparel store in Omaha, followed suit.

The Bernstein brothers, Lou and Mose, originally owned only the grocery department. "It was all delivery in those days. They had a horse and buggy early on and, finally cars, and trucks," says Harold. Eventually, they started the hardware and housewares department in the basement, and come 1924, they sold the grocery section to brothers Sam and Herman Meyerson –– no relation to the Krasnes or the Bernsteins. "My Dad had asthma and he would go in and out of the cooler. He could not handle it."

As the family expanded, the first generation gave way to the second, then the third, and business grew through the years. But as time passed, family members passed proprietorship to their kin: Jake left his holdings to his son Lawrence who ran their departments with his wife Leah and son, Les. Herman, an original founder, left his ownership of the business to his son Millard, Sue Friedman Millward's grandfather, and later partnered with his son Robert. Ike, one of the older Krasne brothers, left his proprietorship to his sons Albert and Clyde. George, another original founder, left the store after many years of ownership. In 1942, Mose left the store, sold his interest to Lou and moved to California. Harold entered the business as partner in 1946.

Harold, born February 21st, 1921, grew up at 222 Frank Street on the Bluffs' east side –– and also at the Peoples Store. "I had been hanging around there all my life," he says. "When I was 12 or 13, I'd walk down there. I'd wait on people…They probably laughed at me, but I did. I was very close with my dad. He was a good businessman, very active in the community and was a big baseball fan." Back then, Council Bluffs had semi-pro baseball teams and the two would catch Sunday games at Broadway Park on 35th and Broadway which was re-named American Legion Park after WWII.

Lou's coming-of-age story differed from Harold's. Like the Krasnes, the Bernsteins emigrated from Poland around 1890. "My dad was about two-years-old," he says. "In fact, I've even got his papers from when they came over. They left from Hamburg, Germany and met up with their cousins who were Levys. Unfortunately, I didn't find out enough from my parents. I didn't know enough to ask certain questions back in those days. He came over here as a young boy and they struggled. My grandfather was a sickly person and he died when my dad was just 12-years-old. But my dad said he was not a man who particularly made a living. When I say 'a living,' in those days they dabbled and did whatever they did. As kids, he and his brother Mose went out and sold newspapers and hustled."

In 1913, Lou Bernstein married Grace Krasne ("How they met I do not know") and had four kids: Rae –– named for Grace's mother Rachael –– Pauline, Harold and Shirley. The only males in their family of five, father and son carved out time together. "I had my bike and I would ride to Hebrew school then ride home with him, throw the bike in the car or whatever…We weren't particularly religious people but we were certainly Jewish people. My dad always attended *yahrzeits* at the synagogue and I'd go with him. People still ask me why I went to the University of Nebraska rather than Iowa and I say, 'I wanted to be in ZBT' (Zeta Beta Tau). That was one of the greatest experiences of my life. It has become my social life. My friends and I still see each other, those of us who are left. Stuart Simon, who was a very close friend of mine and was best man at my wedding, passed away but he was originally from Council Bluffs."

Irv Cohen -- son of Anne and Harry, uncle of Patty Nogg -- was Harold's best buddy. Even today, when Council Bluffians mention Harold's name, Irv's is likely to follow. "We were always acquaintances from the time we were 15, 16. We graduated high school the same year, but then he was going to go to Iowa and I was going to go to Nebraska. So I talked him into going to Nebraska with me. I said, 'You're going to live here, your friends are all going to be here, you can come home on weekends and work once in a while. It's close by, you're going to like it there. It's better than Iowa because people come from all over.' So I talked him into going to Nebraska and we became best friends.

"We went in the army together, took the test together, and he became a B-17 pilot. He got killed in November of 1944, snuffed out at the age of 22. And look at me, I'm 95. I've had a wonderful life, and he had nothing. I'm just saying how fated things are."

Harold had the unique perspective of witnessing the Jewish community increase in number and solidarity over the years. "I counted one day, there were 125 Jewish families and 12 Jewish kids who graduated from A.L. at the same time I did. There was a Jewish community, a Jewish life. You reminisce with certain people, 'You remember so and so?'"

Like his dad Lou, Harold was active in Jewish organizations. He joined a Jewish Boy Scout troupe and B'nai B'rith, a youth organization. "It seemed to be very important to my dad at the time and I just carried it on. I think he made me a member of B'nai Brith when I was 21 in the army. I think I've probably been a member for 70 years! It was a great Jewish organization way back. They fought anti-Semitism and they founded the ADL and spun it off."

During World War II, the Federation bought an old house on South 8th Street which they transformed into the JCC and held B'nai Brith meetings there every two weeks. "When you think about it, the meetings didn't accomplish anything. It was mostly for poker players who wanted to play poker afterwards! They had a grocers' association with Jewish grocers who, even after they weren't grocers anymore, were still active in the association. They met a certain night and played cards."

Council Bluffs even had its own Jewish Federation. "Everyone was president at one point, we had to keep it going." When Israel became a state in 1948, Harold was part of a drive which raised funds they sent to the new Jewish homeland. B'nai Brith solicited new members in small western Iowa towns like Glenwood, Atlantic and Missouri Valley. *Agudas Achim* was a charitable organization which survived because of O. Hochman, a man well-respected in the community.

"They helped Jewish people, Jewish men, who borrowed money for their business, for instance, and paid them back through the years." Inevitably, *Agudas Achum* shuttered its doors. "When certain generations die off, organizations die off with them. You think they last forever but they don't…you just take it for granted." As the years went by, generations moved from Council Bluffs to larger cities like Omaha, Arizona and the West Coast. The Jewish population dwindled down to just a few families. All organizations except the synagogue disappeared.

Harold joined the Krasne/Bernstein bunch at the store in 1946. "We were still selling harnesses for horses. Before the war, the farmers were getting mechanized and tractors were the dominant vehicle they used rather than horses. But during the war, they started using horses again, to an extent, because tractors took gas, they were hard to get and were on allocation," he says. "We still sold cream separators to farmers. Then everything changed! In 1947, the rural areas were still using kerosene lamps to read by. Then the countryside was getting electrified. Electric appliances -- we were big in appliances -- and automatic washing machines came into being. They were hard to get and we sold them as fast as we could get them. TV came in in the late 1940s. They were seven or 10 inches. It was something different!"

Like most Jewish-owned stores in Council Bluffs, the Peoples Store was closed every Yom Kippur. "In the early days when I was younger (this is crazy when I think back now), we'd close on a Saturday and open on a Saturday night after Yom Kippur was over because that was the big night in Council Bluffs for the farmers to come into town and shop. Every store up and down Broadway owned by Jewish people was closed on Yom Kippur, right up 'til the end."

Civic-minded, the Krasnes and Bernsteins contributed to the town which helped them prosper. "Council Bluffs was good to our family." Likewise, their family was good to Council Bluffs. Harold was on the board of The State Bank and Trust and eventually on the First Federal Savings and Loan Board. "I replaced my dad who had previously been on the board," says Harold, who was also very active in the Chamber of Commerce, the Rotary Club and other organizations.

The Peoples Store was a microcosm of the larger community where old-time trust and a handshake were forms of currency. However, as Harold learned through years of experience, everything changes. In the early '70s, the city sold business owners the idea of revitalization. As it turned out, eminent domain (government purchase of property for public purpose) demolished buildings, livelihoods and trust.

"When Urban Renewal was first mentioned, we were very enthused about it and I was active in it. We thought it was going to save Council Bluffs. It was a new concept; we thought it was going to be great. Times were changing; suburban buying (shopping centers) came in. It replaced most of downtown Council Bluffs on Broadway. But it didn't turn out the way it was hoped for."

Harold got out in 1972, but, "not until the very end. I said 'I don't know what I'm gonna do.' I was 52-years-old and I needed to make a living and keep going." Fortunately, a year or so prior, Ben Seldin, Ted's dad, had stepped in. "He kept coming up to me and saying, 'We have Urban Renewal, what are you going to do?' I said, 'I don't know,' and he said, 'I've got a property down on the west end that'll make a good store for you.' The land was terrible and I bought it, and it was one of the best things that ever happened to me. I told him that. It turned out to be a very good location for me. Ben was the guy who had the foresight of all the real estate people in Council Bluffs because he grabbed onto that a year before it happened. I've always been grateful for that!"

In 1974, Harold built Peoples True Value Hardware at 29th and West Broadway which was successful from day one. "Things were good when we opened, and they got better. The late '70s and '80s, those were very good years. The economy was great; inflation raised your values all the time." In 1995, Harold sold out. Twenty years later, the store is still in existence and prospering.

Looking back at decades of success and community, family and friendships, what was Harold's favorite time? He laughs. "You know, you don't realize everything seems like a favorite time of yours. You look back to high school and college and think how wonderful it was, but while you're doing it doesn't seem that. I'd say that when my kids were growing up and probably the '50s and '60s, those were good years. Good business years. And we had a lot of friends," he says. "Council Bluffs made us what we were.

"Good people traded with us, gave us a living, and my family was very close. My mother didn't drive a car, so my aunts (her sisters-in-law) and friends would pick her up to play poker and mahjongg. The store bound us together. Growing up, it seemed I saw my uncles every day. They dropped over at our house…We had no television, so we'd take a ride in the car for entertainment. That was life."

As Harold noted, two decisions he made years ago proved to be wise: joining ZBT ("One of the greatest experiences of my life") and his real estate purchase ("One of the best things that ever happened to me"). But by far, the biggest blessing has been his family. When Harold returned to the University of Nebraska for one semester after the war in 1946, he met Millie Zuber from Hastings, Nebraska, a Sigma Delta Tau who, too, studied at his alma mater. The couple married and had two children: Kay, who married Bruce Goldstein, lives in Minneapolis and has two boys, Aaron and Danny. John, an attorney in Denver, has two kids; daughter Maddie and son Max.

Sixty-nine years of marriage. Two children. Four grandchildren. Says Harold: "Life has been wonderful to me."

125

Louis Bernstein — Sally Paul Abe Esther Lee

Louis Krasne
1839-1912

125. Bernstein, Louis, Sally, Paul Abe Esther and Lee

126. Harold Bernstein's grandfather

127. Grace Krasne Bernstein

128. Shirley Bernstein Kulakofsky (on far left)
129. Louis and Harold Bernstein
130. Shirley K. Bernstein
131. Harold Bernstein, 1940

Harold and Millie Bernstein March 30, 1957

Harold's parents, Grace and Lou in 1963

Bernstein siblings: Harold, Rae, Pauline and Shirley, with parents, Grace and Lou Bernstein

Joanie Lehr with Harold Bernstein's sisters-Rae Brodkey, Shirley Kulakofsky and Pauline Kulakofsky

Family View Report for Harold E Bernstein

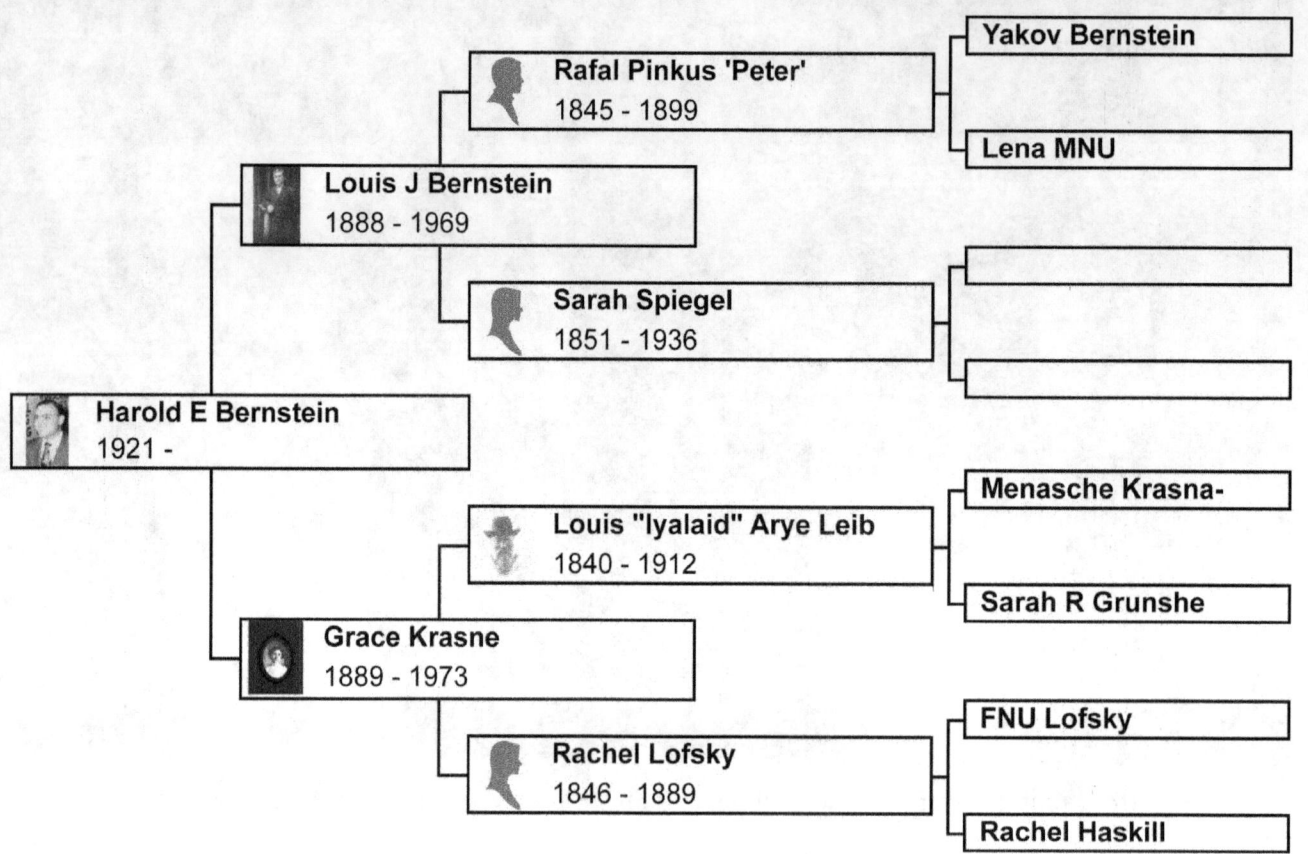

Harold E Bernstein		Millie J Zuber	
Born:	21 Feb 1921	Born:	Jul 1926
	Council Bluffs, Pottawattamie, Iowa,		Hastings, Nebraska, USA
Died:		Died:	

Marriage: 30 Mar 1947 in Hastings, Nebraska, USA

Children:	Sex	Birth	Death
Kay Ellen Bernstein	F	03 Dec 1949 Council Bluffs, Iowa, USA	
John Bernstein	M	28 Mar 1952 Council Bluffs, Iowa, USA	

MARK EVELOFF

SEPTEMBER 18TH, 1948 marked Mark's birth and life in a town so embedded in his DNA, his zip code is still 51503.

While most kids got outta Dodge -- bought a one-way ticket to Omaha or out-of-state -- Mark remained an Iowan. In the fall of 1966, the Abraham Lincoln grad matriculated to the University of Iowa, and upon graduation in 1971, returned home to attend Creighton Law School, only to ricochet to Des Moines for roughly nine years, mostly working as a prosecutor. His fourth and final move? Home, where in 1983, he opened a private practice at 221 South Main Street around Christmastime.

For Jews at Christmas, Chanukah didn't have a prayer, particularly in a town where the Jew:Non-Jew ratio was bent towards the caroling kind. Still, Mark's mother Leona embraced the holiday spirit, no matter it was not their holiday.

"One of the hardest things for me growing up was that the majority of the people I grew up with were not Jewish," says Mark. "When my friends had trees and decorations, I'd go over to their houses and then come back home. Christmas Day, my mom would always be Santa and we'd have our presents in a pile. It was only like three or four each, but we'd always have presents. My mom always wanted us to have something for Christmas because Hanukah might be on the first of December, then you have Christmas break, you go back and all the other kids are talking about Christmas. So, she would always do something like that. We never had a tree, we never decorated; but something like that she wanted to do for us. We'd go to the Brandeis Building, which was a big place to go see Santa as a little kid, and how could we go see Santa and get nothing for Christmas?" he laughs.

Sunday school was hardly Mark's holy grail. "I always pretended to sleep late on Sundays so my mom would let me sleep in. And that would work every once in a while. My brother and sister, Greg and Roz, used to go and I wouldn't; but that didn't work every week. It's school! You just spent five days in school, I was not a great student in grade school, I was a boy and I would screw up a little more than the girls would. You know, at least in grade school. I think most of the top grades in our class were a few girls and I think they were probably the more serious students, and the boys were more into doing dumb boy things. So after going five days of school, on my Sunday off to go back to Sunday school? It just wasn't something I looked forward to. Looking back, I'm sure it was something I needed to do."

Something Mark also needed to do was get Bar Mitzvahed, like it or not, in early October, 1961, before the synagogue's remodel. "I remember it being in the round," he says. "I was kind of in the center and seats were around." Sunday school... Bar Mitzvah...not his choice. So would Mark at least have a say in his Bar Mitzvah party menu?

"My Mom and I had an argument over it. Rock Cornish Hens was the menu. I was just starting eighth grade and Rock Cornish Hens was not one of my favorite meals. They probably got a good deal, and Rock Cornish Hens just wasn't a thing I really wanted to serve to my friends. Rock Cornish Hens? Come on!"

Guess who won.

Mark's parents were religious. "My mom kept 90-plus percent kosher in the house. I always remember during Passover, all the non-Passover foods went in a different cupboard. It meant a lot to her, and my dad, too." Mark's paternal grandmother Esther was, "very religious. When she came up from St. Joe, she made my mom scrub the kitchen up and do a lot."

Sam, Mark's father, born to Esther and Isador, raised in St. Joe, Missouri, was one of six siblings: four boys, then two girls. Though the fourth-born, Sam was the first in his family born in the U.S. after they emigrated between 1910 and 1914 through St. Joe, a pipeline for Jewish families. Interestingly, Mark notes, writer Calvin Trillin has a similar story. In his 1997 memoir, *Messages From My Father*, Trillin, whose family Sam knew, reflects on his Russian-born father Abe who grew up in St. Joe and about the Jewish population who came over from the Russia area to New York City.

Mark's experience growing up in a tight-knit Jewish community echoed that of his father's. "Growing up in Council Bluffs, my high school graduating class had eight Jewish kids alone; now there are eight Jewish kids in the city of Council Bluffs!" His cronies? "Mike Gallner; an attorney in Council Bluffs and still a good friend; Pete Lee, who has been deceased for 20 years; Steve Perlis, a retired attorney in Chicago; and Richard Selo, a urologist in Lafayette, Indiana; Jan Schneider (our fathers were friends; her dad owned the Bargain Spot on the 600 block of West Broadway, my dad had Marcus Department store, about five buildings down from her dad's store. I've known Jan pretty much my whole life"); Judy Cole, a veterinarian, I have not seen her since high school; and Deborah Mezey, a cousin of Mike Gallner. "I'm not sure where she is now. Of the Krasne kids, I'm still close to Gail, who is a few years younger than me, and her sister Susan, one year older."

320 Oakland Avenue, an address forever seared in Mark's mind as it was his childhood home and where his parents lived for over a half-century. "Just before kindergarten, in August, '53, my folks bought the house from my uncle Abe Katelman." Sissy Katelman, now Silber, and Mark's mom were first cousins; she was the baby of that first cousin. Mark's mom, born in 1919 to the Katelman family, was raised in Council Bluffs. When Mark's mom passed away on August 30, 2004, it took him over six months to go through the house.

"It was a large ranch house with a huge basement and I would spend most Sunday afternoons over there, just going through everything, saving everything I wanted to, throwing out a lot of things. This was the house I basically grew up in for over 50 years. It was hard selling it; it really was. I mean, it was not only the house I grew up in when I lived in Des Moines, when I'd come back for weekends, when I moved back here, it was two miles away from where I lived and I'd come back over there. So it was hard. Just going through all the stuff, I came across so many things, and one of the things I did come across was the menu for my Bar Mitzvah."

Before Mark's Bar Mitzvah, Christmases, and 320 Oakland, of course, was his parents meeting. After serving in the military during WWII, Sam worked at Brandeis

Department Store. "My Dad was always in sales; he was home furnishings. My aunt Jeanette Katelman was over there buying stuff from him, and she was a talker and they started to talk...My dad was a salesman, he could talk, too. They started talking and Jeanette says, "I've got a niece I'd like you to meet. She lined them up and it was really a short courtship, I want to say maybe four or five months. They were married four weeks to the day short of 56 years. He died four weeks short to the day of their wedding anniversary in October 2002. So it worked out."

Mark's maternal grandmother Goldie's family owned Marcus Clothing store. "When they got married, they first moved to St. Joe and my dad worked for a department store there, and then my mom's family got back up here and he took over what was then Marcus Clothing Store. I think about '49 or '50. Then in '61, at the end of the block there was Gershun's Department Store, which had men's and women's clothing and shoes in the basement. My dad bought that business when Gershun retired, in 1961 just before my 13th birthday, and he ran that."

A classic family business of the era, everyone pitched in, including 10-year-old Mark, whose first day on the job at Marcus Clothing (the smaller building before it became Marcus Department Store when they merged) proved to be...not one for the books. "I screwed up a big sale that never happened!" he laughs. I accidentally rung up a large sale that did not occur. "My dad, when he was young, was out selling newspapers and he knew old school that you could come down, do this and do that. I guess I wanted to prove to him, "No, I'm too young to go down and do this!"

Sales? Not clearly Mark's thing. "When somebody's haggling me over the price of kids' blue jeans or BVD underwear, it just didn't do anything for me!" he laughs. "If I don't like it, I'll go somewhere else! But that's not good if you want to stay in business. Urban Renewal came through and took the building. The last day he was open was the end of 1982."

For a boy who pretended to sleep late on Sundays and argued over Rock Cornish hens, Mark's Jewish life and relationship to B'nai Israel has come full circle. "I'm on the board now; I've been VP. I'm the only Council Bluffs resident on the board right now, talk about the lack of Jewish families in Council Bluffs. The synagogue burned down and got rebuilt; my mom's grandfathers on each side of her family worked on rebuilding it. That synagogue was always very important to my mother. My dad got a little more religious later in life -- he was always religious, but it meant a lot to him -- so keeping the synagogue open in Council Bluffs was important to me because it's important to my family. I do that to honor my mom and dad because it meant that much to them."

Born at Jennie Edmundson Hospital (roughly $125.00 for one-week's stay), Mark returned to the town where he played, studied and cultivated a Jewish identity. Now, he's a District Court Judge. "Yes, I'm proud of that," Mark says. "My roots are here in Council Bluffs. When I left private practice to get on the bench, I sat down before I applied and did pros and cons. I like to think I'm doing service for our community. I enjoy the work, but it's a way of giving back to the community."

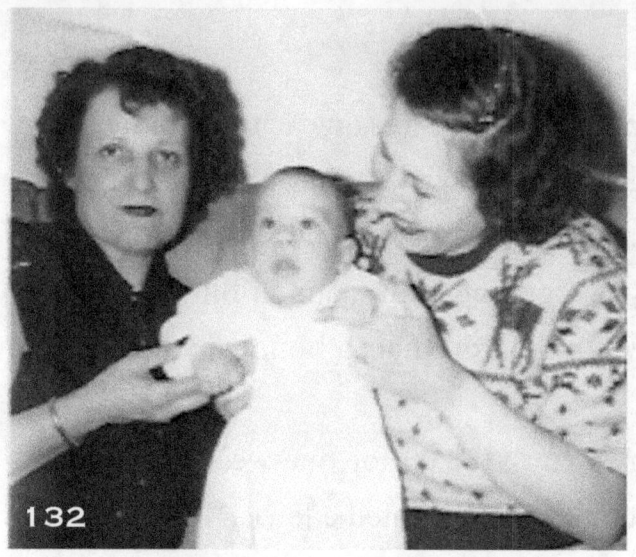

132. Mark, Leona Eveloff, Goldie Katelman (maternal grandmother)

133. Marcus Department Store (Sam Eveloff) & Herman's Clothing Store (Stanley Katelman) late '60s / early '70s

134. Mark Eveloff's Family

135. Leona & Sam Eveloff

136. Lee Katelman (Eveloff), Stanley Katelman (Mark's uncle) and Sam Katelman (Mark's maternal grandfather)

137. Rosalind Hoffman, Leona and Mark Eveloff

YALE GOTSDINER
1922 - 2015

Joey: Yale, you're from Council Bluffs. What do you call yourself, a Council Bluffer?

Yale: That name was given to us by Rabbi Goldstein at Beth El. We used to go there very often for Sunday school, so he called us the Council Bluffers. When it came time for my Bar Mitzvah at B'nai Israel, we took some classes at Beth El, which was more inviting because there were more kids there. We got away with more [laughs] and we had better games: Baseball, football, touch football. In terms of Jewish education, it was very lacking because of the caliber of students we had.

Joey: You and your meathead friends [laughs].

Yale: Right. Before we went to Beth El, we had a tutor, Harry Mendelson, at B'nai Israel. We studied with him, he kept after us, but we played around, didn't take it seriously. We took turns going to the bathroom to get out of studying [laughs].

Joey: So what was it like, not into being Jewish yet having a Bar Mitzvah? Did you just want the presents and the party?

Yale: That was it.

Joey: What did you like most about your Bar Mitzvah?

Yale: Well, mostly I liked when it was over. Alvin Nogg was in my class; he learned about as much as I did. When it was over, what I looked forward to most was the party and picnic in the summertime at Fontenelle Park. I insisted on having a good party, I was looking for gifts.

Joey: Most importantly, what were you favorite gifts? Now we're getting serious.

Yale: I got a nice *tallis*.

Joey: Did you care about a *tallis*?

Yale: Not much. And I got a well-decorated *kippah*.

Joey: Which you didn't care about.

Yale: Which I also didn't care about. But somebody gave me a football which I did care about.

Joey: Did it have a big Jewish star on it?

Yale: No, but actually, the fact I got a *kippah* and a *tallis* I was happy with because everyone that I had when I was forced to go to services, I either lost or they didn't fit. My parents would drag me to a *Shabbat* service every now and then. I got tired of wearing the wrong *kippah* and wearing one that didn't fit. My interest in Judaism waned until I got to Beth El and it picked up a little bit. One of the teachers interested me, an insurance man. He could speak our language. He knew how kids felt and he had a sense of humor. He was not deadly serious and he was a real nice guy, Loyal Kaplan.

Joey: Loyal Kaplan, sounds like a Fiddler character. What was that like being up on the *bima*, did you know what you were doing?

Yale: Not too much, but I got by. It wasn't fashionable for kids from Council Bluffs to be excited about the Bar Mitzvah service. We were interested in Scouts and other programs like AZA.

Joey: AZA was only Jewish and Boy Scouts wasn't Jewish, an interesting split. Did you live a split life in Council Bluffs, your Jewish life and your non-Jewish life?

Yale: No, you could be a non-Jewish person in actuality but it didn't mean that you did not participate. It didn't matter if you were Jewish or not Jewish; you just did what you wanted to do.

Joey: Clearly, Jews were a minority in Council Bluffs. Did you get heckled at all?

Yale: Not as a kid. My folks occasionally ran into it. It was universal. Some of the non-Jews were not happy with Jews in Council Bluffs, although I will say that I never felt any great degree of intolerance. Never. I was welcomed into the kids' homes and we enjoyed each other's company. Scouting, of course, teaches tolerance.

Joey: What did your parents encounter?

Yale: Well, in those days the Ku Klux Klan was active in little old Council Bluffs, somewhere around 1922 or 1924. It wasn't so pronounced as it was in the south, but it was there and I remember a couple of cross burnings, like at Bayliss Park. As a matter of fact, we used to go to Omaha a lot of times on Sundays. We had grandparents there, aunts and uncles, and we would go to spend much of the day. This one time, we were coming back from Omaha to Council Bluffs and we saw the burning of a cross on the bridge which was the old Aksarben Bridge.

The toll was a nickel for the car and a nickel for every passenger. Nickels were scarce in those days, so my sister and I would hide in the back seat, down low, so we didn't have to pay to cross. Sometimes there would be a blanket in the back, and my parents would say, "*Lozan shtill*" "Let there be quiet."

Joey: Did they speak Yiddish to you a lot?

Yale: No. My grandmother did.

Joey: What was her name?

Yale: Her last name was Harmel and her first name was Pearl. They were very devout, my grandparents. They were from *Odessa*.

Joey: What was your grandfather's name?

Yale: Solomon Harmel.

Joey: Solomon and Pearl, good names. Why did they move to Council Bluffs?

Yale: They thought they could make a living, and heard it was peaceful. Basically it was. My grandparents on my father's side, they came over roughly in the early 1900s and got quite an initiation. They settled in Omaha on North Franklin Street. *Zayde*, interesting with him, they decided to go out one day. They had to buy some kind of furniture or bed or something. They had nothing, so they went shopping. They went to a very poor second-hand store and they bought a bed and mattress and so forth. They hired a guy with a wagon to haul it; they had to use the transportation which was available, which wasn't very good. So they got there and my grandmother and grandfather assembled the bed and put the mattress on it and they were told they had to be quiet, make no sound. Just live quietly. They couldn't make any noise;

they didn't want to start anything so they wanted them to be quiet. Don't make any waves, that's the way they lived.

Joey: You obviously changed that.

Yale: We sure did. As Pearl would say, "We damn well did." My parents worked hard and studied the language. Dad got a job when he was about 11 in a grocery store owned by the Christensens.

Joey: Not Jewish.

Yale: No, but they were nice people and my dad would oftentimes have dinner with them because there wasn't much at home. They would make a sandwich for my dad; they had limited funds and had something like 11 children. It was a struggle. My dad was Joseph (Joe) and my mom, Leona. She did quite well. She started out by taking care of the kids mostly, and then they got some relatives taking care of the kids so they could go out and earn some money. She went to school and went to work for the Union Pacific. That was quite a big step and she ended up years later as a secretary for a vice president.

Joey: Impressive! Your sister, what was her name?

Yale: Eileen.

Joey: That's pretty Irish, what's the story with that? I wonder if your parents, when they named her, were trying to fit in, acclimate.

Yale: I imagine, probably. Eileen's Hebrew name was *Hidoba*.

Joey: Yours?

Yale: *Yohan*. I never used it. So, my parents finally found a store that they could afford to buy in Council Bluffs, West Broadway Market. Things blossomed for us to some extent. My folks did well at the little grocery store.

Joey: Did your mom work at the grocery store?

Yale: She helped. Then they accumulated a little money and became friendly with a banker, B. A. Gronstal. My folks got friendly with him, and he looked after them. He told my dad, "If you want to improve your store, see me and I'll try to help you."

So they did and they improved the store and did better. They made it a little larger and added some hardware, which was a flop. They couldn't make it so he threw out the hardware and went back to groceries, made it larger and he did well so then they added some light hardware -- shovels, nails, hammers -- and he sold it pretty well. He, of all things, became a Mason.

Joey: A Mason?!

Yale: Yes, a Jew becoming a Mason. At that time, the Masonic lodge was noted for tolerance, so he and two others got in. It was rather interesting, the lodge got larger to the point they would accept Jews and non-Jews they felt were of decent character. It got so my parents were going to Masonic picnics and they had little social life outside of that, so they were proud of that.

Joey: How did the Jewish community feel about you going to the Masonic temple?

Yale: They got used to the idea. Many of the local Jews were active in Masonic and Eastern Star, the women's branch of the Masonic temple.

Joey: Was your mother a member?

Yale: Yes, for a short time. They accepted them, and my folks did business with a number of them. They got to like each other and sometimes they would have Bridge games at one of their homes. So it all worked out.

Joey: Obviously you love to laugh. Who made you laugh the most?

Yale: The Jews in town, most of them had a pretty good sense of humor. Fortunately most of them did business in an honorable way and they made friends through that. Jews were generally well-respected. When I went to Thomas Jefferson High School, there were just three Jews in the school: Bob Passer, myself and one girl. We played sports and had speech contests, debate and that sort of thing. All three of us were well-accepted, but we were taught from the beginning, "Behave yourself."

Joey: Like in the car when your parents said, in Yiddish, "Be quiet."

Yale: Yes, "*Lozan shtill*." The gentiles thought Jews were a little strange. No Christmas, and Chanukah and some of them still had beards. When time went on we bought a Chrysler and then we were able to go to Omaha a lot. My dad's first car was a Dodge touring car; it had wooden wheels; he treasured that car. Gas was around 13 cents a gallon, around 1926. It meant a lot; the car was a big thing in our lives, getting from here to there, much simpler. Before the car, we had horse and buggy, my parents got it after I was born. The horses lived in a barn near the store for convenience. Our first home was above the store on 34th and Broadway.

Joey: Sounds like you had lots of fun as a kid; you were like Dennis the Menace.

Yale: Yeah, as much as I could.

Joey: What kind of naughty things did you do, listen to people's private party line conversations?

Yale: Oh, yeah. Any time you wanted to be entertained, you could pick up the telephone and see what's going on. People sometimes would indicate that there was somebody else on the line, they could hear the clicks.

Joey: Would people listen to your conversations, and did you know?

Yale: Yes, you would laugh or tell them to mind their own business.

Joey: [Laughs] Speaking of entertainment, going to the movies was big back then. What was your favorite?

Yale: Charlie Chaplin. In the early years, there were three movie theaters: the Liberty, the Broadway and the Strand. It cost something like 15 cents to go; and when I went, my daddy gave me the 15 cents and I wouldn't spend it on that. Sometimes I would sneak into the theater like the rest of the kids, then use that for popcorn or candy. The classiest one was the Strand, maybe a close second would be the Broadway Theater and the Liberty was the cheap-o with the cowboys. I liked that one. All the kids went there and we'd cheer for the cowboys.

Joey: How cheap-o was it?

Yale: A dime.

Joey: So, regarding your sense of Judaism, even though you weren't religious, did you celebrate *Shabbat*?

Yale: Well, my grandparents lived with us, out of respect for them my mother kept a kosher home. That was sort of a given in those days.

Joey: Tell me about the kosher butchers.

Yale: Diamond Butcher.

Joey: Must have been a big deal, going to the butcher. A big outing.

Yale: Yes, it was fun for the kids because it always involved arguments. Part of it was tradition.

Joey: To argue with the butcher?

Yale: To get something cheaper. They tried to "Jew him down." So my grandmother went in and said, "Two pounds of flank," and the butcher would say, "One pound for that, that's plenty for you." He was trying to ration it; he wanted enough left for other customers. So when I was standing there, he would point to my grandmother and say, "*Herst*" "You hear that? He was trying to get a cheaper price. My grandmother, she had a saying, "*Er iz a gonif*" "He's a thief." But she didn't really mean it. She would make a big scene and other customers would listen, but they knew that was part of the show. Then she would buy her pound of flank or whatever it was, and then she would see some other things she wanted. She would tell him to throw in a pickle.

Joey: Would he usually throw in the pickle?

Yale: No, and they would argue about it, the pickle. She didn't want to give him anything and he wanted everything. They would argue about some cut of meat and my grandmother would point to that piece of meat over there, and she would look at that and liked it better, so he would take that knife, turn it around and he said, "You're a butcher, go ahead and cut. I'll charge you." He wouldn't let her get away with anything. The *shtick*.

Yale in front of father's store in Council Bluffs, 1925

138. Yale on tennis team 1937 at Thomas Jefferson High School
139. Yale Gotsdiner and Bob Passer, Thomas Jefferson High School, 1940
140. Yale Gotsdiner

BOB FOX

MY PATERNAL GREAT-GRANDFATHER, Hertz Saltzman, came to Council Bluffs from *Lechovitz*, Ukraine, in about 1900. He had a brother, Moses Saltzman, who settled in Council Bluffs some years earlier. Supposedly, Moses and his family were headed for California but may have been robbed near Council Bluffs. Since they knew of a Jewish family in Council Bluffs, they decided to stay. Hertz's son, *Hazreal*, came in 1901 but died within a few months. Another son, *Beryl*/Ben, came in 1903. Ben had a wife and two children in Russia who joined him later. Hertz's wife, Esther "Rachel" Perlmutter, arrived in 1904 with children; Sarah (my grandmother), Anna, Sam and Mollye. The family lived near the synagogue at 736 Mynster. Several years later, Hertz, Rachel and their younger children moved to 742 Mynster while Ben stayed at 736.

Hertz owned a coal and feed business on the north side of West Broadway in the 1300 block. My grandmother Sarah married David Fox in 1907. The Fox's immigrated to Omaha from *Kremenitz*, Ukraine in 1903 and lived at 2209 Charles in Omaha. In 1908, Dave opened D. Fox Clothing at 140 West Broadway, but it only lasted a short time. He then went to work at the coal yard with his father-in-law. While at the coal yard, he started dealing in scrap metal.

Hertz moved his coal yard a few blocks away to 2nd Avenue and, with son Sam, it became Saltzman & Son. Sam stayed in business until he retired in the 1980s. Dave stayed at the old yard and it became Council Bluffs Parts, dealing in scrap, used auto parts and a few used cars.

There was a duplex at 1310 West Broadway on the old yard property and Hertz let Dave and Sarah live in one half. No plumbing! No electricity! No furnace! My uncles Al and Jack and my aunt Rose were born there. Aunt Pearl was born in a hospital in Omaha. My dad Harold and my uncle Lester were born at Jenny Ed hospital in Council Bluffs. As a kid, I heard stories about this house. In the winter, the main living area was the kitchen because it had a wood stove. The parlor had a coal stove but that was only for company. The outhouse was tipped over every Halloween! Sounded like fun times, sorry us kids missed it…The other half of the duplex was occupied by Rachel's nephew, Willie and Rosie Perlmutter and their kids. The duplex was next to Indian Creek which flooded and caused problems frequently.

Around 1920, Hertz and Dave had a falling out. Dave bought property across the street at 1201 West Broadway and moved Council Bluffs Auto. Along the way, Dave's brother, Oscar Fox, became a partner and later they opened Omaha Gear & Parts in Omaha. In 1932, they sold the yard to Bittner Scrap next door and moved Council Bluffs Auto to 701 West Broadway dealing in new auto parts. After a time, Dave and Oscar ended the partnership with Dave keeping the Council Bluffs store and Oscar keeping the Omaha store. In 1936, the store moved to 134 West Broadway and four years later relocated to 138 West Broadway. After Harold and Jack returned from WWII they came into the business and enlarged the store into 140 and 142 West Broadway. Ironically, 140 was the same building that Dave had for his clothing store in 1908.

After a while, I was born and when old enough to read, my mother decided she didn't want me hanging around the house on Saturdays and school vacations, so I got to go to work with my dad. This was cool. The back of the store was a machine shop where we rebuilt engines. Lots of grease and dirt! What more could a little kid want? I made friends with the mechanic; so in the mornings, he would smear a little grease on my face so I could show my dad that I was working. He was seldom amused. My grandfather always said, "You're going to learn this business from the ground up… here's a dust rag, start cleaning."

Otherwise, I got to do lots of filing. My summer job from the time I was old enough to count was doing inventory. I had no idea how many nuts and bolts would fit in a shoe box! When the weather was nice, I got to deliver small parts to nearby customers. Council Bluffs was so safe they would even send me to the bank, six or eight blocks away, with large deposits. The business people along Broadway may not have known my name, but they knew who I belonged to so there was never any problem.

My grandfather was always called Pa. He was just this little, easy-going guy who looked like a gangster in a straw hat and with a big cigar. He was probably not much over five feet tall. In front of us kids, he and my grandmother and the other adults mostly spoke Yiddish. As a matter of self-preservation, I learned to understand Yiddish fairly well but couldn't speak it much.

My grandmother was a great cook, made fall-off-the-bone roast chicken and pigs in a blanket. Every time one of my aunts tried to copy a recipe by watching my grandmother, something got screwed up. She made world famous poppy seed cookies that everybody fought over. For me she made pans of sweet rolls with white raisins. When she sent them home with my dad, it was with instructions that they were for me only, unless I was willing to share. That part caused a few arguments at home! At my grandparents; the adults would drink hot tea out of special glasses, like a water glass but very thin, and they would tuck sugar cubes in their cheeks for sweetener. Never could master that so the kids just ate the cubes.

On the High Holidays, after Beth El in Omaha, we would go to the Synagogue in Council Bluffs. To me, B'nai Israel was a bunch of old men yelling –– no English —everybody said the same prayers over and over, that's why it took so long. We'd talk and visit quietly. If it got too loud, they'd slam a book down and tell us to "Shut up."

Grandmother Sarah was very quiet, regal in her own way. Didn't laugh or smile a lot but did have a sense of humor, very much the subservient wife, at least in front of us. Grandfather Dave may have run a business, but from what we heard, home was a little bit different. Grandma was the boss, period. Her sons grew up doing the dishes, they may have been men, but for years, even at our house after dinners Dad was up doing the dishes.

Grandpa Dave was kind of strict especially when it came to fasting on Yom Kippur. The kids couldn't make it, so Grandma would sneak us hard candy to get us by until dinner. We just couldn't let Grandpa see us.

We'd all go to Council Bluffs for Passover. My grandmother had these little silver wine cups for each grandkid. Grandpa expected us to follow the service and drink our wine, all of it. Mogen David tasted like grape juice; but after the chopped liver and the matzo ball soup, all of us kids were on the floor out cold. I never realized until I was an adult just how sneaky my grandfather was — a quiet dinner without the kids. He was no dummy!

Some of my cousins and I have been working on our family history. Our biggest regret is that we didn't ask many questions about our ancestors. All grandpa would say about Russia was that they were afraid of the Cossacks. I do remember at Passover, during the reading of the ten plagues, there were a few drops of wine spilled for the Czar. Through our ongoing research we have learned a lot, but a lot has been lost.

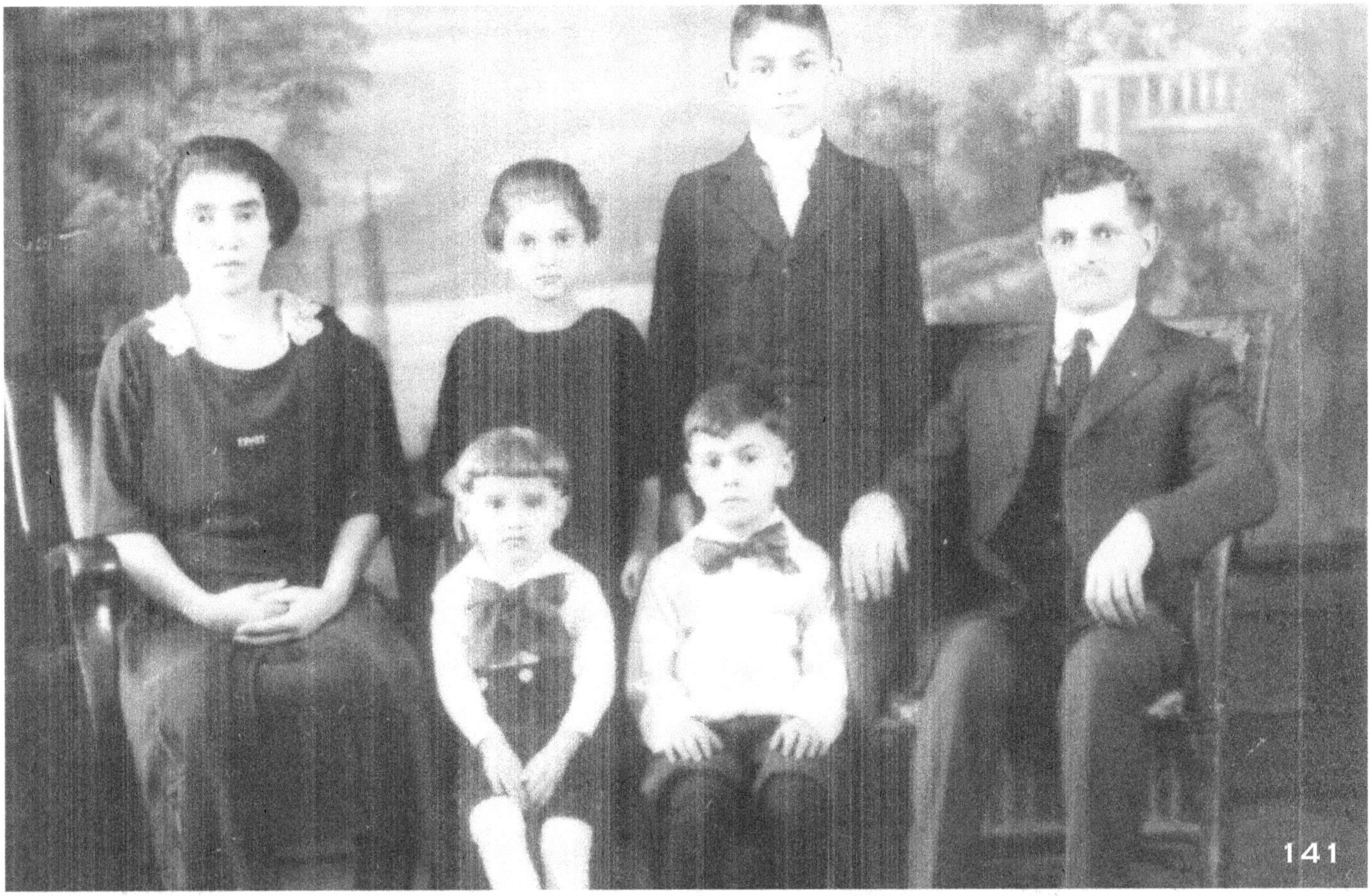

141

Coal

COUNCIL BLUFFS CITY DIRECTORY 1909. 7

IF AT ANY TIME

YOU NEED GOOD COAL

WE HAVE IT

FROM $5.50 TO $10.50

Less 50 Cents for Spot Cash

WALT SMITH COAL COMPANY

1401 South Sixth Street Both Phones 182

Clothing

Complete, Up-to-Date Stock at Very Moderate Prices

WE SAVE YOU MONEY ON EVERYTHING

D. FOX, Clothing

Men's and Boys' Furnishings, Shoes and Hats

VALISES, TRAVELING BAGS AND SUIT CASES

See Fox First (Across from Hafer's) 140 W. Broadway

Contractors

C. P. CHAMBERS

General Contractor and Builder

AND REPAIRING

Estimates Cheerfully Furnished 114 W. Broadway

142

143

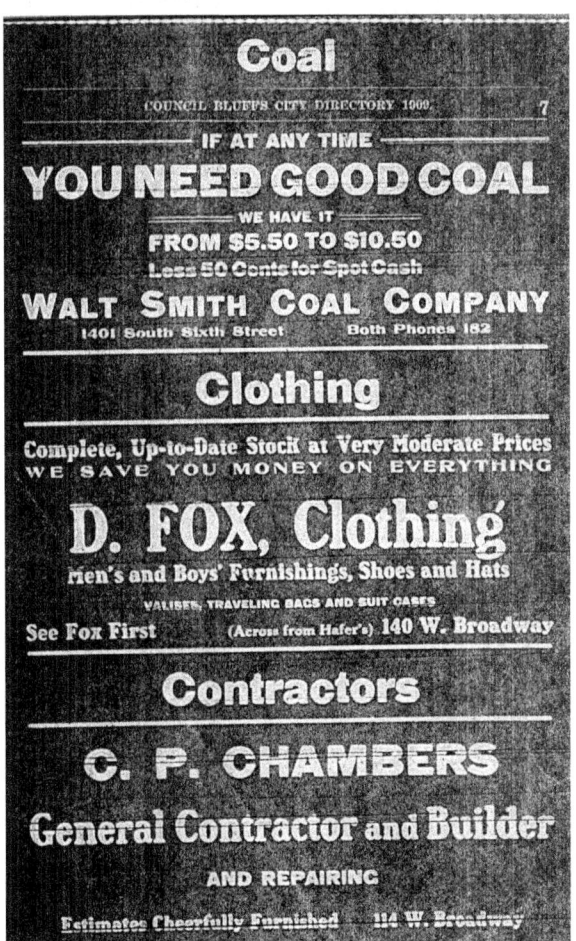

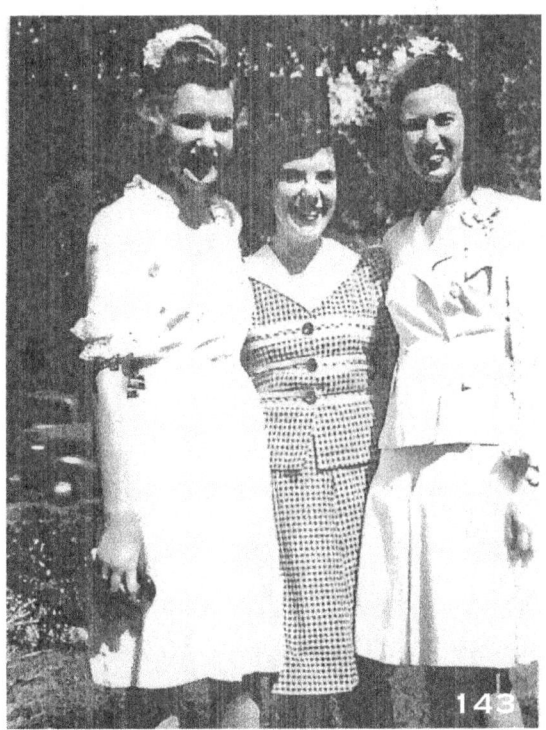

141. Sarah and Dave Fox with children Rose, Al, Harold and Jack, 1920s

142. Sam Saltzman's coal company, Council Bluffs, 1970

143. Bob's mother Ruth Stein Fox with Bev and Darlene Marcus

We Tear Them Down and Sell the Parts **You Save From 50 to 75 Per Cent Off of List Price**

Telephone 2787

Council Bluffs Auto Parts Co.

FOX BROTHERS, Props.

Council Bluffs, Iowa

Parts and Tires for Any Make of Car

OFFICE: 1329 West Broadway.   YARD: 1201 to 15 West Broadway

1918–1921
David, Oscar Fox
(also Hertz coal address)

COUNCIL BLUFFS AUTO PARTS CO
"IF IT IS FOR AN AUTOMOBILE WE HAVE IT"
FOX BROS.
1207 W B'way................2787

1921–1932
David, Oscar Fox
1201–1215 W. B'way
(office 1207)

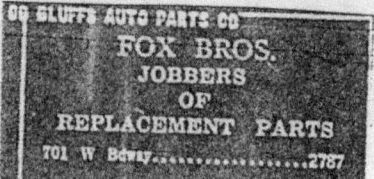

1932–1936
David, Oscar Fox

CO BLUFFS AUTO PARTS CO
FOX BROS.
JOBBERS
OF
REPLACEMENT PARTS
134 W B'way................2787

1936–1940
David, Jack,
Harold Fox

1940–1980
David, Jack,
Harold Fox

138, 140, 142 W B'way
Later phone 323-7171
Omaha phone JA(342)2863

1980–1987
Harold Fox

144. Fox family photo

145. Sam Saltzman had the coal company in Council Bluffs, 1970

146. Bess Fox Herzoff, Ida Fox, Sarah Block Fox, Sarah Saltzman and Dave Fox

JOEL FINKEL

TALK ABOUT MOM AND POP. Joel Finkel's parents, Leonard and Helen, ran a highway-side fruit stand in Atlantic, Iowa in 1943, hawking apples and other fresh produce to passersby. One year later, when their dreams outgrew their inventory, the couple packed up and headed 66 miles west to Council Bluffs, launching a 6,000 square-foot grocery store: Sixth Street Market on Broadway. Flanked by fellow Jewish merchants, Leonard and Helen unwittingly became a part of Jewish history in a town where supporting each other financially and personally was the crux of the community.

"My fondest memories are of all the Jewish merchants in Council Bluffs," says Joel. "Everyone you knew was Jewish on the street. The stores where you bought your clothes, where you bought groceries, they were all Jewish. When I drive up and down the street there now, I think about that. Even though I didn't have Jewish friends, I liked growing up there. If there were Jewish kids there today, they wouldn't have much of a sense of Judaism."

What does a 12-year-old whose parents and grandfather Morris own a grocery store do? "I sorted pop bottles. People would bring in the bottles and get money for them. I was down there, stuck in the basement. It was hot and dirty...Seemed like days and weeks and years," he laughs. "But it was probably an hour on Saturdays."

Around 1985, Sixth Street Market was razed, paving the way for a parking lot. While some might balk, Joel takes it in stride. "It doesn't bother me," he says. "I mean, things have changed and improved there over the years."

Born April 18, 1943, Joel ricocheted from Franklin Elementary, to Bloomer, to Hoover, then graduated from Abraham Lincoln. His first house, located at 31st and Avenue F, was close enough to walk to the store, but why bother when you have a

1952 Chevy? "It was my first car, didn't have a heater. My dad was testing me to see if I could maintain and drive it without crashing into people." Yes, he passed -- no cracked carburetors or human casualties. But ah, Jewish mothers, ever-mindful of their *bubelah's* comfort, and Helen was no exception. Next up: a brand-new, navy '60 Chevy, heater included. "It was a hot car in its day," says Joel, who eventually traded it for a 1957 Corvette, which he and buddy Johnny Banks drove to The University of Oklahoma, his almost-alma mater.

On the east side of Council Bluffs, a hub of Jewish families ("Patty Nogg lived across the street"), Joel lived surrounded by people of his own faith and, of course, knew others through Hebrew school. Still, it was a bubble of sorts, a reminder of his minority status in the larger community. He was the only one in his Bar Mitzvah study class with Rabbi Korb, who he remembers as being, well, not a *mensch*.

"There were a lot of Jews in Council Bluffs; you just happened not to have any others in your class studying. I didn't know any different, just the way it was," says Joel, whose best friend was, "a wonderful Catholic" and still a dear friend. Though not religious, the Finkels attended B'nai Israel services and were always available to pinch-hit when fellow congregants needed a 10th.

"The grocery store was on one corner and the synagogue was right behind it, a block away. When they needed another person for a *minyan*, they called the store. 'Can someone come over?' and they ran over there and did the minyan."

Though it was only roughly 50 years ago, one scene from his childhood sounds Anatevka-like. "I remember being outside the synagogue once. I don't remember what I was doing out there, maybe it was before or after services, but they came outside and needed someone to carry the *Torah*, so they were dragging people off the street."

During college, when family called, Joel headed straight back to Council Bluffs for good. "My dad was going blind and it was a progressive disease that got worse as the years went on, so I had to come back to take over the business, which I was in with him forever. That had a big impact on our lives. He was a very creative, busy entrepreneur and a man who didn't let it get to him the way you'd think. He would get up on a roof with his son."

Get up on the roof, blind?

"He refused to allow it to hold him back when he should have, but he did what he felt he wanted to do. Proud man and I always felt bad that we had to stop him. That was difficult."

When Urban Renewal hit, Sixth Street market took a hit. Prime corner real estate was on the city's radar and, like scores of businesses at that time, they sold out. But their entrepreneurial spirit was high and, thankfully, says Joel of his parents, "I think they were ready to move on."

For their next venture, rather than cater to customers' culinary tastes, they appealed to their tastes in decor. Just 13 blocks away, at 19th and Broadway, Morris and his sons Leonard and Harold opened Home Furniture, which spanned approximately 15,000 square feet –– more than double the market's size –– their little highway-side fruit stand days long gone.

Given Leonard's innovative mind-set, it makes sense they next ventured into real estate. What goes better with furniture than a home in which to put it? But a tire store? Who knows why, but Harold's mind was set, so they subdivided the store, carving out space for Home Auto Center, which they ran for the next five years. They also built apartments and houses and owned commercial buildings.

In keeping with the era when families lived in close proximity, old-world style, Joel's Russian grandfather Morris, father and uncle bought three lots on Elmwood Drive with the intention of being next-door neighbors.

"One-two-three," says Joel. "My grandfather built a house, my uncle built a house and my father said, 'No, I'm not going to do that,' so he bought a house a block away on the same street. He just didn't want to be that close and didn't want to take the time to build, so he sold his lot to someone else. We all lived walking distance from each other's house. I remember walking to my grandparents' house all the time."

Still connected to Council Bluffs –– Joel and his wife Lois have a house on Lake Manawa, and his parents and grandparents, Maurice and Jenny, are buried at Oakhill Cemetery. He enjoys *kibbitzing* with old-timers at Patty's annual ceremony there, reminiscing with his one-time neighbor Patty Lee about his bulldog Wrinkles Finkel.

It brings Joel back to a time when life was a teen dream. "You dated, you had cars, you drove up and down Broadway...My parents always had me work, doing something; but for fun we drove up and down Broadway, went to drive-in restaurants like in any other small town. The main restaurant everyone went to was Ewald's, a drive-in. People parked their cars and everyone went around and waved at each other and got in and out of cars. That's the way we dated, just drove up and down the street, like in some of the old 1960s movies. It was a fun city."

147. Joel Finkel
148. The Finkels
149. Leonard Finkel
150. Helen and Leonard Finkel

LEO MEYERSON
1914 - 2002

Who didn't love *kibbitzing* with a friend using two coffee cans and a string? Leo Meyerson was no exception. Except at nine, this pastime would lead to a career in radio which earned him local acclaim, international recognition and even an Army-Navy "E" Award.

In 1920, Leo's Eighth Street School teacher, Mrs. McIntosh, invited a Great War veteran friend to speak about radio communication and soon-to-be launched broadcast stations. He introduced young Leo to *The Boy Scout Handbook*. That November, when America's first broadcast station launched in East Pittsburg, KDKA, Leo and neighborhood pal Harold Smith built a one-tube regenerative receiving set to hear it.

By golly, it worked!

The budding scientist relied on print media for self-education, savoring his copies of *Popular Mechanics*, *Popular Science* and *National Geographic*. Unwittingly, *The Boy Scout Handbook* proved to be pivotal in his later success. In it, detailed instructions on how to build crystal sets led Leo to scour his house for materials –– and what better places than the bathroom and kitchen? He wound coils around an oatmeal box and toilet tissue roll which allowed him to hear WAAW, Omaha's first station broadcasting from the Omaha Grain Exchange in 1922.

It may be unlikely fellow Council Bluffs kids coveted the small magazine shop two stores up from Owl Grocery on 7th and Broadway like Leo. Stocked with radio magazines like *World Radio* and *Radio Digest,* he was hooked, and gained a friend and mentor, Mr. Freidan, a store employee who introduced him to *White's Radio Log* which listed all broadcast stations, their power and operating wavelengths.

Like a mad scientist (minus the mad), Leo ran a wire roughly six or seven hundred feet long behind his family's house which helped him reach faraway stations. Who else but "The Crazy Meyerson kid" as he was known in the neighborhood, would build a transmitter using his mother's borrowed breadboard attached to a long wire antenna? Or became a self-appointed radio host, playing piano, spinning records, reporting neighborhood news and the weather? His was the first broadcast station in Council Bluffs. It was 1924.

"I found out later that I was broadcasting without a license and promptly got off the air," said Leo, who hit the airwaves three months earlier than the first legal station in Council Bluffs, KOIL.

While a student at Abraham Lincoln, a hardware store in the basement of the Peoples Store where his father Sam worked proved to be a trove of toys (a.k.a. radio parts) and a place where Leo befriended another employee mentor, Victor Nelson, who taught him the ins-and-outs of amateur radio and helped him learn Morse Code. Imagine: a teen, a secret language, communicating with a community of like-minded radio folks, all from a tiny ham shack located by his basement stairwell.

Left-brained Leo, a font of logic and innovation, had the rare distinction of being equally creative. At six, he started piano lessons from Mrs. Waggoner, a German neighbor across the street. On his family's Story and Clark piano, he wrote melodies and loved to sing. In 1927, an impromptu sidewalk meeting advanced his musical and radio ambitions. Ben Harding, owner of the Liberty Theater, approached Leo, asking him to be a theater organist. Leo had yet no organ experience, but no matter. For 15 bucks a week, he was sold, and purchased radio equipment with his earnings.

"Dad always had an interest in music and radio," says his son Larry. "He really wanted to be a professional pianist and got a job while in college at University of Nebraska to go to Chicago and play for the silent movies. They offered him a job there; but around 1935, they came out with the new talking movies. That ended that career.

Score for amateur radio enthusiasts. In the book, *In Tune With Leo: Leo Meyerson, The Last of the Radio Pioneers* (Dageforde Publishing, Inc., 2002), co-author Jim Musgrove, a fellow ham radio operator and Leo admirer, notes: "He is one of the last living pioneers who manufactured amateur radio equipment prior to WWII. Leo Meyerson is recognized by amateur radio operators throughout the world… Meyerson's understanding of the needs of ham operators and his honesty as a businessman account for the recognition by his fellow hams and business colleagues."

Long before he garnered worldwide accolades, Leo started from scratch: fixing people's radios. "He could fix almost anything," says Larry. "He realized there was a real need for electronic parts; people didn't know how to get hold of them. So he formed a little business with the help of his father and started an electronics shop on the cheap, so to speak."

If Leo's father Sam had his way, his son would have joined the family grocery business in the Peoples Store. But Leo's heart was in bandwidths, not bananas. With a $1,000 gift from Dad, a windfall back then, Leo opened a larger electronics shop.

"Son," Sam said. "When you finish, come back to me and we'll get into the grocery business."

Clearly, Leo's first love was radio. Or was it? At a dance in St. Joe, MO, he asked his friend, "Who is that beautiful gal there on the dance floor?"

"Well, that's Helen Wolenski," he said.

"Dad was enthralled with her," Larry says. "He romanced her from Council Bluffs to St. Joe via amateur radio. He bought a little Lafayette Radio receiver, put it in her house, her dad turned it on for her, they'd get on a certain frequency and Dad talked to her in a one-sided conversation on the air, because a receiver is just like radio, yet you can only hear what's coming in. Guys were hearing it from all over the country, hearing my dad romance my mom. He was just a young guy in love."

Later, Leo would find another amateur radio operator in St. Joe who had a higher-tech set-up, so Helen would be driven to the man's house so the two could converse over the air.

Four years later, they married, and eventually had son Larry and daughter, Darlynn Fellman (whom they almost named Crystal). Suddenly, when the war started, the government shut down all amateur radio operators. Virtually out of business yet ever-industrious, Leo knew of a piece of equipment the government needed for walkie-talkies called a crystal: a delicate, simple radio receiver that worked solely from the power of radio waves received by a wire antenna. Leo teamed up with a fellow ham operator and the duo trekked to D.C. with little funds and a few crystal samples.

"They didn't know what they might think when they saw it," Larry says. "They were so impressed, they gave them an order on the spot, $15,000. My dad was flabbergasted!"

Scientific Radio Company was born. They leased a building at 738 Broadway, ("made crystals for Uncle Sam," Larry says) and became one of the top two or three employers in the city. 550 employees, 24/7 shifts; the government even insisted they have guards so people didn't sabotage the crystals. The company became so renowned, at the end of the war they were recognized with the Army-Navy "E" (Excellence) Award. A celebration with over 1,000 people in attendance was held at Council Bluffs' only hotel at the time, The Chieftain.

Post-War, Leo stayed in crystals, yet returned to the amateur radio business. He started manufacturing, engineering and building a few pieces of equipment under the name, "WRL" (World Radio Labs) which eventually became Globe Electronics.

In the late '50s, Leo built the first true walkie talkie called a pocket phone. "He made an awful lot of them," says Larry, who notes Leo also started building Citizens Band or CB Radios. Eventually, an east coast company bought part of the business which absorbed into Textron, which is still in business.

"Then Dad was interested in going back to his first love," Larry laughs. He built a line of equipment called Galaxy Electronics, a mail-order company and Globe Electronics, which engineered and built a line of popular amateur radio transmitters and receivers. Not surprisingly, in the mid-'60s, a company from Lincoln, Hygain Electronics, and a friend of Leo's, Andy Androse, bought that company. Now he was left with just World Radio Labs.

Meanwhile, like Leo, Larry had graduated from the University of Iowa, yet moved to Minneapolis to work as a fire insurance adjustor. Six months later, Dad called.

"Son," he said. "Are you through with that nonsense? Get back here, I need you in our business."

Sound familiar?

"Except that I wasn't building anything and I was starving. Dad always dreamt that I would go into the business and kind of knew I would sometime, but he wanted me to venture out on my own. I didn't want to come straight back to the Bluffs."

Larry did marketing and merchandising for mail-order, phased out of that, then focused strictly on the retail business, while Leo was essentially retired. In 1973, Larry became president of and ran World Radio, a consumer electronics chain store operation throughout the midwest, until the late '80s, when he sold it to his CEO and General Manager.

The Meyerson family story, Council Bluffs portion, started in the early 1900's when Grandfather Sam and his brothers fled the pogroms in Latvia, Russia. They started a grocery business in Omaha, sold out, moved to Council Bluffs and opened Madison Ave Grocery –– formed along with other Jewish friends –– then a grocery in the Peoples Store, started by Sam and Herman Meyerson. Later, Herman would buy out Sam who ran it with his son-in-law, Leon Frankel.

Community service was in their DNA. Sam was President of B'nai Israel and the Jewish Community Center. He was President of The Chamber of Commerce and Kiwanis. "You name it and he was active," Larry says. During the flood of 1952, the city made the Meyerson house the center of communications as they worried the whole lower area of the city would flood.

"Police and civil defense all operated out of our house with my dad's knowledge of electronics, and he was able to give good communications. That's the kind of guy he was. He was pretty terrific."

Leo Meyerson accomplished more professionally, starting at nine, than many do in a lifetime. Still, family came first. And boy, Leo loved to create music. "Chanticleer was very important to my folks. My mom was in a number of little plays; she acted in "Bloomer Girl" while Dad played music. Daughter Darlynn had both Mom and Dad's musical and theatrical talent and still is active in little theater. Piano and organ were important parts of his being for his entire life until he passed away at 100.

"Dad was a gregarious, lovable guy who always liked everybody; he could never see the bad in anyone. He was just that way. He liked people and if someone did him wrong, he'd turn the cheek. He couldn't hold a grudge; he was loved by everyone. That's not just a son talking about his dad. It's true. He was an honorable guy. I tried to emulate as much as I could. I worked with and for him for 29 years; I made plenty of mistakes but was never, ever second guessed. His attitude was, 'Well, we learned from that one, son…'

My entire life, when I'd meet someone and they'd see my last name, they'd want to know if Leo Meyerson was my dad. They all loved him. All of them."

First World Radio in Council Bluffs

151. Leo and Helen Meyerson at costume party
152. Sam (father of Leo) with wife Shirley Wohlner Meyerson in 1970 at wedding at Temple Israel
153. Sam and May Meyerson, Leo and Helen Meyerson, Mr. and Mrs. Al Scheidler of Chicago
154. Leo and Sam Meyerson

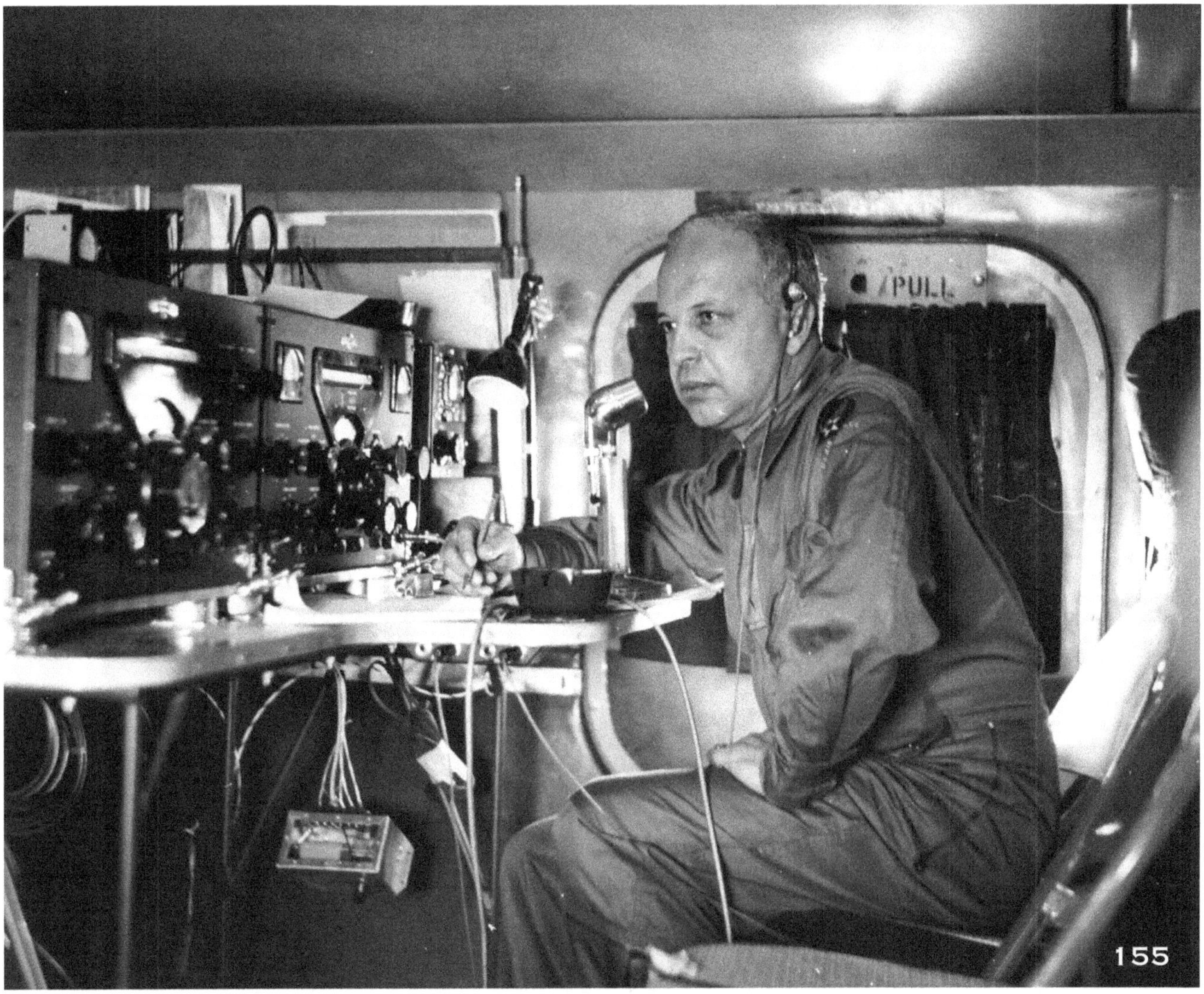

155

156

157

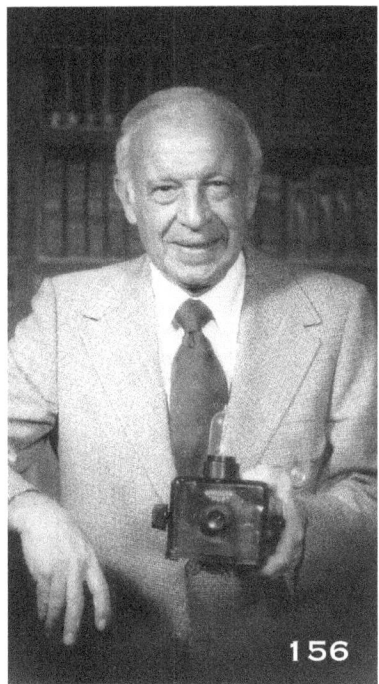

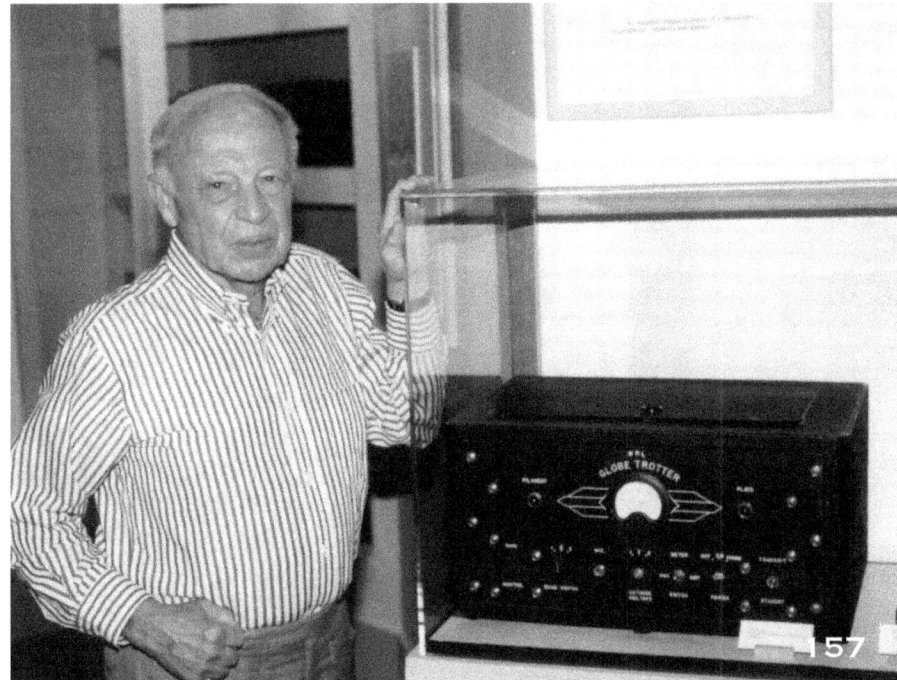

155, 156. Leo Meyerson

157. Leo Meyerson, chairman and founder of World Radio, Council Bluffs, 1980

158, 159. Leo Meyerson
160. Leo, Darlynn and Helen

161. Larry, Helen, Leo and Darlynn
162. Helen and Leo Meyerson
163. Leo, Darlynn, Larry and Helen
164. Darlynn Fellman and Larry Meyerson
165. Helen and Leo Meyerson

Tom Fellman, Leo Meyerson and Larry Meyerson

Leo and Helen Meyerson with Darlynn Fellman and Larry Meyerson

Leo Meyerson Earns Radio Club Honors

Leo I. Meyerson, founder and chairman of the board, World Radio, Council Bluffs, will be elected a fellow of the Radio Club of America, Inc., in ceremonies scheduled for Nov. 21 in New York City.

Mr. Meyerson was selected for the honor for his contributions to the radio electronics industry and his continued leadership, support and international acceptance in that field.

Mr. Meyerson's company was one of the pioneers in the radio amateur equipment field. His company was also one of the first to utilize transistors in producing transceivers.

His interest in amateur radio began more than 50 years ago as a hobby. He obtained his amateur license in 1928 and continues to maintain and use it. (W9GFQ — later WGFQ)

In 1936, Mr. Meyerson opened a radio parts and manufacturing business which served ham radio operators who needed parts and equipment built for them.

During World War II, Mr. Meyerson's company manufactured quartz crystals, an item he had experimented with as an amateur. The company's development of a new method for producing the crystals increased production and quality to 25,000 crystals per month. As a result Mr. Meyerson's company received the Army/Navy E citation in 1944.

Leo Meyerson, chairman of the board and founder, World Radio, Council Bluffs, holds a 1920's vintage one tube regenerative receiver known as a "Crosley Pup."

Later Mr. Meyerson divided the manufacturing and distributing business into two separate companies. In 1958, prior to the CB radio craze, one of his companies created the CB 100 — one of the first citizen's band radios on the market. This product brought the company many orders and helped stimulate the subsequent CB radio craze.

In 1960, Mr. Meyerson's son, Larry, joined the business and the company changed from a mail order parts business to a retail hi-fi and CB business. Today World Radio has 12 stores in two states.

Mr. Meyerson's list of awards, both in the industry and for numerous civic activities is lengthy. One of the most gratifying honors, according to Mr. Meyerson, was the Leo I. Meyerson Emergency Communications Center dedicated to him in 1977 by the Omaha metropolitan area ham radio enthusiasts.

He also is an honorary member of the International Handicappers Association; member AK-SAR-BEN Radio Club; Radio Club of America; Life member International Mission Radio Association; Life member and one of five board members of the Quarter Century Wireless Association and has served as chairman of the scholarship committee for QCWA since 1979; member of the International Amateur Radio Club; first vice president, National Electronics Distributors of America; Life member, American Radio Relay League and Old Timers Club.

He has received a Distinguished Service award from the National Electronics Distributors Association, and the Aztec Award from the Mexico Amateur Radio Club for good relations between the U.S. and Mexico. He is the only outsider to have received a British Honduras license-VIP GFQ.

Mr. Meyerson, who was born in Omaha, but spent his school and business career in Council Bluffs, is now retired and lives in Omaha. He and his wife have two children — Larry and Darlynn Meyerson Feliman, and seven grandchildren.

Omaha World-Herald

Omaha World-Herald, Saturday, October 4, 1980

Auto Crash Turned Bluffs Man's Music Plans Into Love Affair With the Radio

Car Crash Ended Man's Music Plans, Led to Electronics

As a teen-ager in Council Bluffs, Leo Meyerson assumed he would one day become a professional musician.

In his high school days he was a member of a dance orchestra, The Iowans. He played piano and organ accompaniment for silent movies at the Liberty Theater (now the Crest). His piano teacher thought he had a future as a concert pianist.

That, said Meyerson, ended his ambitions for a career in music. He went into radio instead and today is chairman of the board of World Radio. The Council Bluffs-headquartered firm has 12 stores in Iowa and Nebraska, making it the largest retailer of hi-fi and stereo equipment in the two states.

He is to be elected a fellow of the Radio Club of America in ceremonies in New York City Nov. 21.

Long Love Affair

Despite the tragic circumstance that prompted the change in his career plans, Meyerson hardly was an unwilling entrant in the electronics industry. He has had a lifelong love affair with radio.

"I was always awed by the mystery of radio," he said. "I'm still awed by it. I've always been fascinated with the idea that we can hear somebody who is talking from hundreds, even thousands, of miles away."

Now 69, he said his fascination developed early. He "had to be" among the first in the Bluffs to hear a radio signal, he said. He recalled tuning in the early broadcasts of pioneer station KDKA in Pittsburgh, which went on the air in 1920.

Young Meyerson's set was a one-tube regenerative receiver. He helped a fellow enthusiast, an older boy, build it.

"I listened all hours of the night," he said. "I had an overwhelming urge to pick up any new stations that went on the air. I would write to the stations for verification of their broadcasts. Eventually I learned the call letters of 200 or 300 stations."

Soon Meyerson began making his own crystal sets. When he was about 13 he built a 10-watt transmitter, following directions printed in Radio Digest magazine. "It was very crude, of course," he said. "I used my mother's bread board as a base."

Crude or not, the thing worked, and the builder put himself on the air. He played piano, spun an occasional record, and even offered listeners an occasional newscast.

There were no commercial stations then operating in Council Bluffs. "It's quite possible," said Meyerson when asked if his voice might have been the first to be transmitted by radio in the Bluffs.

However the young broadcaster's enterprise was abruptly terminated after a couple of months. "I guess the neighbors reported me," he said. "Up to then, I didn't know you had to have a license to get into the broadcasting business."

Thing Called Ham Radio

In the course of his restless search of the airwaves for new stations, Meyerson picked up a man's voice who was broadcasting from Missouri. Meyerson wrote to him and learned he was a radio amateur, a ham operator.

"I never knew until then that there was such a thing," Meyerson said. "On the card he sent me, he said, 'I hope to see you on the air one of these days.'"

That message proved to be a powerful stimulus. In March 1928, when he was 17, Meyerson did indeed go on the air as holder of ham license W0GFQ.

This new dimension to his hobby made it an all-consuming passion. The chance to talk to other operators, anytime, anywhere, staggered the imagination. "My rig was set up in a closet under the basement stairs," Meyerson said. "I wanted to be on the air all the time. My dad used to get after me. 'You've got to get some rest!' he would say.

"I got into the habit of coming home from school, doing my homework, practicing the piano and then going to bed at 7 o'clock. I would get up at 2 or 3 in the morning and get on the air."

Meyerson with home radio rig... Mystery still awesome

World-Herald/Ed Rath

Airwaves Courtship

When Leo Meyerson met and fell in love with a girl from out of town, Helen Wolinsky of St. Joseph, Mo., he bought her a receiver so he could transmit radio messages to her between visits to her home.

"I would call her by radio every noon," he said. "She couldn't talk back to me because she didn't have a transmitter. But on weekends she would go to a friend of mine in St. Joe, another ham, and then we could have a two-way conversation."

The lovers didn't mind that other hams eagerly listened in on the development of their romance, Meyerson said. Many of them sent congratulatory cards when they were married.

Meyerson operated a small grocery for a time after he gave up thought of a career in music. This was in accordance with the wishes of his father, a Russian immigrant who also was in the grocery business.

DAVID GOODMAN

I WORKED AT my dad's place, Richman Auto Parts, since I was old enough to cross the street. We lived at 2743 West Broadway and the store was across the street at 2748 West Broadway. We started out selling used parts and cars and had a wrecking yard. Prior to the war effort, most of the stuff salvaged from wrecking cars was sold to the state as what was called "riff raff," which was used to hold the banks of the creeks and rivers from flowing over. We used to haul the riff raff to different rivers and creeks in the Council Bluffs area.

It was the late 1930s. I was about nine, too small, so my job was to sit on the guys' laps and steer the trucks. I used to drive on two-lane roads -- there was no interstate and not much traffic -- as far as past Crescent, Iowa. I was their little sidekick. Being with grown-ups was how I learned how to drive a car and how to fix trucks.

Prior to World War I, my maternal grandfather Morris David Reichman lived in Poland, but his business of selling and trading horses was in Germany. When he came home on *Shabbos*, he was king of the house because he was gone all week. He emigrated to America, likely had his name changed to Richman at Ellis Island and settled in Council Bluffs. But the rest of the family got stuck in Poland because the first World War broke out. He went to the Bluffs because his sister was there, she was married to a Kubby. Harry Kubby, his sister's son, was a taxi driver in Council Bluffs. The family said he shouldn't lower himself being a taxi driver so they went into business together: Midwest Auto Parts. Then when they broke up, somewhere in the 1920s, it became M.D. Richman Auto Parts. My cousin Macy and I are named after him.

My father, Morris F. Goodman, came through Ellis Island from Poland in approximately 1922. He had relatives in Chicago who told him to be sure he got to their house in the darkness of the night because they thought he was a typical immigrant with long *payos* and they didn't want the neighbors to see that because they were dignified Americans now. He also had an uncle and cousins who lived in Omaha, that's how he eventually came to this area.

My dad left Poland to avoid being conscripted into the army. The reason I know that is because one time at the store, we used to have these people who went around collecting for the *shivas* and stuff like that. One time there was one who came in the store and wanted to talk to my dad. I told him he'd be in in about an hour, so he stuck around. My dad came in, said hello, and they started talking. They were boyhood friends who left Poland together.

My dad traveled Europe and saw all the big opera houses. Somewhere along the line he met other Jewish people trying to get to America and he connected with someone who helped him get a passport. There's a picture of him when he came to America with no *payos* and no black hat.

My dad got into the dry cleaning business on Cuming Street in Omaha. My mother Eva who was from Council Bluffs went to a business college in the Bluffs, Boyle's College, then got a job working for my father as a bookkeeper. They fell in love and married. My mom Americanized my dad. "Eat Milky Ways," she said, I don't know. Both came from different parts of Poland. Mom near the German border, Dad near the Czech border. Mom always complained about the fact that Dad couldn't pronounce vowels, she'd tease him on that. When Ma's father, who owned Richman Auto Parts, became sick (he passed away in May of 1929), they didn't know what to do with the business, so they got my father to come over from Omaha and run the business.

I was born on September 8th, 1929. As a kid, I'd sweep the floor and roll tires back and forth at the store. I also used to demount tires from the wheels, which was all a manual job at that time. I helped the guys clean up their tools and stuff. My dad bought a couple of places that went bankrupt and they had a lot of stuff all over the place. It was so bad that if you didn't watch out, you'd trip. The guys who worked at my dad's place were characters. All in their teens, maybe in their twenties. At that time, prior to the war effort, jobs were hard to find; most guys were earning like $1 day at our place. Once in a while, the guys would get angry and put me inside a pile of tires stacked to the ceiling. I was eight-years-old and trying to get attention and get in the way. It's a good memory, just getting in trouble, I guess. Sometimes one of the guy's girlfriend, Jessie, would take my younger brother Mickey, my older sister Babette and me down to Lake Manawa to go swimming. That's how we learned how to swim. They just threw you in the water and you'd get a mouthful of water.

We grew up on the wrong side of the tracks, in the west end of Council Bluffs which was the old river bed. When the river overflowed in the spring, that whole area was under water, so they called us "River Rats." Ma was a saver, very resourceful. She learned how to darn stockings, which is a way of mending socks, and she always had to keep the house clean; that was her biggest enjoyment. She'd mop the kitchen floor and, instead of us taking our shoes off, she'd put newspapers on top of it so we wouldn't get the floor dirty.

I talked to my high school buddies in later years. "Were we aware of how bad things were?" No. We didn't know any better. We didn't have to worry about what clothes we were going to wear because we wore the same ones constantly. Before Ma got a washing machine, she cleaned clothes by hand. Rub-a-dub in the tub.

There were very few Jewish families on the west end of Council Bluffs. I think Ben Kubby lived on 5th Avenue, and he took my sister, brother and me to Sunday school with his son Bob. We were a minority, being Jewish. Most of the areas in Council Bluffs were non-Jewish and, therefore, if anything happened, we were the blame for everything. As kids, we were picked on. Not so much in school but mostly on the streets. Today, they call them bullies.

Growing up, the thing is, we knew everybody. I could not go too many places without getting the report the next day of my dad knowing where I was. One time I was stopped by the police and they said:

"Where you going?"

"I'm going home," I said.

"Damn good place for ya."

My mom Eva was one of three Richman girls (Eudice, Eva and Rosalie) who, when they came here after WWI, lied about their ages so they could get into Second Avenue Grade School to learn English. My Aunt Eudice, the oldest, made high school in a year-and-a-half. In fact, Aloysius Bump one of my professors at T.J., Thomas Jefferson High School, came to me one time and said, "Goodman (he always used his finger as a pointer), I'll tell ya one thing, ya ain't as good as your aunt was."

Our social sphere was mostly non-Jews because most of my time was spent across the street in the store; and the other Jewish kids went to a different high school, A.L. When my sister Babette went to T.J. there was only one other Jewish girl in her class, Eleanor Passer. Eleanor's father was in the grocery business, Joe Passer. When I went to T.J., there was Jerry Flatowicz, the Fried boys, Bill and Orville and their cousin Shirley Fried. They're gone. Then Jack and Milt Brown, they're both gone. Jack was a famous attorney in Phoenix, Milt was…I think he was in Des Moines. I think there were at least five families on the west end that had grocery stores: The Maltzes, the Meyersons, the Vilsacks, the Cohns and another family at about 34th and Broadway whose daughter went to T.J. with my sister Babette.

A Jewish organization I belonged to was AZA. We met in an apartment complex that Joe Katelman bought and donated to the Jewish Community Center on 8th Street. Kenny Sacks was mostly in charge of getting AZA off the ground. He used to call me when they'd have meetings, and I went occasionally. They wanted to start a Boy Scout deal at the *shul*, so they called Dad up and said, "Bring your boys up." So we went up, but that didn't take off.

A specific memory I have of our home was when we prepared for *Pesach*. We used to go with Dad to the meat market in Omaha on North 24th Street. And our fish would come out of the Missouri River, carp mostly. Captain Frank had his one-room shack on the river, he'd be out there with his nets fishing. The fish he caught were put into big traps by the dock. The Captain was always happy to see us. We'd get a couple fish, take them home, put water in the bathtub and throw the fish in. Then Ma would pull them out and make us clean the bathtub up because it was filthy. Then she'd cut them up and make gefilte fish. The process of grinding them up was something else. We had a hand grinder, every once in a while pieces of fish would flip onto the floor or the grinder would slip off the counter. In the 1970s, I bought Ma an electric grinder.

The synagogue was very active in the 1940s and 1950s and became more active because of kids having Bar and Bat Mitzvahs. I went to *shul* with my dad on High Holidays. It was old-school with a *bimah* in front, benches around the *bimah*, women and kids upstairs. I did not have a Bar Mitzvah; but in the 1960s my daughter Devra and son Douglas had theirs there. At synagogue, they would put on plays and my mom would always be one of the actors. Maynard Telpner's mother would always direct them. She was a happy, gregarious and outspoken individual. My mother and dad both were in a club that did Yiddish plays at the Omaha JCC at 20th and Dodge.

In approximately 1947, I started working with my dad after high school. I did buying and selling. I had somebody else sweep the floor. During WWII, you couldn't buy cars for salvage because everything was pretty tight, so we started selling new and rebuilt parts. Because of the price of commodities of tin and iron, the market was very low on it.

We didn't make as much money wrecking cars for salvage parts or selling the iron. When the war broke out, everything went up in price because of demand. We sold everything we could; $100 in sales was a good day. Tires were $5 or $7 each, everything was bargain-able at that time. Rubber was at a premium, everything was on an allotment basis from manufacturer. The war helped our business.

I used to call on an account that had a body shop in the east end of town. Red Molgard, the owner, used to call me "Jew Boy." One time, there was another Jewish man in the shop and heard Red call me "Jew Boy." He said to me, "Do you know what he's calling you?" and I said, "I don't care what he calls me as long as he gives me the business." I did whatever I needed to do to get business.

In 1967, we ran out of room so we built a new store about 30 feet east of the old store. We were bought out in September 1998 by Car Quest which was buying up car part stores. The original plan of the Federal Urban Renewal Program in the 1970s was to build behind the businesses on Broadway, but it didn't develop that way. They bought out all of the businesses on Broadway uptown. Many owners didn't re-invest in the business. They just left. They were first- or second-generation and they sold out. We never saw them again. I was the last Jewish-owned business in Council Bluffs.

In the 1970s, I was co-chairman of the cemetery. They wanted somebody younger to help with the cemetery because Abe Katelman had too much to do. He had papers of who-did-what, who was buried where, who bought what plots…all on scrap paper. He had the whole thing, and I was supposed to take it over from him. When he passed away, we held a fundraiser and contacted people who had relatives buried in the Bikur Cholim section of the cemetery. The funds raised were put into a trust at the Council Bluffs Savings Bank that was to be used for perpetual care of the cemetery. Maynard Telpner was named head of the cemetery committee.

The cemetery is so nice, peaceful and quiet. My maternal grandparents Rivke and Morris David Richman are buried in the Bikur Cholim section, as are my parents, Eva and Morris Goodman, my brother *Yankl*

Richman Auto Parts in Council Bluffs

(Jerome Byron Goodman; we called him Mickey because Mickey Mouse was born when he was little) and also my brother-in-law Seymour Martin Blaug. We attend services there twice a year. On Memorial Day Patty Nogg organizes a service and there is one between the High Holidays, usually on the Sunday before Yom Kippur. I go to honor my brother and brother-in-law who served in World War II.

Being charitable has been a value in my family for many years. Growing up, there were rabbis from Israel who came to our store to solicit funds for *Yeshivas* or orphanages. They had lists of places where they could go to get money and my dad was always on the list. When he passed away, I inherited the privilege. I can remember when Dad would give them a car and driver so they could solicit, one of the nice cars he had around. As long as it ran, they didn't care; all they wanted was to go out and collect money to give back to the *Yeshivas*.

In the 1960s and 1970s, Sam Sacks and Sam Saltzman used to come around to our store to collect funds for the *shul*. My dad was always good about giving, so they figured if he could do it, I could do it. There were collectors from *Yeshivas* who traveled from the east to west coast. There were also people who classified themselves as being Jewish or out of luck. They needed funds, a job or came to Council Bluffs and got sick. I'd listen to their stories and give them a check. The *shul* set up a checking account for me so I could distribute funds to these various people.

The thing is, there's an obligation you owe to the community and you owe yourself because you want to be part of the community. It was about dedication, primarily. My close friend Sam Bittner encouraged me to contribute to the *shul*, and he did the same. Jews helping Jews, same way my dad did.

166. Grandma and Grandpa Richman with Rosalie, Eva and Rochelle's mom Udis
167. David 's father, Morris
168. David Goodman, 1929

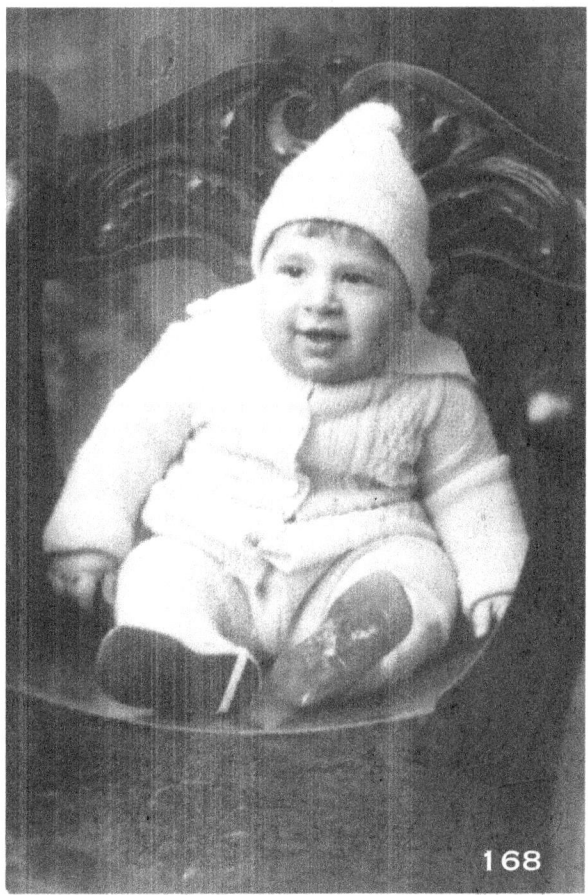

D. GOODMAN | 337

David with son Douglas

David Goodman

DON NOGG

Joey: Don, let's start by talking about your dad.

Don: My dad was Mr. Council Bluffs. He was the kind of guy who, if you needed help, you came to Nate Nogg. If he didn't have enough money himself, he'd get you some money, help you out; he'd try to save your business. That's who he was. He was always doing, active in everything: B'nai Brith, in the little JCC they had, he was on the board of the synagogue in Council Bluffs, he started the Dr. Sher Home for the Aged which was the forerunner of the Blumkin Home. 52nd, just north of Ames.

Dad's big thing was the Council Bluffs Grocers and Butchers Association, he was secretary for 26 years. Why? He knew the grocery business, all the grocers, he was a bright, sharp guy and he needed the extra money. Also, he was Secretary of the Iowa Grocers and Butchers Association. My grandparents had a grocery store on 16th and Broadway, I imagine it was just called Nogg Grocery. They originally lived upstairs. Because of that, he knew so many people in the grocery business. When they redid Bayliss Park, there is an area with plaques on the ground honoring organizations and people in them. Lloyd Krasne, who had been a grocer most of his life in Council Bluffs and was very involved in the Grocers and Butchers Association, said, "I said to the board, we're going to donate there, but the name on the plaque is going to be Nate Nogg because there wouldn't be a Council Bluffs Food Dealers Association –– as it was later named –– if it weren't for him."

Again, he helped out everybody. There was a guy called Harry Kulakofsky in Omaha, and he and his brother owned the big grocery store there, Central Market. Harry got a speeding ticket in Council Bluffs once and was real mad about it. So my dad said, "I'll see what I can do," and he went down to the police station and said to the Police Chief, "Joe/Bill/Fred (whatever his name is), you gave a ticket to

Harry Kulakofsky. Can we get that taken care of?" and he says, "Nate, I can't do that. It's already in the file...I'll tell you what. I gotta go to the bathroom now, and you'll be alone in here." So he left, Dad found it, and tore it up. That's the relationship he had there.

Joey: He sounds terrific! He was born where?

Don: *Kamenets-Podolsk*, in what is now the Ukraine. Whether he was actually born in town or a *shtetl* near town, I have no way of knowing.

Joey: What were the circumstances that made him emigrate?

Don: His father *Moshe*, who became Morris here, came to Council Bluffs before Dad was born. He had a sister *Gittel* who was already in the Bluffs and had been married in the old country, of course. Her husband, *Yeshaia* Cherniss, had relatives in Council Bluffs. He got a job in the stockyards, sent a little money home regularly 'til there was enough. No idea how they came. My dad was only about a year-and-a-half or two-years-old. He didn't know when he was born.

First of all, if they used the local calendar, they used the Julian Calendar there rather than the Gregorian. Secondly, they also used a Jewish calendar, and thirdly, they don't pay attention to dates! "When were you born?" "He was born six days after *Pesach*, four days after *Shabbos*, the day after the cow died!" It just wasn't important! You think they had big birthday parties for everyone in the neighborhood? I don't think so. He had an older sister who died there and an older brother, Sam, so my *Bubbe* –– my grandmother Belle –– and the two boys somehow, with the money *Zada*, my grandfather, sent over, left there.

I have no idea how they came. Did they catch a ship in Odessa? Did they get up to Danzig? Bremen? Nobody knows. Doesn't make a difference. But I do know they came in through Baltimore rather than New York, and there are no records because there was a fire in Baltimore and all the immigration records from about 1890 to 1906 were destroyed. Had no accent, because he was a little child when they came over.

Joey: Did his father come over for economic opportunities or was he fleeing pogroms?

Don: Probably both. That was the beginning of the big immigration. My grandfather had to have come in about 1896, lived in Omaha, but I think by first or second grade my dad was in Council Bluffs. He grew up there –– he was a Council Bluffs kid. As an adult, when he first started working, he worked in grocery stores. He became an accountant, he was always very good with figures and he traveled around helping to keep books for a lot of people. For Abe Baker, who started Baker Supermarkets. Abe had a store in Walnut, Iowa and Dad and he became good friends. He worked for the Newman Brothers in their little store in Benson called Hinky-Dinky, which turned into a big chain all through the midwest. He worked for a while for a place called Omaha Paper and Notion Company. A guy named Joe Cohn ran it. Joe Cohn had only one salesman. Everything was small in those days…the salesman was a Jewish guy as a matter of fact, Frank Hollander, who got drafted during WWI. My dad was there keeping books. Frank didn't have a salesman anymore, so he said to my dad, "How'd you like to be a paper salesman?" My dad says, "I don't know about selling paper." "You'll make more money." "OK." So he goes out and tries it but it didn't work because pretty soon he got drafted also.

After the war, in 1918…he drifted. He worked in grocery stores, he did whatever he could. He and mother got married in 1922 and, in 1923, just after my brother Alvin was born, he and a brother-in-law of his bought a store from one of the Predmestkys (the Pred family in Omaha) and they moved out to Plainview, Nebraska. My uncle and aunt, newlyweds with no children, and my folks with an infant son, moved out there and ran this store. Dad said he learned how to play pitch, the card game, there because they made the mistake of putting in Hart Schaffner & Marx clothes, business suits, which was the big thing in those days; and all those farmers out there wanted was bib overalls! So they sat around doing nothing and went broke in a year.

He came back to Omaha and worked for Max Cohn who had a grocery store on 30th and Avenue B in the Bluffs, and managed the store for him. He said to my uncle Ernie, his younger brother who was working as a salesman for Swift and Company, the packing plant, "Let's start a paper business. I know a little bit about it." Cost nothing to get started. That was 1925. By 1927, they were out of business. Then in a snowstorm, Ernie lost sight in one eye and went to Houston to work for a paper company. Again, Dad's drifting. Max Cohn had a brother-in-law, Sam Bubb, Lloyd Krasne's father-in-law. Everybody was related. The two of them were partners who decided to open a third store, and Dad ran the third store…and it didn't last. In 1930, he writes my uncle in Houston, "Come on back, we'll do it again."

Joey: Talk about perseverance! What was small-town Jewish life like?

Don: It was a very tight-knit community. And as the Council Bluffs Jewish community slowly moved to Omaha, we were even more connected. There was always a group -- what's it called? -- that helped out poor people financially in any way they could. My dad's father was president of B'nai Israel probably in the 1920s. My dad became a Bar Mitzvah there in 1910. I was sent to *cheder* (Hebrew school). I don't remember much about it, we sat outside and played until Rabbi Cassel told us to come in.

I do remember going to services on *Shabbos*, a typical old-world Orthodox synagogue. All the men davened at their own speed, women were up in the *mechitza* and talked, the kids ran around…We had a president who followed my *Zada*, Shy Shyken. He'd stand up there and pound on the lecturn and yell in Yiddish, "*Kinder schweig!*" "Children, be quiet!" Then do a short little sermonette in *Yiddish*. Almost all Jews lived in the east end of Council Bluffs, where the synagogue was. The Noggs and a few other families lived in the west end. It was a long way in those days, 32nd Street to 6th Street, probably three miles. If Dad was around, we drove. If he wasn't, we took the street car.

I used to take Dad, when he got old, to lunch every Thursday. We'd bring him down to the office to try to keep him busy and keep my mother happy. Tuesdays my brother took him to lunch, Thursdays I took him. He always wanted to go to Council Bluffs. That's where his heart was. So we would go to the Bluffs and talk about all kinds of things, and I remember once he started figuring how many Jewish families there were there in, say, in the 1932 to 1940 era. He always came up with about 125 families. Now…that doesn't mean the Krasne family or the Meyerson family or the Yudelson family. That means the Lawrence Krasne family, the Millard Krasne family and so on. A lot of interrelationships. You never dated a Swedish girl, you didn't go out with an Irish guy. You only dated Jews! My dad dated a girl from Omaha who became my mother.

Joey: Was she Jewish?

Don: Very! Her name was a good, old-fashioned Jewish name: Brown.

Joey: Clearly growing up Jewish in Council Bluffs had a big impact on your life.

Don: There's an old saying, "You can get the boy out of Council Bluffs, but you can't take Council Bluffs out of the boy." I feel very Council Bluffs. My very first friends were Council Bluffs. My very first…Jewish-ness was Council Bluffs. My grandparents lived there and my Dad's brother Leo who wasn't married yet lived, with his parents; so I knew him well. My folks owned a lot in a comparatively new area called Keeline, where many Jewish families lived. That's where he thought he'd build. My parents talked and talked about it and finally decided to sell the lot and buy and build in Omaha. His business was in Omaha, his brother and most of their friends lived there, plus my brother Alvin was one of only two Jews at T.J. High School and my mother was scared to death that he'd end up marrying a non-Jew. "Get him into school with Jewish girls." While they were deciding, we lived in the Chieftain Hotel which was the hotel in the Bluffs, for 13 months! Downtown Council Bluffs. Wonderful thing for a kid. Why? The bellboys I got friendly with. No automatic elevators in those days, they had elevator operators and they'd let me run the elevator!

Once in a great while, when my folks went out, I could go to the coffee shop for dinner like a rich person! Across the street from the hotel was a little one square block park, Bayliss Park, and across from that was the Council Bluffs Public Library, and I discovered the library. I fell in love with the library, I fell in love with the librarians. The gal who was at that time the reference librarian, the number two person, Ms. Green would, on cold winter nights, invite me over to her apartment on Sixth and Washington. Dad would take me over there, she'd make cocoa, and we'd sit and talk. My field was geography so I spent a lot of time in the reference department, and we'd talk geography, history or all the stuff I loved.

Joey: The Jewish-ness and how you feel very Council Bluffs, what does that mean to you?

Don: First of all, my wife Ozzie and I don't have many close friends left at our age and they're not from the Bluffs. We have two couples who we're the closest with. Three of them are from Omaha and the fourth is from Winnipeg, so there's no connection there. I went to the University of Colorado at Boulder. We had a fraternity reunion, ZBT, about 10 years ago. Great. And we had a reunion of a bunch of guys I lived with. That's not what it is in Council Bluffs. I'll have lunch tomorrow at Village Inn on 78th and Dodge like we have been doing every Thursday for years and years -- with Harold Bernstein, Sol Kutler and that's all now because my brother Alvin used to be there and he died. But at least there were four of us out of the 12 who came from Council Bluffs. And it used to drive others crazy because what would we talk about? Council Bluffs.

Joey: You talked about your fraternity and you were comparing the fraternity reunion vs. the Council Bluffs reunion every Thursday. It's almost like in Council Bluffs, you had your own fraternity and still do.

Don: Maybe so. I feel for Council Bluffs as well as the people in Council Bluffs. I rode my bike up in the hills. Every summer we'd have a couple picnics in Fairmont Park, the family. I don't know…the Bluffs was…it was just part of me. *Cheder* is where I learned to read Hebrew; that's where I learned to *daven*.

Joey: Is that where you met Sol and Harold?

Don: Harold's nine years older than I am. I was born February 17, 1930. I got to know him either as a kid when I'd go with my dad to the Peoples Store or when I started in the company and called on customers. He was a customer, he had the hardware department at the Peoples Store because his mother was a Krasne.

Joey: I swear, every one's a Krasne. I think I'm a Krasne!

Don: Don't forget, I knew a lot of these people through my brother Alvin, who was about two years younger than Harold. He was the same age as Yale Gotsdiner and they were friendly. They all knew each other, all belonged to AZA. I remember some parties at our house. I remember them coming over and picking on me! They're 16-year-old kids and here's a nine-year-old! They'd like to knock me down, sit on me and tickle me! But Sol lived in a completely different milieu because age-wise he's between Harold and me. Three or four years doesn't mean anything now, but in your teens it means a lot!

Joey: Do they still knock you down and tickle you?

Don: No, I'm too big now!

Joey: You mentioned interrelationships. What others do you recall?

Don: Thursday afternoon was probably when we would go down to my grandparents' house in Council Bluffs. Marsha Tepperman, married name Kushner, her father bought my grandfather's grocery store, which is right across the street from my grandparents' house. So I grew up very friendly with her. I have wonderful memories of that. Incidentally, the Grocers and Butcher's association had a national convention every year and the local chapter would send my folks. That was their vacation every year. Well, what do you do? They'd send my brother over to the grandparents' in Omaha and send me over to my dad's parents in Council Bluffs. I remember it so well because I slept with my unmarried uncle!

We used to have *Pesach* at their house after my grandmother died and my Omaha grandparents would come, too. I remember so well that my mother's father and my father's mother would sit on the porch and speak Russian to each other. Nobody else remembered Russian. I thought it was wonderful they were speaking something that I had no idea what they were saying. *Pesach* included cousins, aunts, uncles... It was set up with a big dining room table where the adults sat, and then there was a smaller table at the front end, and then a card table where the little kids sat. And I probably tasted wine for the first time in my life then, and the food never stopped! Brisket, always chicken too, *tzimmis*, gefilte fish and *knaidlach* (matzo balls).

Aunt Mary never sat down, she served! And the service -- the only part of the service anybody took part in -- when we made *Kiddush*, everybody made *Kiddush*. When you did *hamotzi* over the matzoh, everybody made *hamotzi*. And one of the kids would do the four questions. That was it. Other than that it was a social evening with my grandfather and great uncle Joe sitting at the head of the table going through the entire *Hagaddah* to themselves, every word. Standard. When I got married and went to my first *Seder* at my Orthodox Rabbi father-in-law's house, I wondered, "What the hell?" It was such a pleasure. Everybody took part. He and my brother-in-law would go through everything, but very fast. And then they'd break up and ask questions and have conversations. It was so much different and so much better.

Joey: Did your family speak Yiddish in the house?

Don: My mother spoke a very good Yiddish, Dad fair. All of the men my grandfather knew spoke English because they were in business; they had to. My grandmother in Council Bluffs, Belle, spoke English because she worked in the grocery store with him. But she had a lot of old immigrant Jewish friends who never learned to speak English. All four of my grandparents spoke English, accented of course. You can't come here as an adult and not speak English with an accent.

Joey: You'll never hear that again.

Don: You're right. My mother didn't even like to speak Yiddish with my dad because according to my father-in-law who really knew it, my mother spoke a very grammatically correct Yiddish. Dad didn't, he spoke peasant Yiddish. She was Lithuanian, and just as basic English is London, basic Yiddish was Lithuania. If something wasn't bad, my mother always said, "It's not so *g'ferlach*."

Joey: What was your mother like?

Don: My mother had a baby grand piano and we'd sit around and listen while she played. Dad, because he was a salesman, had to travel in the country. When I was born for instance, my dad was in Logan, IA calling on customers! Did you know my mother was able to have me anyway?

Joey: Wonder Woman!

Don: And she didn't go to the grocery store very often because she didn't have to. My mother would pick up the phone and call Joe Gotsdiner, Yale's father. 34th and Broadway, so that was two-and-a-half blocks from us. She'd say, "Joe, Ruth calling.

I need a box of salt, six white potatoes and a head of lettuce -- make sure you pick out a good head of lettuce -- some calf's liver and whatever the hell else." Then she hangs up and you wait. An hour later, here comes a kid to the door delivering two or three boxes to ya! Bread, milk and ice? You didn't buy those at the store. Robert's or Alamito Dairy were the only ones who delivered. They came by your house every day; you had a box out by the back porch. If you wanted something special, "I'd like some cottage cheese or a pint of ice cream today," you put a note in there. We used to stop at the Kosher butcher, Diamond Butcher, in Council Bluffs one Thursday every month. When Dad called on customers in Woodbine, IA, he'd stop there first because the Smeerins who lived in Woodbine kept kosher. And Dad would pick up their kosher meat and take it out to them.

Joey: Another example of your dad being a *mensch*.

Don: Mm-hmm. And every little town had a Jew or two in it. I don't remember this because it's before my time, but Dad said there was a *minyan* in Missouri Valley. Now there's not a *minyan* in Council Bluffs. I don't think there are ten Jews there.

Joey: Not even a *minyan* in Council Bluffs and when you were there there were 125 families at least.

Don: It was crowded there on the High Holy days. And we didn't call it *shul* because there they had basically Romanians, Ukrainians… we called it *shiel*. The pronunciation of Yiddish is different in other languages. Ever been to Europe? In the South of France, they speak French differently than the North. A good, high German speaker from Bavaria has a hard time understanding the German in other places.

Joey: Like Deep Brooklyn vs. Greenwich, CT.

Don: Yes. And we say *kigel*, not kugel.

Joey: Don, you're a fun guy, what made you laugh back then?

Don: I learned to laugh at myself. Growing up, I was short and fat with big thick glasses and just the epitome of a word that hadn't been invented yet: nerd. I was only 5'6" when I was a senior in high school and I carried that picture of me into my 50s and 60s. So here I am in school as a short, fat, dumpy kid. I wasn't smarter than the other kids, but I had a lot more knowledge.

Joey: Very studious?

Don: Yes. I always liked to say, I don't know how to define "smart." I wasn't necessarily smarter than the other kids, but I knew a lot more things. Jeanine Frye and I used to win every spelling bee. So here I am, the nerd and the only Jew in school, Franklin grade school. The only Jew they ever saw. Most of them I got along with just fine, and with some, they just didn't like Jews. So I learned how to protect myself: be funny and laugh at yourself.

Joey: That's how you survived.

Don: And I survived just fine.

169. Fifth grade class at Franklin School of Council Bluffs in 1940. Don Nogg is the fourth boy from the right in the top row

170. Don Nogg

PATTY LEE NOGG

PARKED IN A booth at Christy Creme -- Council Bluffs's still-hopping hangout open since 1954 -- Patty noshes on extra-crispy crinkle fries (the only way to order them, she swears). It is easy to imagine Patty Lee in the same spot 50 years ago: *kibibtzing* with friends, eating a chocolate-dipped vanilla cone and sporting a Beatles sweatshirt. Today, she's a Council Bluffs girl-turned-unofficial ambassador for Christy Creme and the place she will always call home.

"I live in Omaha, but my heart is in my hometown," she says. "I am fiercely loyal to Council Bluffs and I loved growing up there. Growing up in the Bluffs honestly shaped the person I am today. You couldn't lose yourself in the Jewish community. Everybody cared for each other because we were so small. People can say anything they want about the Bluffs but they'll find out they're talking to the wrong person," she laughs.

Those who know Patty (who doesn't?) are aware she can make an otherwise mundane event a celebration. A Patty Party. Her Council Bluffs tour, with which she has honored countless friends, was no exception for a certain writer. On a blue-skied morning, we rounded the corner past Jennie Edmundson Hospital into the Kenmore/Keeline neighborhood, the one-time enclave for many Jewish families, and stopped at her alma mater as she waxed nostalgic.

"Hoover Elementary did not have a big cafeteria, so if you lived less than a certain distance away (we lived at 334 Kenmore) you had to go home for lunch. We were called Hoover Hikers! My mom would pick us up, then we'd walk back to school. After school, we'd stop at Johnson's Pharmacy on the way home. They had an array of penny candy, I loved peanut butter Kits. They came in a little blocky rectangle and you opened the outside and there were three or four little chewy candies inside. Those were my fave."

Next stop? 118 Plattner, a brown brick fourplex where Patty, born April 2, 1953, lived until about age two with her parents Betty and Sy, older sister Judy and older brother Richard. "Richie," as he was called when he was a little boy, morphed into Pete in junior high or high school when he got a parakeet, named him Pete, and friends made sure the name stuck.

Two streets up the hill from the apartment, Patty parked in front of what was Miss Margaret's Preschool, located in a house that still stands. "There were only about six of us in the class, tiny. I was at Starbucks one day last summer and saw a picture of my preschool class in the *Omaha World-Herald's* "From the Archives" section. Here I am with my bangs two fingers above my eyebrows. I cried with every haircut! Miss Margaret's assistant, we called her Baba, made my favorite snack. She called them button cookies: graham crackers with an M&M in the middle!"

Snacks aside, nothing made Patty feel more joy than spending time with two of her favorite people: her grandparents Anne and Harry Cohen. "I would often go with them to Friday night services at *shul* and that was the beginning of my love for older people. I just loved being with my grandparents' friends. Throughout my life, I think I've had better relationships with older people and small children, better than my peers," she laughs. "All I have to do is think of Friday night and I think of having tea after services at the *Oneg Shabbat* and all of these people who, of course, loved seeing me with my grandparents. That was a special thing."

Anne (née Siegel) and her family emigrated to Omaha from *Bialystock*, which, Patty says, was either a town or a region in Russia at the time. "My grandmother was just sweet, so loving. When I was growing up, she had *Shabbat* dinner every Friday night." Tragically, Anne and Harry's son Irving, a fun-loving guy known for his fraternity pranks, was a World War II pilot whose plane was shot down. He went missing in action.

"Maybe it was after losing her son in the war, but she was kind of a nervous woman. My sister, brother, and I called her 'Grandma Worry.' My cousin Norman Rips tells the story about when my brother Pete and our cousins were having a family dinner at Highland Country Club -- which was built because Jews couldn't get into other clubs -- Pete was swimming in the pool and my grandmother thought he was drowning and ran into the pool fully clothed to, quote, "'save him,'" she laughs.

"On a tastier note, she was a wonderful cook; she made delicious *mandel* bread and poppy seed cookies. We loved the dough and my sister and I would run by and grab a handful of dough and she would yell at us. Her poppy seed or "*mohn* cookies" I really loved. Grandma didn't have a written recipe; so after I was married, I was on the hunt to replicate these cookies because they evoked such fond memories and were delicious. I was in a dentist's office and there was a recipe in *Family Circle* magazine for poppy seed cookies that I adapted a little bit and became my signature recipe, but they aren't exactly the same. My grandmother's were a little less buttery. For Bar and Bat Mitzvahs, I'm always asked to bring my poppy seed cookies."

Harry Cohen –– a.k.a. surrogate Grandpa to local Jewish kids –– grew up in Council Bluffs. His father David, a peddler, rode a horse and buggy through Iowa towns hawking his wares. Harry opened Iowa Clothes Shop in 1919 at 536 West Broadway. Its original façade read, "Correct Dress For Men & Young Men." Harry invited Patty's dad Si into the family business and in 1970, he brought in Pete. In 1974, when Harry passed away, Pete became owner. "I adored my older brother. He went to Arizona State and I followed him. He was just my big brother."

Community consensus? Harry was a mensch. "Much of his clientele were Iowa farmers who would come in after a good season and he would remember the names of their family. 'How's so-and-so?' But the story I think influenced how I live my life is that when the servicemen came back to the Bluffs after the war, he would give them a suit and say, 'Pay me when you can,' because they needed clothes to interview for a job. So many people have told me that story, 'Pay me when you can.'"

Patty worked in the family business at 15 or 16 during busy times, like Christmas and during the summer when the city sponsored "Crazy Days," a big sale day when stores set up tables outside. Through men's shirts and down the stairs were farmers' work clothes plus a shoe department. "Behind the stairs was my grandfather's desk. That's where all the kids knew they could get a piece of Double Bubble gum," she laughs. "You never knew whether he was kidding or not. He had a very cute sense of humor." Every family member worked at Iowa Clothes at some point in their lives. Patty recalls a story her cousin Norman Rips shared. "In his sales technique, he would show this shirt to a customer and say emphatically, 'Oh, this is the finest shirt, it's made from Rips cloth!'" she laughs. "I have great memories of him. The children in the Bluffs loved him. As a little girl, during High Holiday services, my grandfather who had false teeth would sit in front of us, turn around and stick out his teeth! They looked like they were going to fall out of his mouth and the children would laugh hysterically and all of the kids would get in trouble for laughing. He was a great, great guy.

"He could have been a bitter man after losing his own son in the war, but he was just a really good person." Downstairs at the synagogue in Council Bluffs is the Irving Cohen Lodge, dedicated by B'nai B'rith, where a photograph of Irving in uniform is displayed. "I found a diary that my grandmother started in November, 1944. It was written during the year Irving went missing in action. She talked about the most mundane things. She ran a small women's section in the store, so she talked about going into work. They were very social, played cards, had friends over, even during the week, so she wrote about that. Every entry in the diary would end with a prayer: 'Please God, bring our son home to us.'"

When Patty's mom Betty died, her husband Buddy gave her a box of memorabilia full of letters by the bundle: letters written by Anne and Harry to and from Irving when he was either in pilot's training or overseas, and letters written to Anne from other mothers in Irving's battalion. "I heard more stories from Harold Bernstein, his best friend, than from my family. I think it was just too painful. Gene Telpner, Maynard's brother, told me he heard Irving's parachute didn't open and maybe he was the last out of the plane before the crash. I sure wish I had asked more questions when my grandparents were alive."

B'nai Israel was Patty's second home. "When I was really little, there was Rabbi Korb. His English wasn't so good. My sister tells the story…my sister was a troublemaker, I was the goody two-shoes. She and Gail Krasne were in kahootz; they were naughty girls," she laughs. "Not really bad, just typical. I know my brother went to Sunday school and had a Bar Mitzvah, I don't know if he was a troublemaker or not; he was five years older. But Judy was a troublemaker, and she would do this imitation of Rabbi Korb where he would point to the kids making trouble or laughing and say, 'YOU. YOU DOOD IT!' He left and then I remember Rabbi Karzen and his wife Ruby, the *Rebettzin*. I think that was the first time I heard that word. When he left for a better job in Chicago, I think, that was the beginning of the end of the vibrant Jewish life in the Bluffs."

As Jewish life faded, Patty's discomfort increased. Being singled out as a Jew during a time where peer status was paramount became a woeful reminder she was a minority. "I think sixth-grade was the first year six or seven of us had to ride a bus to Beth Israel in Omaha. "I didn't mind it so much at that age. But when I got to seventh grade, it was embarrassing being picked up by a bus. All I wanted to do was quit."

As it turns out, when Patty's children attended Hebrew School, she took refresher courses at the JCC in Omaha and had an adult Bat Mitzvah at 35. She led Tot Shabbat at Beth El and taught preschool and Judaic music at the JCC. What's it like going from Hebrew school drop-out to gung-ho educator? "It's shocking," she says. "And it's shocking that I married a Jewish guy, truly," she says, referring to her husband Steve. "But I always hoped deep in my heart that I would fall in love with a Jewish man."

Rolling through the old neighborhood was like watching a black-and-white slideshow, rapid-fire clips of a girlhood filled with friends and neighbors who did not share DNA, but no matter. "The Jewish community was like one big family. Our neighborhood was idyllic, what you wish for your own kids now. We didn't lock our doors. It was safe. What I remember most is playing outside every night, and the older kids in the neighborhood got games together: kick the can, sardines, capture the flag with the street as the separation. It was wonderful growing up in that atmosphere at that time."

Unlike today, parents have their kids' whereabouts down to a science (there is even a cellphone app which tracks their location), Patty and her pals would walk 20 minutes to downtown Council Bluffs on a Saturday and ricochet around Broadway, shopping at department stores like the Peoples Store, Beno's and Joe Smith's. "Everybody knew everybody. I'd just say my name and say 'Charge it.' When I got my driver's license, we cruised Broadway just like in movies from the '60s. During my brother's time, the cool thing for kids to do was drive through Ewald's to see who was there."

As we inched up Keeline and around Kenmore Avenue, past manicured lawns and well-kept 1950s and 1960s-style homes where Patty's house was located, she recalled a flurry of names: the Suvalskys, the Rudermans, the Finkels, the Mashbeins, the Bernsteins. Rounding Kenmore Circle, we stopped at Kenny and Velma Sacks's home. "I spent more days playing school with Susan and Karen Sacks. They were the first people I babysat for. To this day, they're like little sisters to me. If I wasn't playing school at the Sacks's, I would be playing Little House on the Prairie with Marti Suvalsky."

"Jeri Ruderman, Leah Ball and I had a little summer camp in my backyard. We also advertised our babysitting services by sending out a postcard to families with young children and wrote a poem advertising what we offered. It said something like, 'Summer winter, spring or fall, all you have to do is call.' That's where I developed my love for kids and playing school. On the day of Kennedy's funeral, there was no school and I was just on the cusp of realizing the gravity. Instead of watching the funeral all day, I was playing school in the Sacks's basement. Mrs. Jensen, my favorite teacher, gave me old books to play school with. She had a permanent like ladies used to get, her hair was that blue-gray color and she smelled of baby powder."

A secret that still gets Patty giddy: Kenny was supposed to walk her home six houses away, but it didn't go to plan. "When I saw Camelot for the first time, it reminded me of Kenny. He wouldn't walk me all the way; he told me to yell when I got to my door. It reminds me of King Arthur: "Runnn boy runnn!" she laughs. "Velma never knew, I told her years later."

Across the street from Patty's house lived Alice and Vic Mashbein whose daughter Robin is still Patty's dear friend. "Alice always had a bowl of jelly beans. I'd walk through their garage because it was always open. They had a little eating bar in between the den and kitchen. I'd talk to Alice and eat jelly beans." One memory, however, still makes Patty bitter. "Where the triangle meets at Kenmore and Keeline, more often the boys got to play in the bigger and better park –– we called it The Boy's Park –– while the girls were relegated to the smaller park," she laughs.

Fun factoid: Mayor Joe Katelman lived on Kenmore and when it would snow, so theirs would be one of the first streets to get plowed.

We rounded the corner by The Bayliss Park and parked in front of a limestone ranch set on a hill. Number 405. Anne and Harry Cohen's house. As if on cue, a man working in the yard approached. It was George Russell, the current owner who, it turns out, worked for Harry at Iowa Clothes in high school.

"I'm honored to live in this house. Harry was an inspiration for the rest of my life. He taught me things," George said, referring to an incident where he had apparently once conducted himself in an unprofessional manner. Still, Harry treated him with dignity and gave him a second chance. "He's the man who gave me perspective; you've got to judge the whole person, not just by a single act. The work ethic he taught, early to bed, early to rise…The guy was there at 7 am."

George invited us in for a tour –– a *brokhe*, a blessing, granted to few who have the privilege of returning to a place from childhood which brought such joy. In the kitchen, Patty stood at the peninsula exactly where her grandmother had on Friday nights over a half-century ago. She stretched her arms wide, made three large circles, then covered her eyes, re-enacting a *Shabbos* ritual. "My grandmother would do this. To me, it represents bringing God's love into your heart. Then she would cover her eyes and say the traditional candle blessing:"

Barukh atah Adonai, Eloheinu, melekh ha'olam
asher kidishanu b'mitz'votav v'tzivanu
l'had'lik neir shel Shabbat

On Memorial Day and between the High Holidays at Bikur Cholim/Oak Hill Cemetery, Council Bluffians gather to remember those who came before them. "Probably starting in high school, I'd go with my mother to the cemetery service, then run by Ben Schneider and Lloyd Krasne; there may have been others. My mother went because of her parents and brother being buried there. It meant so much to her and I've continued it. It's different, but it's still remembering the day. We call it a service, but we do more English than Hebrew. It's important to remember all of our ancestors, not just those who died or fought in wars. For all of us, it's a shared history of Council Bluffs."

Afterwards, the group heads to -- where else? -- Christy Creme. "That tradition started a while back when I'd say, 'Gail and I are going to Christy Creme if anyone wants to join.' It's just an unofficial whoever-wants-to-go-to. The funniest thing about Christy Creme is I'm always looking around to see if I see someone I know. The problem is I'm looking for 16 or 17 year-old people!" she laughs. "In my head, I'm still that young girl."

Council Bluffs Sunday School class, 1961

171. David Cohen
173. Rebecca Cohen
172. Harry Cohen
174. Anne Cohen

Harry and Anne Cohen

175

176

177

178

175. Harry Cohen
176. Irving Cohen
177. Anne and Harry Cohen's 40th Anniversary
178. Betty Cohen

Passer & Cohen Family

Harry, Betty, Anne and Irving Cohen

Harry Cohen with grandchildren, Patty, Judy and Richard Lee

Anne Cohen with grandchildren, Richard, Judy and Patty in October, 1957

Dr. Isaac Sternhill from Council Bluffs

DR. ISAAC STERNHILL
1903 - 1970

DR. STERNHILL WAS the best medicine. When Council Bluffs kids were laid up, he knew just how to cure their ills. During house calls or at his office, he'd take the time to listen, nod his head in empathy and assure his patients and their parents all was Ok. He felt like family, which he was. Sort of. The small-town family physician, like the countless families he treated, was Jewish -- an integral part of the community he served for decades. A onetime B'nai Israel synagogue president and Board of Trustees member, Ike Sternhill devoted his time and talents to the *shul* and community he loved.

Like his fellow congregants of a certain vintage, Isaac Sternhill too was an immigrant. At age five, he left Romania for America, grew up in Omaha and graduated in 1927 from Creighton University Medical School. After serving in World War II, Dr. Sternhill practiced medicine in Council Bluffs for over 40 years and, not surprisingly, dedicated himself to causes about which he was passionate and received honors, a testament to his zeal and good nature. He served on the boards of the Council Bluffs Chapter of the Red Cross and United Fund when it was first organized in Council Bluffs, was awarded the Silver Beaver Award from the Boy Scouts of Omaha (having served as the organization's Council president in Council Bluffs) and was active with the National Conference of Christians and Jews who bestowed upon him the distinguished citizen's award.

Citizens of Council Bluffs knew they had a *mensch* in their midst. Dr. Sternhill was a man adored for his warmth, compassion and ability to make it better with the pinch of a cheek.

BETTIE AND LIBBIE GROSSMAN

THE GROSSMAN GIRLS were like Broadway Babies. Mom Lena sang in a choral group and, as Bettie recalls, "I used to sing and opened a dance recital when I was six-years-old. I have some fond memories of being in the operettas, *The Pirates of Penzance* -- which my sister directed -- and *The Mikado*. I was also in a couple of road shows in high school." Libbie's dance, piano, and elocution lessons paid off, earning her entry into Abraham Lincoln High School's Glee Club, Drama Club and plays. Bettie and Libbie even took their act on the road. "We performed a short version of *Midsummer Night's Dream* at the Grocers' Convention. Bettie also did a solo song that was very well-received," said Libbie.

Shabbos at 210 West Washington Avenue was hardly just candles and *challah*. "It was showtime at the Grossmans' every Friday night," Libbien said. Guests included the Sam and Herman Meyerson families, "with Leo at the piano, Bettie and I singing and dancing, and Florence, Pearl, June and Lorraine doing their dramatic readings."

The girls' greatest fan was likely their grandmother, and vice versa. Says Bettie, whose best friend was Betty Lee (Bettie and Betty): "The most powerful influence in my life was my grandmother, Ethel Baila Meyerson. She came from Russia and became modernized very quickly. She was a wonderful cook and I learned some of my Jewish cooking from her and from my mother-in-law, Rose Muskin. Grandma took my sister and me to Omaha to a movie and lunch for our birthdays. She babysat and taught me card games while my mother and father worked in our store. On Friday nights, all her sons and their families met at our house and the children usually put on a show. Her sons also came to lunch at our house as they worked in Council Bluffs at the Peoples Department Store, which was walking distance to our house.

"Our Friday nights were special. Grandma would light the candles and say a prayer. We always had chicken soup, *challah* and other goodies. She also made marvelous *teiglach* (small, knotted pastries boiled in honey syrup) and pickles. Grandma, who was a warm and wonderful woman whom we loved dearly, never got angry with us, and she disciplined my sister and me in a warm and loving way. She lived with us until she died when I was 10."

As Libby remembered, the older generations were "members of all Jewish organizations. Mother was president of *Hadassah* more than once. Grandma was very active in all synagogue activities, and on *Sabbath* afternoon many from the congregation met at our home, hosted by my grandmother. The one thing that impressed me about B'nai Israel was the community's love of my grandmother. As I remember, she was the only woman who had her funeral service held in the *shul* at that time, 1935."

Parents Lena and Morris Grossman together toiled in the family business. But before they owned Grossman's, Council Bluffs' go-to department store, Morris started in Manhattan, Kansas, operating a men's store. After moving to Council Bluffs in 1926, he bought a department store on Broadway with a Mrs. Kramer, recalled Libbie. Shortly, Morris would buy her interest in the business which he operated until the 1940s, then partnered with Ben Gershun -- Shirley Goldstein's dad -- to whom he later sold out. The store was re-named Gershun's Department Store.

"Mother and Dad were noted for having a wonderful reputation in the community for the way they conducted their business," said Libbie. Their reputation at home was surely unmatched. "On Saturday nights, we had our big night on the town which was a ride in the car and A&W Root Beer after closing time." Libbie, now deceased, riffed on more Council Bluffs memories: "No air conditioning…picnics at the park…entertainment was nighttime drives to little towns in Iowa…ten cent movies…meeting at Martin's Drug Store…working when needed at Grossman's Department Store…On the holidays, sitting upstairs with Mother and Grandma…" During that era, if females were permitted to partake in synagogue services, you can bet Bettie and Libbie would have belted from the balcony -- followed by whispers of awe.

Grossman's Department Store of Council Bluffs

Lena Meyerson Grossman with daughters Betttie Muskin and Libbie Olen

Sy and Betty Lee, Dorothy Koren, Bettie and Stuart Muskin

SHIRLEY GOLDSTEIN
1922 - 2017

SHIRLEY EMBODIES THE Hebrew concept of *Tikkun Olam*: to heal, repair and transform the world. Her whimsical nature alone is a balm. Her laugh is like that of a schoolgirl.

Some of what she treasures most? People, cows and Council Bluffs. "I have respect for Council Bluffs, I really do," she says. "I loved every bit of it." Perhaps best illustrative of her love for humanity was how Shirley helped Jews escape Cold War Russia and find refuge in America. "If people would do things when they see it happening, life would be different. If you don't know it, it's one thing. But if you see something is happening, you really have to help."

Father Ben Gershun (born *Gershuny*) came to this country from Poland around 1914 and served in World War I. While overseas, he was injured by mustard gas. "He always had a cough after that and a rash on his arm," says Shirley. "He had a great sense of humor and loved people." Mother Selma (née Wolfson), a Lithuanian girl, had one brother and seven sisters, who all settled here except for one who stayed behind with her family. They were wiped out in the Holocaust.

Devorah and Aaron Wolfson, Selma's parents, remained in their homeland and eventually came to Council Bluffs to live with the rest of their children, but the stay was short-lived. The Bluffs was not religious enough for Aaron, a rabbi, so they moved to then-Palestine with youngest daughter, *Tobka*. Shirley is unsure why her grandmother received this honor, but when Devorah died, "She was buried on the Mount of Olives."

Ben and Selma got their start in the states 80 miles northwest of Council Bluffs in Schuyler, Nebraska, population 3,000, with two Jewish families, including the Gershuns. "Dad had a cousin, Jake Lafsky. They were both Krasnes so the family brought them to the U.S. and set them up in a men and women's clothing store, Lafsky and Gershun," says Shirley, born May 10, 1922, followed 19 months later by brother Teddy. "Most people were bohemians, they were very friendly and we ate lots of *kolaches*. My dad knew how to say in Polish, '*Jak się miewasz*' "How are you?" and the other person would say '*Dubsha*' "Good." My father would yell it all the way across the store."

Lasfsky and Gershun, Shirley recalls, was a one-floor establishment akin to Kilpatrick's, downtown Omaha's onetime higher-end department store. While Ben manned the shop, his kids had other plans. "Teddy and I would go to the top of the steps and slide down the banister. It was some banister," she laughs. In time, like many young immigrant families determined to increase their standard of living, when opportunities arose the Gershuns would pack their belongings and move from town to town. At seven- or eight-years-old, Shirley and her family relocated to Florence, Nebraska in Omaha's north end where Ben opened -- what else? They were Jewish -- a grocery store.

"It was there where I met my very first Jewish girlfriend, Joy Greenberg," Shirley says. A few years later, the family settled just 12 miles southeast in a little town called Council Bluffs, where Ben launched a Pabst Blue Ribbon distributorship. "Everything in our house had logos on it. There was a bar downstairs and we had a neon sign that said 'Pabst Blue Ribbon.' We used to go down there and look in the trunk dad brought from World War I. We'd take out the uniforms and look at all his belongings."

Inside their home at 615 Bluff Street, located one block south of the old A.L. High School, was yet another structure for which playmates Shirley and Teddy found another use. "We had a great banister," she laughs. "We kids always rode a banister." In their neighborhood and at Dodge Street Elementary School, there were few Jews. Yet given the Gershuns were one of only two Jewish families in the entire town of Schuyler, "It didn't make much difference to me because I didn't know. You know what? I can still go into a room and be the only Jewish person and it never bothers me. People are people."

Eventually, Ben returned to his retail roots and, with his wife Selma, joined Morris Grossman in his general store located one block down from the Strand Theater on Broadway. Flanked by fellow Jewish merchants, the department store was, "a family store. We sold a lot of coveralls and overalls like OshKosh B'Gosh… and how! Everybody wanted the name tag on," Shirley says. "My dad was a good salesman; he liked clothing, selling it and picking things out. He liked being with people, you know, coming and going in the store. It's different than living in the city where you go in someplace and don't know them. It makes a difference.

"My dad helped others. Somebody would come in and needed something and they couldn't afford it. He donated plenty. When you see people that don't have anything and you see what they need, that's why you're there. He knew everybody's name that came into our store –– or my mother used to say he pretended he did," she laughs. "He was known for lots of jokes and he spoke with a heavy accent. I remember my mom and dad didn't want us to know what they were talking about, so all of a sudden they'd go into Polish or Lithuanian. Teddy and I knew what they were saying when they thought we didn't know. It's like everything else. You hear enough of it and you get it."

Shirley's favorite place to shop? "The Peoples Store!" she smiles. "They had everything and everybody was friendly and glad to see you." In those days, anyone who got even a whiff of Council Bluffs knew the Peoples Store –– the city's revered go-to department store –– and they knew, or at least heard of, the Krasne and Bernstein families, the original owners from 1907 until it closed in 1972. There, customers felt like family. Fortunately for Ben Gershun, he was family. "I don't know how my dad was related to the Krasnes, but we always claimed each other. It was always fun because they were all relatives."

The basement of any store might not sound like a desired destination, but father-and-son team Lou and Harold Bernstein who owned the hardware department on the lower level created a chummy atmosphere and stocked must-have items which helped them garner a loyal following, Shirley included. "I loved the hardware store, there were always gadgets." Like? "Oh, peelers. I remember we bought the first potato peeler there and I was so excited. It was stainless steel, that was when stainless steel became popular. There were all kinds of gadgets. I always liked the measuring cups that fit inside one another…That was actually when cake mixes first came out and became popular. All you had to do was add the liquid."

Being related to the Krasnes had other added benefits, like built-in friends. "Rhoda Krasne and I were very close. She was about six months older than I was. She was the prettiest girl around, very down-to-earth and the cutest thing in the world," Shirley says, noting Rhoda's parents were George and Toby Krasne. Throughout her childhood, Shirley cavorted with cousins galore. Her mother's side of the family even formed a "Cousins Club," a lively bunch who got together throughout the years at, say, a park in Omaha, to *kibbitz* and "talk about what's happening in the world. I loved to get together with them. The girls were all older than me. There was a lot of beer and I don't think you ever wanted for food."

Selma Gershun had five sisters -- Ethel, Mae, Hannah, Jane and Celia -- who settled in and around Council Bluffs. Some even married local boys, creating interrelationships not uncommon in those days: Mae married Sam Meyerson, Hannah married Hyman Fried, Ethel married Will Solomonow and Jane married Dave Finkel. Sister Celia Fonarow ("sounds Italian but it was very Jewish") lived in Council Bluffs for a short period of time, and a striking event which occurred on the day of Shirley's birth still gets her giddy.

"My cousin Willard and I were born to sisters on the same day in the same hospital in Council Bluffs. Willard and I were very close. We loved to be together. We called ourselves twins. He was fun because he said he was born first. We had building blocks and one of us would always accidentally knock over the others with our elbows," she laughs.

In keeping with the age-old tradition of pestering the older kids, "We would follow the boys around and they hated it," Shirley says. But one boy stood out: Leo Meyerson. Cousin Leo was an especially swell guy, a young inventor-turned ham radio pioneer who honed his crafts in a makeshift "lab" in the Meyerson's house. "He had a studio in the basement. He was unique; he knew what he was doing. Nobody else knew, really. And he was fun. He loved music. He'd say, 'What do ya wanna hear?' He'd come in to the house and see the piano and say, 'Hi honey!'

Then give me a kiss and go to the piano. He'd do things like sing a song with your name in it. I even remember he once sang "Good Morning To You" and then added "Shirley." The kids in that family were all good, they could all do something. To be born with that is pretty good."

During Shirley's Bloomer Junior High years, Ben earned a good enough living to purchase an American icon: a Studebaker. Blue. "I remember when he got it, oh boy! Boy, if there was a mark on that he took his shirtsleeve and wiped it off. If it rained, he'd stop and wipe the windows," she laughs. "We used to go for a ride every night after supper and that's how I became so familiar with cows. Daddy would park by a wooden fence which was low enough for me to climb, and they'd come up to us and I'd pet them. I've been fond of cows every since," says Shirley, whose home is dotted with various inanimate versions. "If I saw one today and there wasn't too much traffic, I'd stop and go up and feed 'em and wait for a 'Moo.'"

As far as Jewish life, Shirley recalls, "There really wasn't a hangout for Jewish people in Council Bluffs. If there was one, it was at the synagogue." Ben went to *shul* religiously. "He was involved in anything he could be and they called him to do various things, like *minyans*. My parents didn't keep kosher yet there was never any *traif* in the house and my mom did light candles every Friday night and had a *Shabbos* dinner. She was a great cook, all my friends liked to come over to eat and the neighbors came over to borrow a cup of this and a cup of that."

Jewish identity was important to both Shirley's parents and her. "When we lived in Florence, my parents wanted to identify with Jewish people and it seemed like we were moving a lot so I needed a core. That's when I became friends with Joy Greenberg." Shirley attended Sunday school at Beth El. "We carpooled with Leo Krasne, the Noggs and the Grossmans. We'd pay five cents a person to cross the Aksarben Bridge. The JCC at 20th and Dodge was bustling on Sundays. All the kids were there. Smitty, I believe his name was, ran the hot dog stand there. If you were lucky, you could buy one." During those years, Shirley added more Jewish friends to her circle. "I was very close with Esther Fox who lived in Omaha. We retained our friendship through the years and we talked every day of our lives, but not back then because a call from Omaha to Council Bluffs was 10 cents. Our folks said we could call each other only so many times a week."

From about ninth-grade on, Shirley was active in a Jewish girl's group, The Emesels. "We tried to get together every Tuesday evening at somebody's house. We put in maybe a dime every week for the club. Once a year we had a dance, usually at the Chieftain Hotel in Council Bluffs. The Omaha group, some from Central, maybe a few from North, would come over and we had a good time with them. The boys wore tuxes and we wore long formals and heels -- and corsages, that was really an important part. A gardenia; everybody wanted a gardenia."

Along with Rhoda Krasne and Esther Fox, Shirley's dear friend was Betty Cohen, a few years her junior. "We spent lot of time together," she says. "I went to work in their store probably starting at Christmastime and when the holidays came up and they needed help. We both worked in the store on Saturdays. She was very sweet." Other friends included Norma Seldin, Betty Grossman and Bernice "Trickle" Himmelstein ("She moved so slowly, they'd call her trickle").

For Shirley "Social Butterfly" Gershun, "dating was interesting. Girls from Council Bluffs would wait until the guys from Omaha all had licenses," she laughs. "Rhoda and I used to double date a lot. There were big dances at Peony Park in West Omaha at 78th and Cass. They had a ballroom and an orchestra on the weekends. That was a big deal."

When Shirley was about 15, the Gershuns bought a home at 427 Forest Drive where neighborhood friends were Edith Bubb, Arlene Krasne and Harold Bernstein. "Harold and I both went to high school at AL. They lived a block from us, he was on Frank Street. We were in the same group of friends and we were friends besides being distant cousins. I could talk to him for advice."

At A.L., Shirley belonged to the Theta Literary Society and acted in plays. "Nobody was looked upon as Jewish or not Jewish, everybody was very congenial and when there were parties, I was always included. I went to every dance and the military ball. There didn't seem to be any distinction between people. Our home was always open to everybody, Mother and Dad always appreciated having people over and a house full."

In high school, Shirley developed a newfound relationship with a boy she had known since grade school, Rhoda Krasne's first cousin on her mother's side, Leonard "Buddy" Goldstein.

"People called him Buddy because he was the youngest of five children and they all babied him." The couple continued their courtship after Shirley graduated in 1940 and headed to Iowa. "It was a wonderful, wonderful year." What did she study? "As little as possible," she laughs. "I probably goofed off more than I should have. I took some human rights classes, it just seemed the thing to do. There was so much going on at that time in the government -- there was always something -- and you'd read and you'd want to get your finger in the pie. I used to read every single thing that came out about how people were treated and I used to call the congressman's office. Whenever I would see something in the paper or hear about it, I remember my dad would say, 'Don't you ever stop calling Washington?' My Emesel friends and I would meet regularly or talk on the phone, so we could keep our congressmen on alert. We wanted the government to know we were aware of what was happening."

Soon, rumblings of war prompted scores of men to be called into the service, Buddy included. In 1941, Shirley returned home to Council Bluffs. "I felt it was my home," she says. The young, budding activist attended Dickinson Business School where she took a course in keypunch operating, the forerunner of computer language, and landed a job at the Federal Land Bank at 19th and Farnam. On November 1, 1942, she and Buddy married in a small service at the Blackstone Hotel, after which they took a train to Chicago where her new husband was stationed. "I went to Chicago with one suitcase."

At one point, while Buddy was overseas, Shirley stayed with her parents and took a job in the personnel department of a bomber plant in Bellevue, working, again, as a key punch operator. "A neighbor drove me, his name was Oliver Oscar Over. I paid him, I think, $2 a week. I think my check every week was $18 or $22 dollars. Every few months, I'd work the three to midnight shift, then 11 to 7 am. I loved it. I liked being one of the first to know the news of what was happening. We got all of it," she says.

When Buddy was discharged from the Army Air Corps, the couple moved to Omaha and, in time, had three children: Donald, Gail and Kathy. Today, Shirley has six grandchildren and four great-grandchildren. Though it has been over 70 years since she has lived in Council Bluffs, "I think it's superior just to say you're from there," she laughs. "I think it's a great town, I loved it. Everybody was friendly and my parents lived a good life there. I still like to go over there and ride around."

After World War II, Ben Gershun helped resettle immigrants in Council Bluffs. "People would come to daddy to find out where to settle or where the jobs were. I don't think he was the only one. The businessmen in Council Bluffs tried to help men who had been in the service and wanted to re-start working. I don't know how they did it or how effective HIAS was at that time, but the Council Bluffs community rented a little house next to the synagogue on Mynster Street and until those people got their feet on the ground I think they would stay there," she says.

Unwittingly, her dad's actions would foreshadow her own. Starting in the early '70s, during the Cold War, Shirley would become a heroine. But tell the unassuming great-grandmother that and she'll cringe. "Nothing's a one-man show," she says. "You can stir things up but you need help in getting it together. I loved it. It makes you want to do more, to speak up, to speak out, let people know what's really happening."

What was happening? Prompted by the suffering of Jews in the USSR, Shirley and her good friend Miriam Simon set out on a humanitarian mission. As part of the Free Soviet Jewry Movement, the activists took on the task of helping Russian Jews earn basic human rights and, ultimately, seek freedom. They enlisted the help of the Jewish Federation, Jewish Family Services, plus private and corporate donations like Nebraska Furniture Mart and Borsheims.

Their work was hardly limited to letter-writing campaigns, rallies or picketing, of which they did plenty. For instance, before a Russian musician was set to play, the group protested in front of the Joslyn. Captured in a January 21, 1976 *Omaha World-Herald* article was a group of men and women standing in front of the Orpheum Theater before an Omaha Symphony concert of a Soviet pianist. They held signs which read: "Let Them Live Or Let Them Leave," "Cry Aloud In Protest," "Russian Oppression Must Stop."

Eventually, they would cross both state and international borders. When Gorbachev visited the U.S., they rallied at the March on Washington. For nearly two decades, Shirley would travel to Russia where she met with refuseniks, activists and dissidents, often in secret. She'd sneak out of her hotel room at night to gather information, to listen, to plan their next move. She would even store, haul and deliver contraband like blue jeans, enlisting the help of Omaha's Russian emigrées to box care packages. Sometimes she would even travel under the guise of a sponsored tour by the *Omaha World-Herald* and the *Jewish Press*. Perfect ploy: a diminutive Jewish mother who, when one arrives at her apartment instantly asks, "Are you comfortable? Would you like a cold drink?"

In a September 5, 2011 *Jewish Press* article, writer Leo Adam Biga published a must-read, two-part series entitled, "Cream of the Crop: One Woman's Remarkable Journey in the Free Soviet Jewry Movement" and "Shirley Goldstein: Activist, Humanitarian, Philanthropist." Shirley's story is recounted in astonishing detail. Take the time she was staying in an Odessa hotel room where she woke to find a man standing inside her door. She was quoted as saying, "I told him to get the hell out. He did. After that, every time I went out of the room I walked backwards and sprinkled baby powder on the floor so I'd know if anybody came in. And, you know what? I was the first person to walk in and mark my own tracks."

Or the time in 1973 during a UNO-sponsored tour of Russia when she toted her daughter Gail who witnessed Shirley being detained at customs in Leningrad. Authorities attempted to confiscate her armful of posters which turned out to be drawings by children from a Jewish day school she intended to bring to Omaha students. After standing her ground, she acquiesced, begrudgingly, then tore the artwork in front of them. "If I can't have it, you can't have it," she said, after which they insisted she pick up the pieces. Ignoring their demand, she walked onto the plane.

Everyone clapped.

Shirley -- a woman on the KGB's radar -- always took steps to ensure protection from government interference. In the article, she said, "Before leaving for the USSR each time, I'd go to my congressmen and have them write letters of referral to the authorities that said I was seeing people I knew and that the U.S. government would appreciate it if I were not bothered. When KGB or customs agents wanted to see my papers, those letters always came out first."

Biga wrote: "Ask Buddy if Shirley's someone to trifle with, and he says, "Oh boy…"

Her story could be a book, or a movie, which in fact, it was. The documentary, *Let My People Go* by filmmaker Laura Bialis and producer Stephanie Howard --Ted and Sarah Seldin's daughter -- chronicles the astonishing tale of courage and *chutzpah* of a woman who dared to film and photograph the oppression she witnessed, images which were published around the world.

Shirley's last trip to the USSR was in 1989. The Soviets finally revoked her Visa. Of course she attempted, in vain, to re-enter the country. But no matter. She and her cohorts' actions sparked human rights reform in Russia. Borders reopened, and they helped sponsor refugees in their flight to freedom, including setting them up with jobs, housing and English lessons.

Shirley's parents behind Eleanor Roosevelt

In the 1980s, Shirley won the Jewish Federation's Humanitarian of the Year Award and in 1996, became an honorary Doctor of Humane Letters from UNO, "for her tireless efforts on behalf of Soviet Jewry and the cause of human rights worldwide, for her conviction and example that one person can make a difference in the lives of others, and for her ability to inspire compassion and humanity, both near and far."

What sparked Shirley Goldstein, a girl from Council Bluffs who loved to slide down banisters, fraternize with cousins and attend black-tie dances, to risk her life helping others?

"Knowing both my parents had come from that area and reading how bad it was; and once they got here, how great it was. People were leaving the vicious circles over there and you'd hear about them. I thought, 'Somebody should be able to take advantage of it and others can't? That's not fair.' People don't want to know. Maybe it's depressing. I knew what was happening. If you can make it better, make it better.

"It made me feel good when people were getting out and they'd come here and you could help them, for instance if they needed a night or so in our home or someplace. I had a great husband who helped me. If I needed something he'd see to it. You can let people know what's happening, but you can't do the whole thing by yourself. It was a community event. We got donations for homes and apartments and we'd take them places. I think the Jewish community has been great in helping the Russians. I'm lucky I could do what I did. They remember what we did together. If they needed something, they'd call and ask for it. That means we were helping. Isn't that what the Jewish community is for?"

ADD NEW BEER LINE

—Nonpareil Photo.

Ben Gershun, manager of the Iowa Distributing company, 1215 South Main street, holds a bottle of Gluek's beer from the first shipment of Gluek's Brewing company. Gershun, who has just added Gluek's to his products, receives all his shipments by rail. Next to Gershun is G. G. Schleicher, Sioux Falls, S. D., agent for the company; Blaine Thomas and Ted Gershun, both distributing company employes.

179. Shirley Goldstein's father
180. Shirley Goldstein
181. Shirley and Teddy, 1927
182. Selma Gershun with Shirley and Teddy

Shirley Goldstein's family

Shirley with Harold Bernstein

183. Shirley & Betty Lee

184. Ben and Selma Gershun, Shirley's parents

185. Shirley in early years was involved in Russian resettlement programs

186. Documentation on Shirley's house
187. Shirley G. and Henry Jackson
188. Shirley's house in Council Bluffs
189. Shirley at 427 Forest Drive

Gershun's Department Store in Council Bluffs

Shirley with Soviet dissident, Natan Sharansky, now Israeli politician

Shirley Goldstein

www.ingramcontent.com/pod-product-compliance
Lightning Source LLC
Chambersburg PA
CBHW060257240426
43661CB00060B/2812